CRITICAL INSIGHTS

Contemporary Latin American Fiction

CRITICAL INSIGHTS

Contemporary Latin American Fiction

Editor
Ignacio López-Calvo
University of California, Merced

SALEM PRESS
A Division of EBSCO Information Services, Inc.
Ipswich, Massachusetts

GREY HOUSE PUBLISHING

Publisher's Cataloging-In-Publication Data
(Prepared by The Donohue Group, Inc.)

Names: López-Calvo, Ignacio, editor.
Title: Contemporary Latin American fiction / editor, Ignacio López-Calvo,
        University of California, Merced.
Other Titles: Critical insights.
Description: [First edition]. | Ipswich, Massachusetts : Salem Press, a division
        of EBSCO Information Services, Inc. ; Amenia, NY : Grey
        House Publishing, [2017] | Includes bibliographical references
        and index.
Identifiers: ISBN 9781682175613 (hardcover)
Subjects: LCSH: Latin American fiction--20th century--History and criticism. |
        Latin American fiction--21st century--History and criticism
Classification: LCC PQ7082.N7 C66 2017 | DDC 863.640998--dc23

First Printing

Contents

Critical Contexts

Critical Readings

The Labor of Gender: Cristina Rivera Garza,
    a Feminist Pedagogy, Laura J. Torres-Rodríguez   217

Resources

To my friend José I. Suárez

About This Volume

Ignacio López-Calvo

With four original introductory articles as well as nine essays on specific Latin American authors that provide critical and descriptive overviews (all previously unpublished) of their oeuvres and careers, this volume revisits the present situation of contemporary Latin American literature. It offers readers a survey of recent Spanish-, Portuguese-, and English-language Latin American and Caribbean fiction writing that may complement larger anthologies, such as Will H. Corral, Juan A. de Castro, and Nicholas Birns's 2013 *The Contemporary Spanish-American Novel. Bolaño and After*. Instead of offering a list of names and asking the critics to choose one, as is often done with this type of anthology, I chose to give the critics the freedom to think of a contemporary Latin American author whom they find relevant and then explain why they think that this writer is representative of today's heterogeneous Latin American belles lettres. As a result, the oeuvres of twelve authors, six female and six male, are analyzed: Costa Rican Anacristina Rossi (1952-), Cuban Daína Chaviano (1957-), Argentine Claudia Piñeiro (1960-), Colombian Juan Gabriel Vázquez (1973-), Peruvian Carlos Yushimito del Valle (1977-), Brazilians Milton Hatoum (1952-) and Bernardo Carvalho (1960-), Chileans Roberto Bolaño (1953-2003) and Camila Gutiérrez Berner (1985-), and Mexicans Bárbara Jacobs (1947-), Daniel Sada (1953-2011) and Cristina Rivera Garza (1964-). Except for Roberto Bolaño and Daniel Sada, these authors are still alive, with a chronological span from Bárbara Jacobs, born in 1947, to the youngest author, Camila Gutiérrez Berner, who was born in 1985.

Because of space restraints, the anthology is inevitably limited and fragmented, with numerous absences in terms of both authors and countries. The Further Reading section, however, provides an idea of the wealth and diversity of recent Latin American literature, as well as of the large number of authors who could have been included, were it not for space limitations. This list includes, besides authors who write in Spanish, Lusophone writers from Brazil as well as English-language Latino writers residing in the United States. Authors such as the Dominican Americans Junot Díaz[1] and Julia Álvarez,[2] for example, could be framed under different levels: US, Latina/o, Caribbean, and Latin American writing. Indeed, their works deal with both US and Caribbean cultures, as well as with the transculturation or cultural exchanges suffered by Latina/o immigrants in the United States, a prominent topic, for instance, in Álvarez's novel *How the Garcia Girls Lost Their Accents* (1991) and Díaz's *The Brief Wondrous Life of Oscar Wao* (2007). Among the main topics appearing in their works, we find those of life under the Trujillo dictatorship, male chauvinism, and migration. Interestingly, one could argue that Álvarez and Díaz have achieved more international acclaim than any novelist born in the Dominican Republic.

This volume, as well as similar ones, should help offset the tendency among American critics and presses to essentialize and tropicalize Latin American literature by identifying it almost exclusively with stereotypical magical realism, a literary mode that has been, for the most part, rejected by newer generations of Latin American authors. The variety, diversity, and heterogeneity of today's Latin American fiction should be self-evident in the essays collected in this book and, even more, in the list of authors and works included in the Further Reading section. Moreover, given the renewed interest in the region's literature thanks to the impressive success of Chilean Roberto Bolaño's novels, we hope to provide a guide to prominent names of his generation as well as younger ones.

Opening the volume, Melissa Fitch's chapter addresses how new technology has radically transformed the way we understand notions of text, authorship, and readership within the field of Latin American literature. It provides a historical context for understanding such new developments in light of work done in the last century by writers in the region. It also discusses the pioneering scholarly work done on the topic over the last twenty years. Finally, it traces briefly the work of four notable writers/bloggers: Alberto Chimal (Mexico

1970), Juan B. Gutiérrez (Colombia 1973), Cielo Latini (Argentina 1984), and Daniel Galera (Brazil 1979).

My essay, dealing with critical reception, revisits possible reasons for the amazing success of Bolaño's literature and its sudden entrance into world literature. It also problematizes how the constant publication of the author's posthumous novels without his explicit consent may eventually alter his literary reputation. Finally, it considers the consequences of Bolaño's entrance into the World Republic of Letters for younger generations of Latin American writers.

Next, Shigeko Mato examines the unveiling of the unconscious desire for cultural Westernization in contemporary Lima through the short story "Rizoma" ("Rhizome," 2013), by Peruvian writer Carlos Yushimito del Valle (1977-). The story depicts the feverish climate of a gourmet boom in Lima, in which the upper classes have a constant urge to be mindlessly entertained by new cutting-edge dishes. An ambitious entrepreneurial French gourmet chef tries to discover "something marvelous," using Peruvian indigenous culture and food through "techno-cooking" techniques imported from Europe, attracting clients through the exoticization of indigenous culture and food. Both the chef and his clients are too absorbed in their entertainment to be aware of the meanings as well as the traditional, regional, and communal values of the foods that they are co-opting. Because of the lack of critical consciousness, they eventually turn into rabid cannibalistic zombies. Setting up a mindless consumer society, Yushimito portrays the gruesome outcome of the nonstop fetishization of Europeanized gourmet food. That is, he describes the decomposition of human society into a cynocephalic (dog-headed and human-bodied) dystopia. Mato's study, therefore, analyzes how and why this futuristic dystopian story can serve, not only as a warning sign of the degradation of society caused by the incessant pursuit of entertainment and consumerism, but also, perhaps more importantly, as a criticism against the manipulation of the masses by a long-lasting repetition of the colonial global power system that Aníbal Quijano calls the "coloniality of power."

Closing the Critical Contexts section, Gene H. Bell-Villada offers a comparative study of *Historia secreta de Costaguana* (2007; *The Secret History of Costaguana* 2011), by Colombian author Juan Gabriel Vásquez (1973-), and *Nostromo* (1904), by Polish-English Joseph Conrad. *Historia secreta de Costaguana* is a complex novel that seamlessly integrates three different plots. It tells first of all about some key events in nineteenth-century Colombia's Department of Panama: the construction of the trans-Isthmian railroad, the vast but failed French Canal project, the civil wars and secessionist rumblings, and the US intervention that led promptly to Panamanian separation and to the beginnings of the American Canal venture. The entire history in turn is narrated (and partly lived) by one José Altamirano, whose father Miguel was posted as a journalist on the Isthmus; José for his part ends up marrying Charlotte, the widow of a French engineer who had died of yellow fever. (The couple will have and raise a Panamanian daughter named Eloísa.) Finally, as the book title implies, the novel references and relates to Joseph Conrad, whose seafaring cum literary biography serves as a third plotline, and who figures as a character-interlocutor to whom the anguished narrator José, exiled in London, will pour out the unfortunate history of Colombia. The Polish-English writer then shamelessly appropriates this hearsay material for his *Nostromo*, a novel set in a conflict-ridden republic that he calls *Costaguana*. Vásquez's *Secret History*, a sophisticated work of intertextual artifice, thus qualifies as a kind of historiographic metafiction.

Opening the Critical Readings section, Rudyard Alcocer looks at the fiction of Costa Rican author Anacristina Rossi (1952-), who has consistently sought to expose and challenge her country's social norms. These norms (or contradictions), we learn, have varied in substance and focus, ranging from issues of gender, environmentalism, and political corruption, to ones of race and ethnicity. Oftentimes, her fiction is able to syncretize several of these issues simultaneously. While challenging both societal norms and narrative conventions, her novels never lack courage and occasionally unlock pronounced and rare societal responses that have led to practical changes in how Costa Rica is governed. As such, Rossi's oeuvre sheds important light on the variable dynamics that can exist between fictions and their readers. More to the point, Alcocer argues that this oeuvre demonstrates that in the 1990s, at least, politically oriented fiction could still effect transformative change in a society. The essay undertakes a critical examination of Rossi's most important novels; never far from the surface throughout is the basic contention that Rossi and her fiction deserve our attention and interest.

In turn, Paula C. Park examines how the novels and short stories that Daína Chaviano published in the 1980s in Cuba secured her a spot as one of the most important science-fiction writers within the Spanish-speaking world. The chapter, however, analyzes the works Chaviano produced after leaving Cuba in 1991, especially her highly acclaimed and commercially successful novel *La isla de los amores infinitos* (*The Island of Eternal Love*, 2006), a family saga that pays homage to the symbolic union of the Spanish, the African, and the Chinese in Cuba. Although *La isla de los amores infinitos* responds to market demands for mainstream fantasy and love stories between "exotic" multicultural characters, Park argues that Chaviano employs a distinct archival style through which she inserts historical documentation on the Chinese in Cuba, the repression and hunger suffered by Cubans in Havana in the 1980s (as evident also in her 1998 novel *El hombre, la hembra y el hambre* (*Man, Woman, and Hunger*), and the psychological dilemma of those who, like the author, left Cuba after 1991. In doing so, Park demonstrates that although Chaviano has become a mainstream writer, she is still committed to developing an intimate relationship with her readers, whether science-fiction fans or completely alien to Cuban history.

David William Foster turns to a feminist view of recent Argentine history as represented in Claudia Piñeiro's opus. As he explains, Piñeiro has established a solid inventory of feminist interpretations of Argentine social history since that country's return to constitutional democracy in 1983. Against the backdrop of neoliberal economic policy and its fissures and ultimate collapse in 2001, Piñeiro's highly successful works of fiction provide an interpretation of the instability and moral relativism carried along with a process not always willing or successful in dealing with its often monstrous collective imaginaries. As Foster points out, while not all of Piñeiro's fiction privileges female characters, it does privilege women's consciousness in the face of a society that remains intransigently masculinist.

Antonio Luciano Tosta looks at the opus of Milton Hatoum, one of Brazil's major contemporary authors, discussing his four novels, his *crônica* collection, and his short story collection. The chapter explores Hatoum's narrative plots, protagonists, most common themes, and the ways in which his work serves as a reflection on the relationship between locality and globality.

In her essay, Sandra Sousa explains that while Bernardo Carvalho acknowledges the ubiquity of violence in Brazilian daily life, he resists the tendency to reduce literature to a mechanically mimetic function, claiming that literature is not an exercise in sociology. He also distances himself from the social and aesthetic values of postmodernism, affirming instead much of the legacy of Western modernity, including core aspects of modernist aesthetic practice, such as art's ability to bring about truths in the world. Carvalho's literary project has largely been based on the idea of traveling to write, which is more complex than simply taking a trip to other regions in Brazil or to other countries in order to find inspiration for writing. Since Carvalho's fictional geographies are biographically unfamiliar to him, his experiences of them arise as much from his imagination as from practical encounters. In the end, Carvalho is interested in the truth that can only be known through fiction.

Moisés Park's essay focuses on theodicy through the writings of Chilean writer Camila Gutiérrez Berner (1985-), whose social media writings were turned into a film and later adapted into an autobiographic book, *Joven y alocada* (2013), and a second novel, *No te ama* (2015). In spite of the first novel being an out-of-religion coming of age, containing more religious content, the second novel, about a bisexual love triangle, tackles the topic in its more traditional form, reformulating the theodical form. Sororal (sisterly) apostasy is highlighted as a means of finding freedom and love outside the closed religious circle.

Traci Roberts-Camps's chapter examines the writings of Bárbara Jacobs, including *Florencia y Ruiseñor* (*Florencia and Ruiseñor*, 2006), *La dueña del Hotel Poe* (*The Owner of Hotel Poe*, 2014), and *Hacia el valle del sueño* (*Toward the Valley of Sleep*, 2014). This analysis focuses on the following topics: multiple languages, linguistic analysis and wordplay, literary theory, the world of publishing, self-awareness, and self-analysis. Gérard Genette's concepts of narrative discourse complement Jacobs's emphasis on language, literature, and the writing process. According to Roberts-Camps, Jacobs's attentiveness to the formal aspects of writing is at once playful and earnest.

Mark Anderson focuses on Daniel Sada, renowned as one of Mexico's most innovative writers of the turn of the twenty-first century. His chapter examines Sada's trajectory beginning with his first novel, *Lampa vida* (1980), up through *Albedrío* (1989), *Porque parece mentira la verdad nunca se sabe* (1999), and his final, posthumously published novel, *El lenguaje del juego* (2012). It analyzes three key recurrent themes in Sada's works: migration, the unknowability of the other, and violence. It also takes a close look at Sada's distinctive writing style, which has often been compared to a "baroque" aesthetics.

Closing the volume, Laura J. Torres-Rodríguez's chapter explores the contributions of Mexican writer Cristina Rivera Garza (1964-) to the understanding of literature as a contemporary writing practice. It argues that her fiction proposes writing and reading as forms of collective production—not organized solely by the figure of the individual author or reader—that entail in turn other forms of social labor. Moreover, the attention that Rivera Garza's work devotes to the collective conditions of reproduction inscribes it within a broader feminist tradition. The chapter thus analyzes three specific aspects of Rivera Garza's vast literary work: the historical novel and the revision of Mexican history, the critique of crime fiction as a genre that pretends to represent contemporary violence, and the practice of rewriting important figures and moments of the

Mexican literary history through the perspective of the present. Finally, the chapter concludes with the assertion that the complexity of her experimental literary work is not an obstacle to the practice of pedagogy, but rather offers a vantage point from which students can engage with literature as a collective form of understanding and producing an alternative present.

Notes

1. Besides the novel *The Brief Wondrous Life of Oscar Wao* (2007), Díaz has published the short story collections *Drown* 1996) and *This Is How You Lose Her* (2012).

2. Álvarez has received numerous awards and has published the following novels: *How the García Girls Lost Their Accents* (1991), *In the Time of the Butterflies* (1994), *¡YO!* (1997), *In the Name of Salomé* (2000), *How Tía Lola Came to ~~Visit~~ Stay* (2001), *When We Were Free* (2002), and *Saving the World* (2006). She is also the author of several collections of poems: *Homecoming* (1984), *The Housekeeping Book* (1994), *The Other Side/El otro lado* (1995), *Homecoming: New and Collected Poems* (1996), and *Seven Trees* (1999), and has edited the collection of poems *Old Age Ain't for Sissies*.

Work Cited

Corral, Will H., Juan A. de Castro, and Nicholas Birns. *The Contemporary Spanish-American Novel. Bolaño and After.* Bloomsbury, 2013.

On Contemporary Latin American Fiction: From Engaged Literature to Depoliticized Autofiction

Ignacio López-Calvo

In an interview with Javier Rodríguez Marcos, Peruvian Nobel Prize winner Mario Vargas Llosa, after providing some exceptions, describes today's Latin American literature as "less engaged and more self-absorbed."[1] Valerie Miles, founder of the Spanish edition of *Granta* magazine, shares the same assessment about the newer generations of Latin American authors: "The ideas about politics are not so obvious in their writing as they were in the writers of the boom: politics becomes something more intimate that comes out from the daily life with the partner, children... not from the state" (Sánchez Díaz n.p.). The reason for this depoliticization, in Vargas Llosa's view, is the evolution toward democracy in the region. Today, following worldwide trends, younger generations of writers tend to reject the political engagement that, for decades, was a staple among Boom and post-Boom writers.[2] Instead, Vargas Llosa adds, younger Latin American writers are more inclined to write autofiction: "A mixture of fantasy and autobiography in which the author becomes a character."[3] (Rodríguez Marcos n.p.) Indeed, perhaps even more than previous generations, these authors resort to their own life, identity, or reading experiences as a source of inspiration to create their characters. As Puerto Rican author Mayra Santos-Febres explains, in the autofiction genre writers assume that "'truth' is always slippery and objectivity is inevitably subjective. The logic, coherence, and beauty of a literary text are more important than political correction, shyness, or loyalty to family."[4]

This rejection of "committed" art has to be understood within the context of the Cold War cultural interventions and tensions between political art and nonpolitical academic aestheticism. The institutionalization of aesthetic modernism in the United States during the 1940s and the endorsement of "pure art" in Latin

America, which were meant to counter rigid Soviet programmatic realism depicting class struggle, also have to be understood within the context of the Cold War, as Jean Franco has posited:

> But the continent was also a battlefield of another kind as both the United States and the Soviet Union carried on covert activities to influence the hearts and minds of Latin Americans. Thus abstract universalism and freedom were values disseminated by CIA-funded journals against the universal teleology of revolution, behind which lurked the Soviet national project. . . . In the United States itself the turn from public art to abstract expressionism, from a politicized avant-garde to a depoliticized avant-garde art, from realist to experimental writing . . . was based on claims of artistic autonomy. (Franco 2)

In other words, for some critics the new attitude of young generations of Latin American writers is reminiscent of the dictum of anti-Communist Cold War politics espoused by the United States.

Going back to Rodríguez Marcos's interview with Vargas Llosa, the Peruvian author also points out significant thematic changes. For example, the archetypical figure of the Latin American dictator, which became the protagonist of key novels of the Latin American canon, such as Miguel Ángel Asturias's *El señor presidente* (*The President*, 1946), Alejo Carpentier's *El recurso del método* (*Reasons of State,* 1973), Augusto Roa Bastos's *Yo, el supremo* (*I, the Supreme,* 1973), Gabriel García Márquez's *El otoño del Patriarca* (*The Autumn of the Patriarch*, 1975), Tomás Eloy Martínez's *La novela de Perón* (1986), and Mario Vargas Llosa's *La fiesta del chivo* (*The Feast of the Goat*, 2000), has ceased to be so prominent, also because of democratic changes in Latin America. Vargas Llosa wonders whether today's replacement for the character of the Latin American dictator is the drug trafficker: "It is possible that violent and corrupt power has passed from the dictator to the drug baron."[5] Yet he argues that the widespread presence of political corruption and drug dealers in Latin America, which has been translated into political, social, and cultural influence, has yet to produce a key novel on the topic. In any case, several Latin American writers have adhered to the so-called narcoliterature, a type of narrative subgenre exploring the ultraviolent socioeconomic, cultural, and political phenomenon of drug trafficking in the Western Hemisphere, including Mexican Élmer Mendoza, who has been considered the father of narcoliterature, with novels such as *Un asesino solitario* (*A Lone Murderer, 1999*), *El amante de Janis Joplin* (*Janis Joplin's Lover*, 2008; winner of the José Fuentes Mares National Prize for Literature), *Balas de plata* (*Silver Bullets*, 2008), and *La prueba del ácido* (*Acid Test*, 2010).[6] As will be seen, in her chapter, Laura J. Torres-Rodríguez questions, as other critics have done, the ethics of this type of genre when she states: "To read the present violence, we need ways of writing that do not spectacularize violence without analyzing it—like narconarratives—."

A third change in literary tastes, according to Vargas Llosa, is the rejection of the total novel that became a trademark among Boom writers. Indeed, Ignacio Padilla, in the Crack manifesto, declares: "No one writes novels any more, or rather, no one writes total novels. But, I wonder, novels for whom? Total for whom."[7] The Nobel Prize laureate wonders whether this skepticism toward the "great novel" (à la Honoré de Balzac) responds to a lack of literary ambition. Instead, he explains, recent generations of Latin American writers have withdrawn into a more intimate and private world, similar to Franz Kafka's writing, which they find more authentic. Indeed, as Alberto Fuguet and Sergio Gómez suggest, "the great theme of Latin American identity (who are we?) gave way to the theme of personal identity."[8] This new intimate approach perhaps explains that fact that, with a few exceptions, such as Bolaño's novels *Los detectives salvajes* (*The Savage Detectives,* 1998) and *2666* (2004), recent Latin American novels tend to be considerably shorter than those typically published by Boom authors. As Will H. Corral points out, "today the novelistic emphases are on concision, easy wit, fairly straight narrative flow, vernacular insights, a continuing discovery of new masters, and even bittersweet perspectives on emotions and moods" (12). In any case, Bolivian Liliana Colanzi has questioned this idea of ambition presented by Vargas Llosa: "But why that obsession with having the theme define how ambitious a work is? They also called Rubén Darío and the *Modernistas* afeminate because they talked about swans and kings. Perhaps the ambition may be to shake up sensitivity. The form is as political as the themes."[9] Equally rebelling against the only surviving forefather of the Boom, Peruvian Jennifer Thorndike argues that the intimate is political "because it investigates the structure of what we are and the labels imposed on us: woman, white, Peruvian... There are novels that are supposed to be dealing with the great themes, but do nothing more than following the official history of the great themes. Literature must always question things."[10] Likewise, Carlos Fonseca, born in Costa Rica and raised in Puerto Rico, wonders "whether ambition doesn't mean globalization: *2666* would be the global novel today because it is built not in the classic way, but through points of intensity that, like Ciudad Juárez, could seem peripheral."[11]

Vargas Llosa's reflection on the evolution of Latin American literature over the last three decades continues by pointing out that the admiration for Argentine master Jorge Luis Borges that characterized his generation continues today, but now one must also add the influence of Chilean author Roberto Bolaño. Furthermore, reflecting Latin American reality, the Latin American novel has become more urban. Vargas Llosa points out that in contrast with *indigenista* literature, which began during the 1930s in Peru with writers such as José María Arguedas and was commonly set in the countryside, nowadays peasants are drawn to large cities where they can often find better living standards. Likewise, feminist advances in the region have also been reflected in its literature, according to Vargas Llosa. It is telling, for example, that half of the twenty Latin American authors born in the 1980s invited to the Guadalajara's Feria Internacional del Libro (FIL) in 2016 were women (as are half of the writers chosen by the critics in this book). Yet persistent challenges remain, as reflected in the hundreds of femicides and disappearances in Ciudad Juárez, Mexico, famously portrayed in Bolaño's monumental *2666*. Chilean "ochentera" Paulina Flores, for example, has cited the widespread femicides in Latin America as one of her main concerns: "The indifference with which we see the assassination of women is worrysome."[12] This concern is also reflected in Argentine Selva Almada's chronicle collection *Chicas muertas* (*Dead Girls*, 2014).

Some of these changes pointed out by Vargas Llosa, including the increased preoccupation with the self and the tendency to be less politically involved or less openly Leftist, were already evident with the creation of the McOndo literary movement in 1996, which embraced popular culture (often mixing high culture with American pop culture), mass media, as well as urban and suburban life, thus presenting a more globalized vision of contemporary Latin America. Although the McOndo and Crack literary movements have sometimes been dismissed by critics as mere self-promotion or collective self-identification gimmicks or the typical Oedipal struggle against previous generations of writers, I still think it is worth revisiting their proclamations and manifestos, as they do echo an increasing change of paradigm in Latin American fiction.

Inspired by the success of their *Cuentos con Walkman* (*Short Stories with Walkman*, 1993), a Chilean short story anthology, Chilean writers Alberto Fuguet and Sergio Gómez decided to publish *McOndo* (1996) in Barcelona, an anthology of seventeen urban short stories by Latin American and Spanish men born after 1959. In the introduction, they embrace pop culture: "For us, the Chapulín Colorado, Ricky Martin, Selena, Julio Iglesias, and soap operas are as Latin American as candomblé and vallenato."[13] The anthology's title makes a pun with the names of the fast food chain McDonald's and Macintosh computers—symbols of globalization and Americanization, and its book cover already announced "There is no Magical Realism here, there is virtual reality."[14] The editors sought to counterbalance this mode of narration, which, in their view, exoticized, caricaturized, and essentialized Latin America, as well as what they saw as the tropicalized, rural, and backward vision of Latin America sometimes presented by Boom authors, as noticeable, for example, in the description of the fictional town of Macondo in Colombian Nobel Prize Laureate Gabriel García Márquez's masterpiece *Cien años de soledad* (*One Hundred Years of Solitude*, 1967) or in the "banana republics" depicted on the novels of the dictator. In Fuguet and Gómez's own words: "it is not possible to accept reductionist essentialisms, and believe that here everyone wears a sombrero and lives on trees."[15] Instead, the McOndo writers preferred more realistic narratives depicting urban life, globalization, consumerism, as well as the economic and class disparities in Latin America: "To sell a rural continent when, in reality, it is urban (in spite of the fact that its overpopulated cities are chaotic and do not work) seems an aberration to us, easy and immoral."[16] This urban turn has a predecessor in the Mexican literary movement La Onda, which, during the second half of the 1960s also rejected pastoral representations of Mexico and chose more realistic and urban representations of city life, popular culture, and modernization.[17] Their irreverent, urban literature was considered countercultural by some critics. The La Onda writers indirectly opposed PRI governmental politics and often resorted to a realistic, sometimes coarse language to challenge tradition by addressing taboo topics, including sexuality, drugs, rock and roll, and the Vietnam War.

McOndo writers (besides Fuguet and Gómez, the most prominent ones are Bolivian Edmundo Paz Soldán, Puerto Rican Giannina Braschi, Chilean Pía Barros, Cuban Pedro Juan Gutiérrez, Colombian Jorge Franco, and Chilean Hernán Rivera Letelier) also challenged the expectations that international publishers and critics had from Latin American writers: a magical realist mode, cultural self-exoticization, and the portrayal of regional economic underdevelopment. Instead, they protest: "Our country, McOndo, is bigger, overpopulated and full of pollution, with freeways, subway, cable tv, and slums. In McOndo there are McDonald's, Mac computers and condominiums, besides five-star hotels built with laundered money and gigantic shopping malls."[18]

The McOndo literary movement has often been associated with "La generación del *crack*" or The Crack Generation (Jorge Volpi, Ignacio Padilla, Eloy Urroz, Pedro Ángel Palou, and Ricardo Chávez Castañeda), which emerged in the Mexico City of the mid-1990s and published their *Manifiesto Crack* (*Crack Manifesto*; also in 1996 and one month before *McOndo*), along with five novels: Pedro Ángel Palou's *Memoria de los días*, Eloy Urroz's *Las Rémoras*, Ricardo Chávez Castañeda's *La conspiración idiota*,

Ignacio Padilla's *Si volviesen sus majestades*, and Jorge Volpi's *El temperamento melancólico*. This heterogeneous group of Mexican writers born around 1968 also advocated for realist literature away from the Magical Realist literary conventions that characterized the commercial writings of García Márquez's Post-Boom epigones, opting instead for a multiplicity of voices as well as complexity of plots and styles that challenged the active reader. In the late Ignacio Padilla's words, the Crack movement responds to "weariness from the fact that the great Latin American literature and the questionable Magical Realism may have become, for our literature, tragic magicism."[19] These young authors, most of whom had begun their careers in literary workshops, typically went away from Mexican settings and issues, opting instead for international geographical frameworks. As Padilla explains,

> dislocation in these Crack novels will not be, after all, but a remedy against a crazy and dislocated reality, the outcome of a world taken by mass media to an end of the century that, in terms of times and places, is shattered, broken as a result of an excess of ligaments. . . . What the Crack novels are looking for is managing to create stores whose chronotope, in Bakhtinian terms, is zero: the no place and no time, all the times and places, and none of them."[20]

Incidentally, this attempt to locate the plots in a no time and a no place has been pursued by Peruvian-Mexican author Mario Bellatin in *El jardín de la señora Murakami* (*Ms. Murakami's Garden*, 2000) and other works. Crack novels were also characterized by their pessimistic and, coinciding with the end of the century, even apocalyptic overtones, full of despair and broken ideals.

Regarding newer generations of writers (I am aware of the limited critical use of the concept of literary generations), some critics have talked about the Ochenteros, that is, those Latin American writers born in the 1980s, such as Mexicans Óscar Guillermo Solano, Ave Barrera, Pedro Acuña, and Joel Flores; Guatemalan Arnaldo Gálvez Suárez; Nicaraguan José Adiak Montoya; Costa Rican-Puerto Rican Carlos Fonseca; Cuban Carlos Manuel Álvarez; Venezuelan Enza García Arreaza; Peruvian Jennifer Thorndike; Bolivian Liliana

Colanzi; Ecuadorian Marcela Rivanedeira; Chileans Paulina Flores, Camila Gutiérrez Berner, and Francisco Ovando; Brazilians Carol Bensimon and Carol Rodrigues; Uruguayan Damián González Bertolino; and Argentines Mauro Libertella and Camila Fabbri, all of them invited to Guadalajara's Feria Internacional del Libro in 2016.

Among the many topics one can read in their fiction, some of the most prominent ones are marginality, violence and crime (as evident in Joel Flores's novel *Nunca más su nombre* [*Never again her name*]), apocalyptic visions (Francisco Ovando's *Acerca de Suárez* [*About Suárez*]), the effects of neoliberalism, as well as stories dealing with borders and migration, such as those by Yuri Herrera. Other commonalities are the hybridization of literary genres and their tendency to look beyond the national, opting instead for transnational worldviews. Other topics that are also recurrent are the persistence of memory, the recollection of Jewish family histories and of life under dictatorship (also evident in the works of authors born in the 1970s, such as Peruvian Santiago Rocagliolo's 2014 *La pena máxima* [*The Maximum Penalty*] and Mexican Patricio Pron's 2014 *Nosotros caminamos en sueños* [*We Walk in Dreams*]). Along these lines, mass culture is no longer a theme, according to Mexican Ave Barrera, but part of their education. Regarding the theme of violence, the Peruvian Jennifer Thorndike ponders: "I don't know if it comes from video games and being exposed to violence, but ours is a very explicit and crude literature. Things are intense, violent, as if there were a need to constantly strike the reader."[21]

A commonality for many of these writers is that, even though it is still considered prestigious to be published by a large Spanish publishing house, many have opted instead for submitting their book manuscripts to independent Latin American small presses, many of which are flourishing thanks to the new editing, publishing, and commercialization technologies. According to Amir Valle, in Latin America "more than 60 percent of literary works are published by these independent publishers, who provide more accessible prices."[22] New open-access platforms have also contributed to the wider dissemination of new Latin American literary works. After all, as Argentine born in Mexico Mauro Libertella claims, "Our parents had the Cuban Revolution; we, the digital revolution. . . . The Internet arrived to us when we were fifteen years old and left our analogical childhood encapsuled, that's why we write about it with a certain nostalgia."[23] This development has perhaps influenced the blurring of lines between high and popular culture, as many of these writers express their love for Faulkner or Bolaño, as well as for video games.

Overall, the vibrant plurality of Latin American literature is today unquestionable. And as happened with Crack authors, younger generations of multifaceted writers are also opting for international themes and geographical frameworks beyond their native countries. Part of the reason for this transnational outlook—beyond the nation and the so-called "national literatures" that, according to Bolaño, are inexistent—is that many of them do not live in the country where they were born. From their particular speaking positions in the Global South or the countries where they emigrated, these writers react in their own personal ways to issues often related to today's globalization and neoliberalism, the political philosophy often associated with it. But, no longer overwhelmed by censorship, exile, or political oppression, like their predecessors, they often do so by focusing on the personal, on quotidian life, rather than engaging in total novels responding to ethical goals. A recently increased interest in the translation into English of young Latin American authors, such as the Chilean Alejandro Zambra among many others, promises a wider dissemination of these writers' works worldwide. Likewise, the abundance of small presses all over Latin America, despite their challenges with distribution, has also opened the door for the appearance of new voices. And as Melissa Fitch explains in her chapter, new media such as Twitter, Tumblr, and blogs provide wider readerships and experimental venues for authors willing to take risks. The future indeed looks bright for many of these authors.

Notes

1. "Menos comprometidas y más ensimismadas" (Rodríguez Marcos "Una literatura" n.p.).

2. Among many others, some of the Post-Boom writers listed by Donald L. Shaw are the Chileans Antonio Skármeta, Isabel Allende, and Ariel Dorfman; the Mexicans Elena Poniatowska, José Agustín, Gustavo Sainz, José Emilio Pacheco, and Jorge Aguilar Mora; the Puerto Rican Luis Rafael Sánchez; the Argentines Mempo Giardinelli, Luisa Valenzuela, Ricardo Piglia, Manuel Puig, Juan José Saer, and Eduardo Gudiño Kiefer; the Cubans Reinaldo Arenas and Miguel Barnet; the Colombian Óscar Collazos and Rafael Humberto Moreno Durán; the Nicaraguan Sergio Ramírez (12).

3. "Una mezcla de fantasía y autobiografía en la que el autor se convierte en personaje" (Rodríguez Marcos "Una literatura" n.p.).

4. "'La verdad' es siempre resbaladiza, y la objetividad inevitablemente subjetiva. En este género, la lógica, la coherencia y la belleza de un relato pasan antes que la corrección política, pudor o la lealtad familiar" ("Con A" n.p.).

5. "Es posible que el poder corrupto y violento haya pasado del dictador al narco" (Rodríguez Marcos "Una literatura" n.p.).

6. Many other *narcoliteratura* authors are the following: the also Mexican Luis Humberto Crosthwaite's *Estrella de la calle sexta* (2000), *Idos de la mente* (2001), *Instrucciones para cruzar la frontera* (2003), and *Tijuana: Crimen y olvido* (2010); Daniel Sada's *El lenguaje del juego* (2012); Alejandro Páez Varela's *Corazón de Kaláshnikov* (2009), *El reino de las moscas* (2012), and *Música para perros* (2013); Orfa Alarcón's *Perra brava* (2010) and *Bitch Doll* (2013); Yuri Herrera's *Trabajos del reino* (2004); Gabriel Trujillo Muñoz's *Mezquite Road* (1999); Jesús Alvarado's *Bajo el disfraz* (2003), Pablo Serrano's *Diario de un narcotraficante* (1967); Víctor Hugo Rascón Banda's *Contrabando* (2008), *Volver a Santa Rosa* (1996), *Los ilegales* (1979), *El baile de los montañeses* (1982), *Voces en el umbral* (1983), *Teatro del delito: La fiera del Ajusco, Máscara contra cabellera, Manos arriba* (1985), *Tina Modotti y otras obras de teatro* (1986), *Guerrero Negro y Cierren las puertas* (1988), *La daga, más teatro joven en México* (1988), *La banca. Doce a las doce* (1989), *Armas blancas* (trilogía: *El abrecartas, La navaja* y *La daga*) (1990), *Playa azul* (1991), *Cierren las puertas* (1992), *Sabor de engaño* (1992), *Escenario del crimen, Guerrero negro* y *Fugitivo* (1999), *Los ejecutivos* (2003), and *Creencias e increencias* (2006); Juan Pablo Villalobos's *Fiesta en la madriguera* (2010); Eduardo Antonio Parra's *Parábolas del silencio* (2006), *Nostalgia*

de la sombra (2002), *Nadie los vio salir* (2001), and *Tierra de nadie* (1999); Heriberto Yépez's *A.B.U.R.T.O.* (2005), *Al otro lado* (2008), and *Made in Tijuana* (2006); Óscar de la Borbolla's *La vida de un muerto* (1998); Sergio González Rodríguez's *El hombre sin cabeza* (2009), *Huesos en el desierto* (2006), and *Campo de Guerra* (2014); and Bernardo Fernández's *Tiempo de alacranes* (2005) and *Narcocuentos* (2014); Gerardo Cornejo's *Juan Justino Judicial* (1996); Homero Aridjis's *La santa muerte* (2003), *Sicarios* (2007), and *La zona del silencio* (2002).

7. In Colombia, where the term "Novela del sicariato" (Hitman Novel) is normally preferred, many other narcoliteratura works, often dealing with the picaresque-like adventures of sicarios (hitmen or hired assassins), have been published and sometimes turned into films and television series, including Fernando Vallejo's *La virgen de los sicarios* (1994), Gustavo Bolívar Moreno's *Sin tetas no hay paraíso* (2007) and *El Capo* (2009); Laura Restrepo's *El ángel descuidado* (1997), *Delirio* (2004), and *Leopardo de sol* (1993); Jorge Franco Ramos's *Mala noche* (1997), *Rosario Tijeras* (1999), *Paraíso Travel* (2001), *Melodrama* (2006), *Santa suerte* (2010), and *El mundo de afuera* (2014); and Arturo Alape's *Bogotazo: Memoria del olvido* (1983), *El Bogotazo: La paz, la violencia. Testigos de excepción* (1985), *Ciudad Bolívar. La hoguera de las ilusiones* (1995), and *Sangre ajena* (2004).

8. The Chilean Eduardo Pérez Arroyo has also published *El lugar donde los pájaros lloran* (2015) and the Puerto Rican Gean Carlo Villegas, *Osario de vivos* (2012) and *Cuentos post retro* (2009).

9. "Ya nadie escribe novelas, o bien: ya nadie escribe novelas totales. Pero, me pregunto, ¿novelas para quién?, ¿totales para quién?" (n.p.).

10. "El gran tema de la identidad latinoamericana (¿quienes somos?) pareció dejar paso al tema de la identidad personal (¿quién soy?)" (n.p.).

11. "Pero ¿por qué esa obsesión de que sea el tema el que define la ambición de una obra? También a Rubén Darío y a los modernistas los llamaron afeminados por hablar de cisnes y reyes. Tal vez la ambición sea revolucionar la sensibilidad. La forma es tan política como los temas" (Rodríguez Marcos "Ochenteros" n.p.).

12. "Porque investiga en la estructura de lo que somos y de las etiquetas que se nos vienen encima: mujer, blanca, peruana... Hay novelas que

creen tratar los grandes temas y no hacen más que seguir la historia oficial de los grandes temas. La literatura debe cuestionar siempre" (Rodríguez Marcos "Ochenteros" n.p.).

13. "Si ambición no significa hoy globalización: "*2666* sería la novela global de estos tiempos porque se construye no a la manera clásica sino mediante puntos de intensidad que, como Ciudad Juárez, podrían parecer periféricos" (Rodríguez Marcos "Ochenteros" n.p.).

14. "Es preocupante la indiferencia con la que vemos asesinar a las mujeres" (Rodríguez Marcos "Ochenteros" n.p.).

15. "Para nosotros, el Chapulín Colorado, Ricky Martin, Selena, Julio Iglesias y las telenovelas (o culebrones) son tan latinoamericanas como el candombe o el vallenato" (n.p.).

16. "Aquí no hay realismo mágico, hay realismo virtual."

17. "No es posible aceptar los esencialismos reduccionistas, y creer que aquií todo el mundo anda con sombrero y vive en árboles" (n.p.).

18. "Vender un continente rural cuando, la verdad de las cosas, es urbano (más allá que sus sobrepobladas ciudades son un caos y no funcionen) nos parece aberrante, cómodo e inmoral" (n.p.).

19. Among the members of La Onda are the following authors: José Agustín, Gustavo Sainz, Parménides García Saldaña, René Aivlés Fabila, Federico Arana, Héctor Manjarrez, Hugo Hiriart, Margarita Dalto, and Armando Ramírez.

20. "Nuestro país McOndo es más grande, sobrepoblado y lleno de contaminación, con autopistas, metro, tv-cable y barriadas. En McOndo hay McDonald's, computadores Mac y condominios, amén de hoteles cinco estrellas construidos con dinero lavado y malls gigantescos" (n.p).

21. "Cansancio de que la gran literatura latinoamericana y el dudoso realismo mágico se hayan convertido, para nuestras letras, en magiquismo trágico" (n.p.).

22. "La dislocación en estas novelas del Crack no será a fin de cuentas sino remedo de una realidad alocada y dislocada, producto de un mundo cuya massmediatización lo lleva a un fin de siglo trunco en tiempos y lugares, roto por exceso de ligamentos . . . lo que buscan las novelas del Crack es lograr historias cuyo cronotopo, en términos bajtinianos, sea cero: el no lugar y el no tiempo, todos los tiempos y lugares y ninguno" (n.p.).

23. "No sé si procede de los videojuegos y de la exposición a la violencia, pero la nuestra es una literatura muy explícita, muy cruda. Las cosas son intensas, violentas, como si hubiera una necesidad de golpear al lector todo el rato" (Rodríguez Marcos "Ochenteros" n.p.).

24. "En América Latina, por ejemplo, más del 60 por ciento de las obras literarias que se publican, son editadas por estos sellos independientes, que venden a precios más accesibles" (n.p.).

25. "Nuestros padres tuvieron la revolución cubana; nosotros, la revolución digital. . . . "Internet nos llegó con 15 años y dejó encapsulada nuestra infancia analógica, por eso escribimos de ella con cierta nostalgia" (Rodríguez Marcos "Ochenteros" n.p.).

Works Cited

"Con A de América, con B de... De afrodescendiente a violencia. 30 autores latinoamericanos definen el mapa de la literatura de un continente diverso y mestizo." *El País*.www.elpais.com/cultura/2016/11/25/babelia/1480084093_844089.html?rel=mas Accessed 26 Nov. 26, 2016.

Corral, Will H., Juan A. de Castro, and Nicholas Birns. *The Contemporary Spanish-American Novel. Bolaño and After*. Bloomsbury, 2013.

Franco, Jean. *The Decline and Fall of the Lettered City: Latin America in the Cold War*. Cambridge, Massachusetts: Harvard University Press, 2009. Print.

Fuguet, Alberto, and Sergio Gómez, editors. *Cuentos con Walkman*. Editorial Planeta, 1993.

_____. *McOndo*. Grijalbo Mondadori, 1996.

Padilla, Ignacio. "Manifiesto del Crack." Confabulario. *El Universal*. Web. 26 Sept. 2017. http://confabulario.eluniversal.com.mx/manifiesto-del-crack-1996/

Rodríguez Marcos, Javier. "Ochenteros: nueva sensibilidad para la gran novela." *El País*, Dec. 3, 2016. www.elpais.com/cultura/2016/12/03/actualidad/1480787848_355398.html. Accessed 1 Aug. 1, 2017.

Rodríguez Marcos, Javier. "Una literatura despolitizada." *El País*, Nov. 26, 2016. www.elpais.com/cultura/2016/11/24/babelia/1480014723_069953.html. Accessed Nov. 26, 2016.

Sánchez Díez, María. "Beyond Bolaño: These are the Latin American authors you should be reading this summer." *Quartz* 28 June 2015.

Web 26 Sept. 2017. https://qz.com/430787/these-are-the-latin-american-authors-you-should-be-reading-this-summer/

Shaw, Donald L. "The Post-Boom in Spanish American Fiction." *Studies in 20th & 21st Century Literature* Article 3 19.1 (1995): 1-17. 1 Jan. 1995. Web. 26 Sept. 2017 http://newprairiepress.org/cgi/viewcontent.cgi?article=1359&context=sttcl

Valle, Amir. ¿Nuevo boom de las letras latinoamericanas? *DW Cultura* 9 Sept 2014. Web. 26 Sept. 2017 http://www.dw.com/es/nuevo-boom-de-las-letras-latinoamericanas/a-17911051

CRITICAL
CONTEXTS

Latin American Literature and New Technology

Melissa Fitch

Timeline

1969: Creation of ARPANET at UCLA
1971: First email sent
1971: Gutenberg Project launched
1982: First use of the term Internet (replaced ARPANET)
1991: World Wide Web goes public
Mid 1990s: First digital literature created
1996: Juan B. Gutiérrez first creates *El Primer Vuelvo de los Hermanos Wright* in Colombia.
1998: Google created
1999: Biblioteca Virtual Miguel de Cervantes launched
2004: Facebook launched
2005: YouTube launched
2006: Twitter launched
2017: Facebook announces 2,01 billion users in the world each month

> Contemporary global society stands at a crossroads with regard to the book and the literary culture it engenders. At once, we face an increasing disappearance of the physical book and other print media, while different forms of writing convulse and populate our daily interactions. Indeed, it is difficult to fathom the rapid flows of textual information channeled through the Internet at any second of any given day, as our personal interactions become evermore textualized in instant messaging formats and in social media platforms. (Bush and Gentic, *Technology*)

To say that new technology has changed the way that we understand not just literary genres but also the notions of text, authorship, and questions related to readership over the last twenty years is a vast understatement. It is, some say, a love-and-hate relationship between the literary world and technology. While many decry the "death of the book" (which harkens back to Roland Barthes's seminal 1967 essay "Death of the Author"), it was beyond the scope of our imagination at the time of his essay to think that the book, in and of itself, as a material object, could ever die. And yet that death, as Mark Twain once famously said (referring to a report of his own death), has been "greatly exaggerated." The death is not, in fact, that of reading. On the contrary, one could argue that we are living in a veritable golden age with regard to the wealth of material available instantly to read and comment upon as well as new possibilities for literary creation. It is, rather, the aesthetic experience of the material object itself that is on a deathwatch. It is the smell of the paper, the notes in the margins, the tactile experience of reading, the beauty of books themselves, sitting on shelves and desks in our homes and offices, that are at risk.

Literary content, however, is not only surviving, it is thriving. In Latin America this is no exception. Authors and readers are now in continual conversation. Books come to life as never before, and are often the result of collaborations among myriad authors. Literary supplements historically found exclusively in print are now found online and discussion flows freely among readers. Literary websites, goodreads.com, YouTube channels, and Facebook pages allow individuals around the world to debate online and in real time what they are reading, or for that matter to "attend" events that are live-streamed, where they can interact with authors and other readers. Much like in the way that both radio and television have somewhat surprisingly thrived as a result of technological changes (after both had also suffered dire "the death of...." predictions), there has never been, perhaps, a better time for reading than now.

Digital literature may be divided into those texts that were originally in print form and then became digitized, and those that were, in essence, born into the digital realm, starting in the mid to late 1990s. One of the most positive aspects of the former is that books that were written and published many years ago and passed into relative obscurity shortly thereafter are now getting a digitized second life, made widely available for the very first time to vast new audiences. The Gutenberg Project, initiated in 1971, has been putting into electronic format books that have passed into the public domain; thus the rich literary history of the world is now accessible online and for free (although, obviously, one has to have access to a system that enables one to go online, and the books digitized, to date, have been primarily in English).

A second dimension to this renewed interest in "old" literature is a result of social media and online communities based around shared affinities. When a member of a community "shares" or "likes" a book or essay with their own social network or reviews it on a public site, it can lead to a surge in interest, a phenomenon referred to as "The Long Tail" in the now classic 2004 article by Chris Anderson in *Wired* magazine. In the essay, he traced the impact of amazon.com reader recommendations on sales. In other words, in some ways the much-lamented "death" of the book has instead led to its resurrection.

These positive aspects notwithstanding, it is a challenge to even classify digital literature beyond the two areas listed above, essentially a "before and after" demarcation, those created before the web versus those created directly on the web. There are many different names for this new form of literature and for new genres comprised within it, many of which often describe the same thing or have minor variations and concomitant variants in Spanish and Portuguese. For the sake of simplification, I have elected to use the term *digital literature* to mark the distinction with print-based literature, which is the focus of this brief introduction to the topic. This essay is primarily focused on web content created after the mid 1990s. In many cases the texts mentioned in this introduction that were created online by Latin American authors later took either a printed form, YouTube videos, or even feature-length films (or all three). Although there are multiple names, and indeed, variations, of this second form of "native-born" digital literature, there is one question that must be addressed: is this new form of literary creation in Latin America really all that new? Perhaps surprisingly, the answer is no.

Historical Antecedents

The first digital literature in Latin America emerged toward the end of the 1990s and it has increased markedly in popularity in subsequent years, with a huge surge in interest and availability by the mid 2000s after the creation of Twitter and Facebook, which was also buoyed by the decrease in cost for mobile phones, tablets, and laptops. Digital literature has become popular not just with younger generations of writers, as one might expect, but also with mainstream canonical writers who typically still publish their work in print media (newspapers, magazines, and books). Brazilian author Paulo Coelho is one such example. Digital literature created online can be divided between that which allows readers to modify or extend the work, and one that only allows the readers to read (but still post comments and otherwise engage with others). In most digital novels, the reader has to make a series of decisions that will change the story as it progresses. In essence, reading a digital novel becomes much like a video game. It is a labyrinth that delivers a different story depending on who is reading. The reader decides which hyperlink to pursue, based on his or her own interests.

For fans of Latin American literature, this sounds very similar to Argentine writer Jorge Luis Borges's 1941 story "El jardín de los senderos que se bifurcan" ("The Garden of Forking Paths"), in which there are different paths to pursue, offering endless possibilities. It is also reminiscent of Argentine author Julio Cortázar's novel *Rayuela* (*Hopscotch*), published in 1963, long before the advent of the Internet. Instead of selecting one path with which to read the novel, Cortázar offers several alternative paths as well. With the advent of digital literature, the reader is able to pursue a dizzying number of variants all of which will transform the story, making it in many cases a multisensorial and individualized experience.

Cortázar also seemed to anticipate the nature of the blog itself when he wrote, with the help of artist José Silva, *La vuelta al día en ochenta mundos* (*Around the Day in 80 Worlds*, 1967), the title a play on the famous *Around the World in 80 Days* (1873) by French author Jules Verne (1828-1905). The book is a collection of illustrations, newspaper clippings, drawings, photographs, poems, essays, and fragments of news, much like the assortment of disparate elements one might find in a personal blog today.

One of the most popular forms of literature found online has often been called *twitterature*, literature created within the 160 characters permitted for each tweet. And yet, this form of writing had a longstanding tradition in Latin American literature. Brazil, in particular, has a rich history of flash fiction, ministories or *microcontos* in Portuguese (also called *minicontos*, *nanocontos*, *relatos hiperbreves*), that predates Twitter, many written by famed writer Dalton Trevison (1925-). Mexico also has a rich history of the genre. But perhaps the most famous author of this literary form in Latin America was Guatemalan Augusto Monterroso (1921-2003), whose "Cuando despertó, el dinosauro todavía estaba allí" ("When he awoke, the dinosaur was still there," 1969) *microrrelato* or *minicuento* is well known.

While this type of literature has existed in the Spanish- and Portuguese-speaking regions of Latin America for much of the last century, the novelty is that new technology has enabled it to be created and consumed by many more individuals online. New technology has also offered the capacity to push these genres to new heights of creativity, to make them available on a much wider scale, and in far greater complexity, and to open up the challenge to embark on the pursuit of literary creation to all who have online access, instead of leaving it to be exclusively the domain of established authors in the printed realm.

In the case of microstories, the most important dimension is their evocative power. There is a particular artistry that is on display by the author. He or she must know the cultural referents of the audience, which words will enable the reader to supply the missing information with his or her own imagination. The reader must be able to envision the story untold. Precision is required, obviously, but also what is necessary on the part of the author is the use of words that will stimulate the curiosity of the reader.

Mexican writer Alberto Chimal (1970) explains that it is not just the writing that has changed because of new technology, but also the way that readers read. He stated: "It is a fragmentary kind of reading, looser, more disperse. This isn't really a good time for deep reading or anything that requires concentration, as was the case for the great novels of the nineteenth century. This type of literature continues to be written, we have best sellers that are thousands of pages long . . . but new generations are being formed that are different." (n.p.)[1] In addition to being a writer himself, Chimal is also a leading expert on digital writing and the Internet in Mexico. He won the 2002 Premio Nacional de Cuento San Luis Potosí given by the Instituto Nacional de Bellas Artes, was a finalist for the Premio Internacional de Novela Rómulo Gallegos and the winner of the Premio de Narrativa Colima in 2014. He is the author of numerous collections of short stories and plays. He has two novels that were published as a result of multiple postings of microfictions over time on Twitter, *83 novelas* (*83 Novels*, 2011) and *El viajero en el tiempo (The Traveler in Time)*. *83 novelas* was immediately made available free online via Kindle or pdf and just 150 printed versions were made, not meant to be sold, but rather for the author to distribute himself. According to CNN in Spanish, Chimal is considered one of the most creative and energetic authors in his country today. In addition to being active on Twitter, he maintains a blog and the Spanish-language literary website *Las historias* (las historias.com.mx).

In terms of the intellectual lineage and antecedents related to the role of digital technology in Latin America, Matthew Bush and Tania Gentic point out that

> the idea of digital technology as tied to progress and futurity is a continuation of discourses of modernity that circulated throughout the late nineteenth and early twentieth centuries in Latin America relating to industrialization, economic development, and foreign investment. Conceptualizing the Internet, video games, Microsoft Office, or other technologies as new and therefore capable of changing society returns to a long archive of techno determinism that views industrial innovation as somehow linked to an idealized future. (10)

Thus, these seemingly brand new developments in Latin American intellectual and creative forms are in many cases simply a new phase of what has come before, a new twist in the story, but not a new story.

Entering Latin American Literary World(s)

The field of Digital Humanities has exploded recently, and editorial houses are also beginning to publish books and journals directly online. The number of websites related to digital literature in the Spanish- and Portuguese-speaking worlds today is extensive and easily found online. Some sites are longstanding and contain a wide assortment of features, including literary criticism, works by new authors, film clips, debates, and interviews with authors. Probably the best known is the Biblioteca Virtual Miguel de Cervantes, a digital library that started in 1999. A website that serves as a clearinghouse for Latin American literature and culture online is http://www.clubcultura.com/suscriptores/ok.php, the cultural portal of the FNAC (Fondo Nacional de Arte y Cultura), in which many writers have links to their work. ClubCultura began in 2005 and Bolivian author Edmundo Paz Soldán (1967-) wrote the first entry. There are numerous other websites dedicated to the diffusion of the work of young authors in the Spanish-speaking world, including *Puntos de Partida, Círculo de Poesía, HermanoCerdo, Destiempos, La otra revista, Periódico La Manzana, Los Nóveles,* and *Palabras Malditas.* In many cases, as mentioned above, famous canonical authors from Latin America who also maintain websites are electing to have special sections devoted to promoting new authors from the region. There is also a social media platform devoted to Latin American writers and readers where they are able to read, collaborate, and share stories, as well as learn of the latest happenings the literary realm, such as *Wattpad,* www.wattpad.com/tags/latinoamericana._

Blogs and the *Blogueros*

Today Latin American authors will often publish their work online first on their own blog. This has provided them also with a unique way to gauge the popularity of their work with their fans and to engage in conversations related to their work, something previously only possible at literary events. Some of the most popular authors who work in both online and print forms in Latin America include Peruvian Iván Thays (*El viaje interior, La disciplina de la variedad*), Argentine Eduardo Berti (*Todos los funes, Agua*), Venezuelan Slavko Zupcic (*Barbie, Giuliana Labolita: El caso de Pepe Toledo*), and Puerto Rican Yolanda Arroyo Pizarro (*Ojos de luna, Los documentados, Transmutadxs*). Still others present their work exclusively online, such as Alejandro Zambra (Chile), César Aira (Argentina), and Belén Gaché (Argentina-España). There are also numerous Facebook pages devoted to specific authors where readers can engage the texts and often interact with the authors themselves. In the XVIII Feria International del Libro en Bogotá, Colombia, there were numerous stalls devoted not only to bloggers but also booktubers (web personalities who focus their programs on literature).

Among the bloggers who have won some of the most important literary prizes in Latin America and Spain, there is Andrés Neumann (Argentina, 1977-), who won Spain's Premio Alfaguara de Novela in 2009, one of the country's most prestigious awards, for his novel *El viajero del siglo* (*The Traveler of the Century*). From Colombia, Daniel Ferreira (1981-), received the Premio Clarin de la Novela in Argentina in 2014 for his novel *Rebelión de los oficios inútiles* (*The Rebellion of Useless Trades*, 2014) the first non-Argentine writer to win the distinction. Prior to that, he had received an award for Mejor Blog de Difusión de la Cultura en Español in 2014 among almost 1,000 competitors, given by the Instituto Cervantes in Spain.

In Spanish-speaking Latin America, among the many cases of best-selling novels that began as blogs we have *Abzurdah* (*Absurd*, 2006) by the Argentine author Cielo Latini (1984-), and *Diario de una mujer gorda* (*Diary of a Fat Woman*, 2006) by an Argentine residing in Spain, Hernán Casciari (1971-). The book *Buena leche* (*Good Temper*, 2006), written by Lola Copacabana (Inés Gallo de Urioste) also began as a blog).

There is yet another new category to mention here related to technology and literature, and that is of famous Latin American star videobloggers (or *vloggers*) of YouTube, most of whom publish short weekly videos, often humorous, and who later turned their vlogs into books that became bestsellers, such as werevertumorro (Gabriel Montiel, 1989-) and yuya (Mariand Castrejón Castañeda, 1993-), both Mexicans, and holasoygermán from Chilean Germán Garmendia (1990-). These books are not exactly literary fare, but rather just a different format of the material seen and known widely from the shows. What must be underscored, however, is that these programs, usually aimed at a teenage audience, have millions of views online and from every corner of the Spanish- and Portuguese-speaking world, far beyond any sort of reach that a print publication might have.

Transformations in the literature of Spanish- and Portuguese-speaking Latin America has been revolutionary. For the purposes of this introduction to the topic of Latin American literature and new technology, I will now turn to a critical overview of scholarship connected to the theme and after that, I will offer a brief discussion of three authors whose literary work is principally found online. These are Colombian Juan Gutiérrez (1973-), Argentine Cielo Latini (1984-) and Brazilian Daniel Galera (1979-).

Theoretical Approaches to Understanding Latin American Literature and New Technology

Scholarship on literature has historically rested on something being fixed in time, space, and material form. This is what enabled literary scholars to offer critiques. And yet, because of new technology, this is no longer self-evident. As a result of the web, there are narratives that are constantly re-elaborated in which previous versions are no longer available. In some cases, the online narrative is a collective and ongoing creation, as readers online supply their own additions to texts. There is a blurring of lines between readers and authors, producers and consumers, and each subsequent modification or addition is in some way often a response to previous ones. There is a convergence of artistic and media forms online as well, making it difficult to isolate and separate a particular genre. This has presented literary scholars with an enormous challenge: how to intellectually approach such dramatic transformations when the lines between author and reader, producer and consumer have become blurred, and when the cultural manifestation analyzed is in a state of near constant change, or worse, it could simply disappear overnight.

In this section, we seek to underscore that it is not only authors and readers who are engaged in this new revitalized online conversation, but also scholars who work in the field of Latin American literature who are grappling with the frustrations as well as exciting possibilities that digital literature presents. More and more scholars who began their careers in the area of traditional print literature are now crossing over to analyzing literature created online. Doctoral students working the area of Latin American literature are writing dissertations on bloggers, websites, and different forms of digital literature. As these scholars enter the field in greater numbers, they will be changing the nature of what is taught in the classroom.

Within Latin America, writers such as Beatriz Sarlo have been examining the role of technology in society since the 1990s with *La imaginación técnica: Sueños modernos de la cultura argentina* (*The Technical Imagination: Modern Dreams of Argentine Culture*, 1992) and *Escenas de la vida posmoderna* (*Scenes of Postmodern Life*, 1994). In her work, there is a skepticism regarding the neoliberal mass-mediatized society (well founded, it turns out). A pioneering text in the field published in the United States was Jerry Hoeg's *Science, Technology and Latin American Narrative in the Twentieth Century and Beyond* (2000), in which the author sought to evaluate the impact of science and technology on Latin American literature because it was something that he noticed had been previously ignored by literary scholars. The book is not focused on Internet culture, but it points to a general opening of the field of literary scholarship related to the theme of technology. One year later, in 2001, Edmundo Paz Soldán and Debra Castillo edited *Latin American Literature and Mass Media*, which did, in fact, begin to focus the conversation on the transformations in the field, including Castillo's Chapter 14, titled "Lack of Materiality in Latin American Media Theory", and Carlos Jauregui's "Writing Communities on the Internet: Textual Authority and Territorialization," both dealing with recently formed (at the time) online literary communities. The editors underscore how new generations of writers are utilizing technology to "challenge a Latin

American narrative imaginary" (16). And yet there was no way for the authors to know just how dramatically literature would change within a few short years of the publication of their book with the creation of Facebook (2004) and Twitter (2006). In terms of other scholarship, Josefina Ludmer and Luz Horne, in their respective works, argue that new technology is changing the perception of reality and discuss how it is represented in contemporary society, something that is understood as a given today. In turn, Claire Taylor and Thea Pitman, in *Latin American Identity in Online Cultural Production*, make it clear that the Internet has transformed markedly the ways in which one conceptualizes Latin America, becoming, in some ways, "post regional" (21). According to Martín-Barbero, media creates a form of global citizenship in which people of different countries interact with one another based on shared interests as opposed to nation, religion, political affiliations, or other groups. This is, in fact, part of the premise of Barry Wellman and Lee Raine's *Networked: The New Social Operating System* (2012).

Perhaps the most comprehensive book related to Latin American digital literature that has emerged is the *Technology, Literature, and Digital Culture in Latin America: Mediated Sensibilities in a Globalized Era* (2015), edited by Matthew Bush and Tania Gentic. It is focused on videogames, blogs, and electronic literature, as well as on social networking sites. The central question that all essays seek to answer is how the global networked subject has affected political and cultural concerns. As the editors put it in their Introduction,

[we] focus on the ways in which an imagined concept of a networked subject penetrates both the digital platforms through which new media circulate, and the contemporary literatures that engage with technology in their narratives. . . . It rests on some central concepts: 1) people and communities have changes as a result of technological advances; 2) subjects are more connected—to each other and to the public sphere—than they were before, and this connection is mediated through texts and visual images; 3) subjects living in the digital era move and change "faster" than in previous eras; and 4) as subjects become more wired to each other through these networks, affective relationships are replaced by a data-driven subjectivity. (2)

The editors also sought to call into question one of the biggest "lies" of new technology: that somehow it has created an even playing field among people in different countries (or within them). It has not. New technology requires knowledge, time, and access. But who has access to the systems needed to read or produce digital literature? The answer is, generally speaking, those who have the most money. We cannot escape that fact, and as a result the digital divide looms large. Beyond that, operating systems change and are updated regularly, and one must have the capital to upgrade with them in order to continue to have access. The networked subject is not uniformly the same across countries of Latin America or within them.

Another problematic aspect that the editors highlight in the Introduction is that it is a common practice among scholars to view the Internet in one of two ways: either as a space of free labor and thus exploitative, or as a space of resistance from global capitalism. Carolina Gainza argues exactly that in 2017, stating that online "social relationships and networks of cooperation among different people can pose a threat to mechanisms of control used by informational capitalism" (7). Bush and Gentic argue that such formulations are problematic because they do not take into account the role of pleasure or affect in the equation. Use of the Internet often stems from desire as opposed to coercion.

The Internet is, ultimately, the convergence of any number of different factors, used for a wide range of reasons, and involves all sorts of exchanges, and types of media, in multiple spheres, across multiple platforms, which each individual cobbles into his or her own personal mythology to add meaning to daily life, as Henry Jenkins makes clear in his *Convergence Culture: Where Old and New Media Collide*. Again, this is what makes it a particularly daunting topic to engage as a scholar.

Bush and Tantic's objections notwithstanding, Gainza makes some very important points that cannot be easily discounted or dismissed. She states that because digital texts are produced collectively, "the result of a collective intelligence, a group composed of writers, designers, computer programmers, software specialists, plastic artists, photographers, and other creative minds" (3), no individual can take all of the credit, it belongs to all, thus in many ways it subverts the cult of individualism that capitalism is reliant upon. She situates her discussion about collaboration, appropriation, and property directly into the context of the Latin American Cultural Studies tradition: "Technologies are being used as platforms of creation, a process in which writing and politics become connected in the formation of spaces for subverting the imposed forms of creation of, as Ángel Rama called it, the *lettered city*. The resignification of technologies in the context of Latin American digital literature relates to the development of actions of resistance and construction of identity (5). For Gainza, the notions of the *author* in any traditional sense are subverted, as are those related to intellectual property. In this sense, it is connected to the larger movement of Creative Commons or Free Culture or, as Lawrence Lessig famously said, "all culture is remix."

What all of the books and essays related specifically to Latin America and digital literature seem to share is the overriding belief that, in the words of Bush and Gentic, "Latin American literature embraces an increasingly mediatized social milieu and adapts the mechanisms of a visually dominant media culture" (14). Everyone is in agreement on this point, but the other debates loom large on the horizon among Latin Americanists.

Latin American Digital "Native" Authors: Three Examples

Juan B. Gutiérrez (Colombia, 1974-) was a pioneer. In 1997 he published his *El primer vuelo de los hermanos Wright* (*The First Flight of the Wright Brothers*), considered the very first digital novel in the Spanish-speaking world. He also wrote *Condiciones extremas* (Extreme Conditions, 1998), while his colleague Jaime Alejandro Rodríguez wrote another two digital novels, *Gabriella infinita* (*Infinite Gabriella*, 2002) and *Golpe de gracia* (*Coup de Grace*, 2005). Taken together, these four texts signal the start of digital literature in Latin America.

Gutiérrez, a mathematician at the University of Georgia, has worked with digital narratives since the mid 1990s when he was a student in Colombia. He is a writer who bridges the distance between the humanities and the sciences, having been trained in both areas. Thematically, his electronic texts are a reflection of many things happening not only in his native country but also in other parts of Latin America. In 1996, the Ministry of Culture in Colombia gave him a grant to embark on his digital literary project. At the time, he was devoting himself to print media as much as to digital media, working in multiple capacities. The first version (it would eventually have three) came out in 1996, *El primer vuelo de los hermanos Wright*. What made it distinctively Latin American was his focus on the "almost eternal vices of Latin America" (Gutiérrez 2005). At the same time, it is a loving portrayal of small town life in Colombia, very much an homage, in terms of the detailed descriptions of the town of Villapintada's inhabitants, to the country's Nobel Prize winner, Gabriel García Márquez. In it, he traces the reaction and incredulity of townsfolk to the first flight, making a clear parallel to current responses to the technological revolution. Gutiérrez shows the irrational and very humorous ways in which the townspeople responded. Some decide to go immediately to the church to pray, convinced that it was time to make an accounting of their sins. Couples living together in sin decided to marry. Married people confessed to having lovers. Everyone swore they would be good and decent and live without sin from that moment forward.

The reader/viewer must go back and forth between the characters of the town to be able to understand completely what is happening. For *Los hermanos*, the author explains at the start that the reader may elect to do as she or he pleases. All of the parts of the novel connect. Or the reader can take advantage of the author's attempts to "help." The novel deals with the role of the church, class divisions, and the changing role of women. In a way, the text is like a scavenger hunt. Gutiérrez has said that his desire in his digital novel was to transmit the richness of Latin American literature because they "saw narration and technology as instruments to stimulate the imagination and to disseminate the loved and feared idiosyncrasies of Latin America."[2]

Cielo Latini (Argentina, 1984-) has two novels that in large part originated online, *Abzurdah* (2006) and *Chubasco* (2010). *Abzurdah*, largely autobiographical, chronicles the protagonist's obsession with Alejandro, a man ten years her senior. Insecure, lonely, and desperately trying to win him over, she develops eating disorders and also creates a blog, "Me como a mí" (I eat myself), in which she inspires other young girls to become similarly obsessed with their weight. Latini wrote about the experience from the age of twenty looking back and incorporating large portions of her online material. In Argentina, she became a celebrity, and a 2015 film based on the book was also a huge success at the box office. Latini's subsequent novel, *Chubasco*, also dealt with teenage angst and the Internet, this time again in terms of the protagonist's obsession with a boy, and again, extreme insecurity, in this case such that it causes her to engage in a cat-and-mouse type of adolescent games that are now so commonly fueled by sexting, sending sexy photos and videos in a desperate attempt to earn his affections.

What Latini does well is to capture the seemingly contradictory connected isolation that characterizes social media use, in which online "friends" and "communities" serve to paradoxically help people feel less, and more, alone. While no one would accuse Latini of being a literary master in the style of fellow online writers Colombian Gutiérrez or Mexican Chimal, discussed above, nor Brazilian Daniel Galera that we discuss briefly below, Latini does, nonetheless, capture the current moment—the confusion, hope, solitude, and insecurities of a certain class of young women grappling with new technology.

Daniel Galera (Brazil, 1979-) is a writer widely known for promoting digital literature in Brazil and for his work with the microconto or micro short story. His 2003 *Até o dia em que o cão morreu* (*Until the Day the Dog Died*) became a feature film *Cão sem Dono* (*Ownerless Dog*, 2007), which was nominated for two national film awards. His work has been translated into English, Spanish, and Italian and he has won numerous literary prizes, including one for the Publishing House of the Year in Porto Alegre in 2003, the Machado de Assis award for the novel *Cordilhera* in 2008 and a 2012 *Granta* magazine recognition as one of Brazil's emerging young novelists. In 2013, Galera received the São Paulo

Prize for literature for his novel *Barba ensopada de sangue* (*Beard Drenched in Blood*), which won for book of the year. His personal website may be found at www.ranchocarne.org. Brazilian scholar Antonio Carlos Viana considers Galera's work among the current line of short stories in Brazil that take their cue for oral traditions. Galera's *Dentes guardados* ("Saved Teeth," a wink to readers with a reference to something written by famed Brazilian author Hilda Hilst), first published online, displays the full force of his creative imagination and brevity of descriptive adjectives, using a "an agile, modern language, without any fear of words."[3] In almost all of Galera's characters, there is a similar incapacity to connect to others in any real or genuine way. Like Latini, Galera underscores the profound solitude of his characters, many of whom spend large amounts of time online "connecting" with others but without any depth.

Galera was one of the first writers in Brazil to realize the potential of the Internet and to devote himself to using it for his work and for promoting the work of others. During the process of writing *Cordilhera* in 2010, Galera was one of a group of Brazilian authors sent around the world to live for one month in another city and write a novel that takes place in the location. He was sent to Buenos Aires. While there, he made regular blog posts and a documentary was filmed around his experience and posted to YouTube. Finally, after the publication of the book, the film rights were sold. Thus, *Cordilhera* provides the perfect example of Henry Jenkins's "media convergence," where all parts are interrelated and often simultaneous, as opposed to a more linear development in the past, in which a book became a movie. *Cordilhera* was made into a movie in 2012 directed by Carolina Jabor.

The three Latin American authors very briefly profiled here all have created digital literature that was "born" and widely circulated on the Internet before coming out in print or on film. All of the authors were born after 1974. For the two male authors, Colombian Gutiérrez and Brazilian Galera, as well as Mexican Chimal, mentioned earlier, there has been a conscious decision to establish a connection between their own digital writing and the Latin American literary masters. In the case of Argentine Latini, her digital writing is less connected to literature, or for that matter Latin America, than it is tied to similar concerns expressed by middle and upper middle class urban teens and young women around the world. For all of the writers, new technology is present both in the form and the content of their writings. What the cultural critic Beatriz Resende has said regarding young writers in Brazil can be equally applicable to those of the entire region: that they are creating a literature that is in "in synch with contemporary time, trying new subjectivities, of tensions between the local and the global, of deterritorialization and the end of any barrier between what is considered high culture versus mass culture,"[4] in which, as Resende further pointed out, there is a "immediate fleeting present, liquid and solitary"[5] characterized by a "disconcerting individualism or lost subjects who suffer a constant identity crisis."[6]

What we hope the reader takes away from this brief foray into Latin American digital literature are two things: 1) the vast richness and scope of the current online cultural production found in Latin America, and 2) the concomitant complexity with regard to the development of critical tools that will enable us to intellectually understand and assess the present moment. The challenge of bridging the traditional split between the humanities and the sciences is what is in order, so that we may all fully grasp the effects of the technological revolution in the Latin American literature.

Notes

1. "Es una lectura más fragmentaria, es más suelta, mucho más dispersa, esta no es una buena época para las lecturas profundas y concentradas, como las de las grandes novelas del siglo XIX, se sigue dando esa posibilidad de lectura, tenemos *best sellers* que miden miles de páginas . . . pero las nuevas generaciones se están formando de otra manera" (Gómez n.p.).

2. "Percibieron en la narración y la tecnología instrumentos para estimular la imaginación y difundir las amadas o temidas idiosincrasias de Latinoamérica" (Sasson-Henry 152).

3. "Linguagem ágil, moderna, sem medo algum das palavras" (Viana 280).

4. "Sintonia com os tempos contemporâneos, tratando de novas subjetividades, da tensão entre o local e o global, da desterritorialização e do fim da barreira entre a considerada alta cultura e a cultura de massa" (27).

5. "Presente imediato fugaz, líquido e solitário" (82).

6. "Um individualismo desconcertante de sujeitos perdidos e em constante crises identitárias" (82).

Works Cited

Aarseth, Espen. *Cybertext: Perspectives on Ergodic Literature.* Johns Hopkins UP, 1997.

Alejandro Rodríguez, Jaime. *Gabriela infinita. Un hypermedia narrativo.* 1999-. La Pontifícia Universidad Javeriana. Bogotá, Colombia. http://www.javeriana.edu.co/gabriella_infinita/portada. htm (accessed September 29. 2017)

_____. *Golpe de gracia.* Pontifícia Universidad Javeriana. 2006- Bogotá, Colombia. *Electronic Literature Collection. Vol 2.* Cambridge, Massachusetts, February, 2011. *http://collection. eliterature.org/2/works/rodriguez_golpedegracia.html* (Accessed September 29, 2017)

Anderson, Chris. "The Long Tail." *Wired Magazine* 12, Oct. 10, 2004. www. wired. com/wired/archive/12.10/tail. Accessed July 1, 2017.

Arroyo Pizarro, Yolanda. *Blog Boreales.* www.narrativadeyolanda. blogspot.com. Accessed Aug. 14, 2017.

_____. *Ojos de luna.* Terranova, 2007.

_____. *Los documentados.* Situm, 2005.

Assis, Laura. "A essencialidade dos 'detalhes inúteis': estratégias de representação em dois romances de Daniel Galera." *Brasiliana-Journal for Brazilian Studies* 3.1, 2014, pp. 120-38. www.tidsskrift. dk/bras/article/view/16734. Accessed July 15, 2017.

Berti, Eduardo. *Bertigo: Blog del escritor Eduardo Berti.* www. eduardoberti.blogspot.com.Accessed Aug. 17, 2017.

_____. *Todos los Funes.* Anagrama, 2004.

_____. *Agua. Agua.* Tusquets, 1997.

_____. *Un padre extranjero*. Tusquets/ Impedimenta, 2016.

Borges, Jorge Luis. *Ficciones*. Grove, 1962.

Brescia, Pablo. "La estética de lo mínimo." *Ensayos sobre microrrelatos mexicanos*. Universidad de Guadalajara, 2013.

Bruns, Axel. *Blogs, Wikipedia, Second Life, and Beyond: From Production to Produsage*. New York: Peter Lang 2008.

Bush, Mathew, and Tania Gentic. *Technology, Literature, and Digital Culture in Latin America: Mediated Sensibilities in a Globalized Era*. Routledge, 2015.

Casciari, Hernán. *Diario de una mujer gorda*. Debosillo, 2006.

Cavanagh, Allison. *Sociology in the Age of the Internet*. Berg, 2005.

Chiappe, Domenico. "Hipermedismo, narrativa para la virtualidad." *Alicante: Biblioteca Virtual Miguel de Cervantes*, 2009. www.cervantesvirtual.com/nd/ark:/59851/bmch4274. Accessed Aug. 1, 2017.

Chimal, Alberto. *Las historias: Textos, opiniones, descubrimientos. Sitio de Alberto Chimal*. www.lashistorias.com.mx. Accessed July 15, 2017.

_____. "Subir, desde abajo: el cuento mexicano en internet." *Tierra Adentro* 117.118, 2002, pp. 76-82.

_____. *83 novelas*. 2010. *Las historias: Textos, opiniones, descubrimientos. Sitio de Alberto Chimal*. www.lashistorias.com.mx/index.php/archivo/83-novelas. Accessed Aug. 5, 2017.

_____. *El viajero del tiempo*. 2011. www.lashistorias.com.mx/index.php/textos/el-viajero-del-tiempo. Accessed July 20, 2017.

Constante, Alberto, Alberto Chimal, Elva Peniche Montfort, Gabriela Álvarez, Ninel Valderrama, Elisa Schmelkes, Paola Uribe et al. "Arte en las redes sociales." (2013). Edition: primera, Publisher: Facultad de Filosofía y Letras, Universidad Nacional Autónoma de México, Editor: Estudio Paraíso. https://www.researchgate.net/publication/299437595_Arte_en_las_redes_sociales

Cortázar, Julio. *Rayuela*. Sudamericana, 1970.

Deleuze, Gilles, and Felix Guattari. *A Thousand Plateaus. Capitalism and Schizophrenia*. U of Minnesota P, 2009.

DiMaggio, Paul, et al. *Social Implications of the Internet, Annual Review of Sociology* 27, 2001, pp. 307-36.

Ferreira, Daniel. *Una hoguera para que arda goya.* www. unahogueraparaqueardagoya.blogspot.com. Accessed Aug. 14, 2017.

_____. *Rebelión de los oficios inútiles.* Alfaguara, 2014.

Gainza, Carolina. "Networks of Collaboration and Creation in Latin American Digital Literature." *CLC Web: Comparative Literature and Culture* 19.1, 2017. doi.org/10.7771/1481-4374.2918. Accessed July 28, 2017.

Galera, Daniel. *Barba ensopada de sangue.* Companhia das Letras, 2012.

_____. *Cordilhera.* Companhia das letras, 2008.

_____. *Until the Dog Died.* Porto Alegre: Livros do mal, 2003.

García Carcedo, Pilar, and Begoña Regueiro. *El reto de escribir. Entre papeles y pantallas.* GEU, 2015.

Gómez, Jorge Eduardo. "El cuento, ¿El nuevo género literario de Internet y las redes sociales?" *Micropolis: Una alternativa necesaria para todos los lectores.* Lima, Peru. Feb. 16, 2013. www.micropolis. pe/?p=4049. Accessed Aug. 14, 2017.

Gordon, Samuel. *Mito, fantasía y recepción en la obra de Alberto Chimal. AlterTexto: Teoría y crítica.* Universidad Iberoamericana, 2006.

Gutiérrez, Juan B. *El primer vuelo de los hermanos Wright.* Hipernovela. 1996-2006. *Literatrónica: Narrativa Digital Adaptiva.* www. literatronica.com/wright/el_primer_vuelo.htm. Accessed Aug. 14, 2017.

_____. *Condiciones extremas.* 1998-2006. *Literatrónica: Narrativa Digital Adaptiva.* www.literatronica.com/src/Nuntius. aspx?lng=HISPANIA&nuntius=OPUS_ABOUT_1&opus=1. Accessed Aug. 14, 2017.

Hayles, Katherine. *Electronic Literature: New Horizons for the Literary.* U of Notre Dame P, 2008.

Hine, Christine. *Virtual Methods: Issues in Social Research on the Internet.* Berg, 2005.

Hoeg, Jerry. *Science, Technology, and Latin American Narrative in the Twentieth Century and Beyond.* Lehigh UP/ Associated University Presses, 2000.

Horne, Luz. *Literaturas reales: transformaciones del realismo en la narrativa latinoamericana contemporánea.* Beatriz Viterbo, 2011.

Jenkins, Henry. *Convergence Culture: Where Old and New Media Collide.* New York UP, 2006.

_____. "The Cultural Logic of Media Convergence." *International Journal of Cultural Studies.* 7.1 (2004): 33-43.

_____, Sam Ford, and Joshua Green. *Spreadable Media: Creating Value and Meaning in a Networked Culture.* NYUP, 2013.

Landow, George P. *Hypertext. The Convergence of Contemporary Critical Theory and Technology.* Johns Hopkins UP, 1992.

_____. *Hypertext 2.0.* Johns Hopkins UP, 1997.

_____. *Hypertext 3.0: Critical Theory and New Media in the Age of Globalization.* Johns Hopkins UP, 2006.

Latini, Cielo. *Abzurdah: la perturbadora historia de una adolescente.* Ámbar, 2006.

Ludmer, Josefina. "Literaturas postautónomas 2.0." *Propuesta Educativa* 32, 2009, pp. 41-45.

Martín-Barbero, Jesús. *Al sur de la modernidad: Comunicación, globalización y multiculturalidad.* U of Pittsburgh P, 2001.

Martínez, Samue,l and Edwing Solano, editors. *Blogs, bloggers, blogósfera. Una revisión multidisciplinaria.* Universidad Iberoamericana, 2010. www.ibero.mx/web/filesd/publicaciones/blogs-enero2010.pdf. Accessed Aug. 14, 2017.

Mignolo, Walter. *The Darker Side of Western Modernity: Global Futures, Decolonial Options.* Duke UP, 2011.

Monterroso, Augusto. "El dinosauro." *La oveja negra y demás fábulas.* Era, 1969. *Centro Virtual Cervantes.* www.cvc.cervantes.es/actcult/monterroso/antologia. Accessed August 2. 2017.

Montoya Juárez, Jesús. *Narrativas de simulacro: Videocultura, tecnología y literatura en Argentina y Uruguay.* Universidad de Murcia, Servicio de Publicaciones, 2013.

Moreno, Isaí, Alberto Chimal, and Daniel Espartaco. "Escribir en Twitter es como hacer un misil: debe llevar potencia y puntería." *La Jornada. Espectáculos* 1 de abril, 2013, p. 12.

La jornada en línea. www.jornada.unam.mx/2013/04/01/espectaculos/a12n1esp. Accessed Aug. 14, 2017.

_____. *Chubasco.* Planeta, 2010.

Neuman, Andrés. *El viajero del siglo.* Alfaguara, 2009.

Nielsen, Gustavo. *Milanesa con papas: Gustavo Nielsen Blogspot*. www. milanesaconpapas.blogspot.com. Accessed Aug. 3, 2017.

_____. *La flor azteca*. Planeta, 1997.

_____. *El amor enfermo*. Alfaguara, 2000.

Pajares Toska, Susana. "Las posibilidades de la narrativa hipertextual" *Espéculo. Revista de estudios literarios* 6 (1997). https:// pendientedemigracion.ucm.es/info/especulo/numero6/s_pajare. htm. Accessed September 29, 2017.

Paz Soldán, Edmundo, and Debra Castillo. *Latin American Literature and Mass Media*. Hispanic Issues 22. Garland, 2001.

Piscitelli, Alejandro. *Ciberculturas 2.0: en la era de las máquinas inteligentes*. Paidós, 2002.

Resende, Beatriz. *Contemporâneos: expressões da literatura brasileira no século XXI*. Casa da Palavra, 2008.

Sánchez Mesa, Domingo. *Literatura y cibercultura. Selección, introducción, traducción, y bibliografía*. Arcos Libros, 2004.

Sanz, Amelia, and Dolores Romero, editors. *Literatures in Digital Era: Theory and Praxis*. Cambridge UP, 2007.

Sarlo, Beatriz. *Escenas de la vida posmoderna: Intelectuales, arte y video cultura en la Argentina*. Seix Barral, 2011.

_____. *The Technical Imagination: Argentine Culture's Modern Dreams*. Translated by Xavier Callahan. Stanford UP, 2008.

_____. *La imaginación técnica. Sueños modernos de la cultura argentina*. Nueva Visión, 1997.

Sasson-Henry, Perla. "Metamorfosis literaria en la era digital: El primer vuelo de los hermanos Wright." *Cuadernos de Literatura* 12.23, 2007, pp. 142-52.

Taylor, Claire, and Thea Pitman. *Latin American Identity in Online Cultural Production*. Routledge, 2013.

_____. editors. *Latin American Cyberculture and Cyberliterature*. Liverpool UP, 2007.

Thays, Iván. *Moleskine Ò Literario: Blog de noticias literarias & Asesorías literarias dirigido por Iván Thays*. http://ivanthays.com. pe/. Accessed July 25, 2017.

_____. *El viaje interior*. Peisa, 1999.

_____. *La disciplina de la vanidad*. Fondo, 2000.

Viana, Antonio Carlos. "O conto Brasileiro hoje." *Interdisciplinar: Revista de Estudos em Lingua e Literatura* 5.10, 2010, pp. 271-82. www.seer.ufs.br/index.php/interdisciplinar/article/view/1272. Accessed July 20, 2017.

Virilio, Paul. "Velocidad e información. ¡Alarma en el ciberespacio!" *Le monde Diplomatique*. August 1995. www.infoamerica.org/teoria_textos/virilio95.pdf. Accessed Aug. 14, 2017.

Wellman, Barry, and Lee Raine. *Networked: The New Social Operating System*. MIT UP, 2012.

World Literature and the Marketing of Roberto Bolaño's Posthumous Works_____

Ignacio López-Calvo

Coinciding with the publication of *El espíritu de la ciencia-ficción* (The Spirit of Science-Fiction, 2016), which Chilean Roberto Bolaño (1953-2003) wrote in 1984, Peruvian author Santiago Roncagliolo ironically wondered in an article published in the Spanish journal *El País*:

> Since he died, Roberto Bolaño does not stop working. . . . One wonders why geniuses edit those works after dying, considering that they did not do it while still alive. Perhaps it is because it is not they who do it but an army of agents, editors, producers, and heirs. Bolaño has a contract of 500,000 euros and has generated big judicial and mediatic fights among the administrators of his memory. But he cannot give his opinion. Shouldn't we allow artists to control their life while they're still alive, instead of deforming it after they die?[1]

Roncagliolo jokes that, in comparison, while still alive, Bolaño seemed to be quite lazy, and then compares him with Russian-American Vladimir Nabokov and American Truman Capote, whose oeuvres also continued to grow after their death. Indeed, since Bolaño's untimely death from liver failure, the astonishing number of nine posthumous works have been published in thirteen years: the novels *2666* (2004), written in 1999-2003 and translated in 2008; *El Tercer Reich* (2010; *The Third Reich,* 2011), written in 1989; *Los sinsabores del verdadero policía* (2011; *Woes of the True Policeman,* 2012), begun in the 1980s and written through 2003; and *El espíritu de la ciencia-ficción,* which takes place in Mexico City, like much of *Amuleto* (Amulet, 1999), *Los detectives salvajes* (*The Savage Detectives,* 1998)*, 2666,* and *Sepulcros de vaqueros* (Cowboy Sepulchers [three novellas], 2017); as well as the short-story collections *El gaucho insufrible* (2003; *The Insufferable*

Gaucho 2010); *Diario de bar* (Bar Diary, 2006), cowritten with A. G. Porta 1983 and published together with a new edition of *Consejos de un discípulo de Morrison a un fanático de Joyce* [1984; Tips from a Disciple of Morrison to a Fan of Joyce]); and *El secreto del mal* (2007; *The Secret of Evil,* 2012); and the collection of essays, articles, and speeches from 1998 through 2003 *Entre paréntesis* (2004; *Between Parentheses,* 2011).

Moreover, Bolaño's literature has also attracted the attention of film directors: Alicia Scherson directed *El futuro* (The Future, 2013), based on *Una novelita lumpen* (*A Little Lumpen Novelita,* 2002); Valeria Sarmiento is planning to film *La pista de hielo* (1993); and Gael García Bernal's company, Canana, is planning to have David Pablos direct a film based on *Los detectives salvajes,* a novel based on the experiences of the adventures of two poets of the avant-garde *infrarrealista* movement that Bolaño cofounded (called *visceral realists* in the novel), how they sabotage the literary establishment of the Mexico of the 1970s and Octavio Paz in particular, and how they search for a 1920s fictional poet named Cesárea Tinajero. In 2016, there was also a five-hour stage adaptation of *2666,* directed by Seth Bockley and Robert Falls, the artistic director of the Goodman Theater in Chicago.

Additional publications of new manuscripts by Bolaño have already been announced: *La virgen de Barcelona* (The Virgin of Barcelona, 1980), and *Diorama* (1984), as well as some of Bolaño's letters. And many more titles may be published in the near future, if we keep in mind that the *Arxiu Bolaño: 1977-2003* (Bolaño Archive), a 2013 exhibit in Barcelona's Centre de Cultura Contemporània (Center for Contemporary Culture), listed, besides his poems, the following titles: *Lento palacio de invierno* (Slow Winter Palace, written in 1979), *Tres minutos antes de la aparición del gato* (Three Minutes before the Appearance of the Cat, written in 1979), *Las alamedas luminosas* (The Luminous Poplar Groves, written in 1979), *Las rodillas de un autor de ciencia-ficción, atrás* (The Knees of a Sci-Fi Author, Behind, written in 1979), *El náufrago* (The Castaway, 1979-1982), *Ellos supieron perder* (They Knew How to Lose, 1979-1982), *La virgen de Barcelona, El contorno del ojo* (The Outline of the Eye, written in 1979-1982), *El espectro de Rudolf Armand Philippi* (The Specter of Rudolf Armand Philippi, written in 1982), *Adiós, Shane* (Goodbye Shane, written in 1983), *D.F., La paloma, Tobruk* (DF, The Pigeon, Tobruk, written in 1983), *Diorama* (written in 1983-1984), *El maquinista* (The Train Engineer, written in 1986), *Última entrevista en Boca-cero* (Last Interview in Boca-cero, written in 1995-1996), *Sepulcros de vaqueros* (written in 1996), *Todo lo que la gente cuenta de Ulises Lima* (Everything People Say about Ulises Lima, written in 1996-1997), *Vuelve el man a Venezuela* (The Man Returns to Venezuela, written in 1999), *Corrida* (Bullfight, written in 1999-2000), *Comedia del horror de Francia* (Comedy of Horrors in France, written in 2001), and *Dos señores de Chile* (Two Gentlemen from Chile, written in 2001).

One cannot help but wonder whether the Chilean writer had actually planned to publish all these books or whether some or all of them were simple drafts that did not fully satisfy him. Will this rush to publish most of what he wrote eventually affect his reputation as a writer or will it increase his aura as a master writer, as happened with the publication of the posthumous *2666*? After all, *El Tercer Reich* and *Los sinsabores del verdadero policía* received mixed reviews, with *The New York Times* actually describing the latter, perhaps unfairly, as "a collection of outtakes." As is well known, Bolaño had attained a minor success with his second novel *Pista de hielo* (*The Skating Rink*, 1993) and three years later, some critical acclaim (albeit a failure in sales) with *Estrella distante* (*Distant Star*) and *La literatura nazi en América* (*Nazi Literature in the Americas*). But his literary cachet in Spain and Latin America would grow dramatically after receiving the 1998 Herralde Award and the 1999 Rómulo Gallegos Prize for *The Savage Detectives*, published a year earlier. After his death, and especially after *Time* magazine chose *2666* as the best book of 2008, *The New York Times* declared it one of "The Ten Best Books of 2008," and then it won the National Book Critics Circle Award for Fiction, the Chilean author's acclaim attained a global reach, with a special impetus in the English-speaking world. In recent years, after the translation of several of his texts into English, Bolaño's literary reputation has made him one of the most acclaimed writers in any language and an indisputable member of the World Republic of Letters, to use Pascale Casanova's term.

But to what do we owe this Bolañomania and the ensuing rush to publish his manuscripts? Apart from the obvious economic benefits to certain publishers and Bolaño's heirs, there is no question that his warm reception by both critics and readers has turned him into a cult writer. Neither the self-proclaimed successors of the Boom writers, the Crack and McOndo writers, nor best-selling Latin American writers from the 1980s and 90s, such as Isabel Allende and Laura Esquivel, ever reached Bolaño's universal acclaim. As a result, the vacuum left by the Boom writers (Gabriel García Márquez, Mario Vargas Llosa, Julio Cortázar, and Carlos Fuentes) had to be filled by someone: Roberto Bolaño. As Nicholas Birns puts it,

> Bolaño was a post-Boomer who had more to offer than *just* coming after the Boom. He seemed a weightier and more highbrow figure than Fuguet or even Volpi. Yet he was not simply these writers trussed up and made less obvious: Bolaño had a history with leftist politics and literary insurgency the younger writers did not, and his generational status made him more than a young man in a hurry or part of a new cohort, oedipally overthrowing their predecessors. ("The Part," 53)

Regarding Bolaño's success in the United States, Sara Pollack has speculated that along with the successful marketing campaign, the persistence of cultural stereotypes about Latin America among US publishers has also had a powerful effect:

> Unwittingly—or perhaps with provocative deliberation—*The Savage Detectives* plays on a series of opposing characteristics that the United States has historically employed in defining itself vis-à-vis its neighbors to the south: hardworking vs. lazy, mature vs. adolescent, responsible vs. reckless, upstanding vs. delinquent. In a nutshell, Sarmiento's dichotomy, as old as Latin America itself: civilization vs. barbarism. Regarded from this standpoint, *The Savage Detectives* is a comfortable choice for U.S. readers, offering both the pleasures of the savage and the superiority of the civilized. (362)

Along these lines, the Spanish writer Javier Cercas has suggested that, beyond the unquestionable literary value of his works, his canonization as a writer has something to do with his premature death:

> The fact that Bolaño died young and at the summit of his creating power and his prestige prevented, I guess, any other possibility; the incurable mythomaniac tendency of our literary medium, added to our hypocritical and equally incurable tendency to speak well about the dead—because they no longer bother us and can be easily manipulated, or perhaps because we want to compensate for how badly we spoke about them when they were alive—has done the rest.[2]

Indeed, it is possible that his tragic and untimely death, coupled with the public's awareness that after finding out about his liver disease in 1992, Bolaño wrote feverishly to ensure his family's economic security until he published eleven novels in thirteen years, turned him, as Cercas puts it, into a sort of literary James Dean. Readers suddenly associated him with an aura of rebelliousness, which, incidentally, Bolaño himself helped propagate through his literary alter-egos, as well as through his autobiographical accounts delivered in several interviews and essays. This information, however, is in many cases full of inaccuracies, since in reality, as has been repeatedly pointed out in recent years, during his most productive years Bolaño was a prudent family man, devoted to his children, who did not drink alcohol, was never a heroin addict, and had become a moderate leftist in politics.

In any case, since Bolaño became the most influential writer of his generation and the only Latin American author in the last twenty-five years to have become canonical in the United States and to have achieved world literary status, the number of posthumous publications and the marketing campaign does not seem to reach an end, which has brought about the perhaps inevitable concern about whether economic motivation is being prioritized over aesthetic and literary value.[3] This publication of posthumous novels seems particularly problematic when some of the works, such as *Los sinsabores del verdadero policía*, were still unfinished at the time of Bolaño's death. Comments such as the following one made by the notorious literary agent Andrew Wylie about Penguin Random House (the group to which Alfaguara belongs), regarding the publication of Bolaño's posthumous books, do not help appease the skepticism of critics and readers alike: "As a good American, I am a capitalist. The market has its rules and what it says about Bolaño is that his latest works have been the most valuable ones. I would also say that some of these books should not be considered at the same literary level as *The Savage Detectives* or *2666*."[4] (Marcial Pérez n.p.) Wylie's candid acknowledgment that these new publications do not match the literary value of Bolaño's masterpieces adds little information, however, about whether or not it is worth publishing them beyond the economic benefits they may bring to the publishing house he works for.

More reassuringly, Carolina López, Bolaño's widow, has underscored the—according to her—rigorous criteria used to decide whether the manuscripts should be published. Thus, in an interview with Josep Massot, she avers:

> When a writer is world renowned, as is Bolaño's case, readers appreciate it when his diaries or correspondence are published, as well as certain documents and texts (as long as they have literary value) that could have remained unpublished. Everything is publishable, provided one applies certain criteria. The main one: to respect scrupulously the text left by the author, as well as to contextualize it so that the reader may have the necessary information, and to incorporate it to the corpus of his oeuvre without damaging it. . . . Besides these criteria, we have worked with texts that at some point Bolaño considered finished; we have carried out a rigorous study in the author's archive of all the documentation related to the text, guaranteeing the maximum information and veracity.[5] (Page 13)

In spite of the Spanish literary critic (and Bolaño's close friend) Ignacio Echevarría's criticism about how she is managing her late husband's posthumous works, López has repeatedly stated that she would never allow the publication of a work that would damage her late husband's prestige as an author.

A posthumous novel by Bolaño that seemed to be finished by 1984 is *El espíritu de la ciencia-ficción*. The manuscript was taken from his seemingly endless archives, this time from neatly handwritten notebooks, and was published by the prestigious Spanish publishing house Alfaguara (which, incidentally, rejected Bolaño's book manuscripts on several occasions before he achieved worldwide fame), instead of Jorge Herralde's Anagrama, where the Chilean author's oeuvre achieved world literature status. Pilar Reyes, the Alfaguara editor, frankly admits: "We cannot speculate about whether for Bolaño it was a finished manuscript or not, publishable or not. The manuscript has a date and it is signed, and it is contained in three notebooks, in three writing stages: notes, first draft, and final transcription."[6] Therefore, the fact that the Chilean author bothered to date, polish, and copy the manuscript in a final transcription seems to satisfy her requirements for publication, an argument that could easily be debated.

Furthermore, there is speculation that the fact that part of it, titled "Manifiesto mexicano" (Mexican Manifesto), had already been published with some minor variations in the journal *Turia* in 2005 (two years after his death), then two years later in the collection of poetry and prose *La universidad desconocida* (*The Unknown University*, 2007), and finally in 2013 in *The New Yorker*, may be indicative of the fact that Bolaño did not intend to publish the rest of the book manuscript. As Elena Hevia points out, "That he only typed this fragment in his computer seems to suggest that Bolaño wanted to rescue this story alone, which can be read as an independent account, and left behind in the manuscript—which he had cleaned up, that is true—the rest of a novel that probably did not satisfy him."[7] Hevia adds that Bolaño, in his 1980s correspondence with his friends A. G. Porta and Bruno Montané, repeatedly expressed his dissatisfaction with this work, which he sometimes described as a "shitty novel"[8] or as "abominable," also pointing out that some of the scenes did not match the rest of the plot. By contrast, Valerie Miles argues that if "he truly had not wanted the novel to be published, he would have left explicit instructions to his widow."[9] (Hevia n.p.) One may quickly respond, however, that neither did

Bolaño leave instructions for his widow to publish the novel. At any rate, one must admit that in the case of *2666*, it was a good idea not to follow Bolaño's instructions of publishing it in five separate books for economic reasons.

Be that as it may, it is still interesting to note how in early works such as *El espíritu de la ciencia-ficción* and *Sepulcros de vaqueros* one can already take a glimpse at some of the Chilean author's main narrative techniques (metaliterature); tone (irony, humor); alter-egos, characters (embryonic versions of Arturo Belano, Ulises Lima, and Auxilio Lacouture); themes (the literary initiation of young poets in Mexico City); and obsessions (the archeology of evil and violence). Furthermore, *El espíritu de la ciencia-ficción* and *Los sinsabores del verdadero policía* have the added value—at least for literary critics and Bolaño fans—of potentially representing the drafts or embryos of *Los detectives salvajes* and *2666*, respectively.

International Reception and Bolaño's World Literary Status

Beyond any type of marketing strategy (let us not forget that not long ago some critics also unfairly ascribed the success of the Boom to marketing campaigns), there is no doubt that Bolaño's writing touched a generation of readers and writers who admired him as a leader and as a model to emulate. Besides the admiration of his peers, Bolaño entered in record time the conventional literary world-system, all the while becoming an international bestseller. In fact, the also Chilean Isabel Allende (whose work Bolaño openly denigrated, as he did with the oeuvres of several of his Chilean peers) is the only Latin American author who sells more novels in the United States than Bolaño.

In this context, David Damrosch has famously defined world literature in the following way:

> I take world literature to encompass all literary works that circulate beyond their culture of origin, either in translation or in the original language . . . a work only has an *effective* life as world literature whenever, and wherever, it is actively present within a literary system beyond that of its original culture . . . world literature is not an

infinite, ungraspable canon of works but rather a mode of circulation and of reading, a mode that is applicable to individual works as to bodies of material, available for reading established classics and new discoveries alike. (*What* 4-5)

Damrosch later adds that "literature stays within its national or regional tradition when it usually loses in translation, whereas works become world literature when they gain on balance in translation, stylistic losses offset by an expansion in depth as they increase their range" (*What* 289). In the case of Bolaño's opus, it has been successfully translated to dozens of languages and, as stated, no other Latin American author since the Boom authors has had a more triumphal entrance into the World Republic of Letters (to use Pascale Casanova's concept). Tellingly, in October 2016, *Babelia*, the cultural magazine of the prestigious Spanish newspaper *El País*, included two of Bolaño's novels among the three best ones published in the last quarter of a century. Some of the terms coined for this literary phenomenon, "The Bolaño tsunami," "Bolañomania," "The Bolaño effect," and even "Bolaño fatigue," attest to the level of his international success among readers and critics alike.

The worldliness in Bolaño's works, however, responds not only to their global circulation, multiple translations, success in the English language (it is often said that less that 3 percent of literature published in the United States is fiction in translation), and the fact that they may very well gain in translation, but also to the cosmopolitan consciousness and non-Eurocentric worldview of his works, whose settings often cross national and continental borders. These transnational settings facilitate the "transcultural comparisons" that Damrosch considers another indispensable category for a text to attain world-literature status. As Nicholas Birns and Juan E. De Castro point out, "Not just Bolaño's recognition but also his material is global. As a writer he covers the entire world" (8). Indeed, the postnational, transnational, and global cognitive mapping of Bolaño's literary journey—incidentally, the author himself was globally oriented beyond his writing, as he seemed reluctant to consider himself only

Chilean—may have helped his works to be recognized beyond the national borders of the country where they were written (Mexico and, since 1977, Spain). Bolaño's ouevre, therefore, could be considered world literature, beyond market events, because of its non-Eurocentric, planetary consciousness beyond national projects. Of course, Bolaño was not the first Latin American author to propose anti-eurocentrist critiques against pretensions of European universalism, as they are also present in authors from previous generations, such as Miguel Ángel Asturas, Carlos Fuentes, and Julio Cortázar. In this context, Oswaldo Zavala has emphasized Bolaño's proposal of an alternative Latin American modernity that exceeds the frameworks of what is normally understood by *world literature*, all the while pointing out the limitations of the world literature paradigm due to the scarcity of translations. He argues that the Chilean author disrupts world literature paradigms with "a constant interruption of the logic of symbolic capital as the result of a productive reactivation of key European and Latin American avant-garde poetics in a politically conscious intellectual project that in combination lead to other formations of the modern" (82). Along these lines, Benjamin Loy argues that "lying at the core of Bolaño's oeuvre is a reworking of Modernity and the issues surrounding the global literary field. Based on operations of intertextuality and humor, whose role is fundamental in Bolaño, his writing questions the cartographies formulated by the self-designated 'western center'" (156).

Chilean Ricardo House's documentary film *Roberto Bolaño: La batalla futura III* (Roberto Bolaño: The Future Battle III, 2017) unveils Bolaño's international outlook in both his literature and his personal worldview. Born in Chile, where he lived until the age of fifteen (and then returned briefly in 1973), he spent extended periods of time in Mexico with his family, where he cofounded the Infrarrealista literary group, and then in Spain, where he spent the last twenty-six years of his life. Carlos Labbé, for this reason, argues that "Bolaño was not Chilean, he was a Mexican-Catalan born in Chile. That is evident in his lexical decisions and in his literary politics."[10] These international experiences marked his life and career, finding a homeland mostly in the Spanish language in which he wrote his works. In fact, in a radio interview with Chilean writer Pedro Lemebel, Bolaño declared that his only tradition is his language and then chastised the critic Raquel Olea's defense of national literatures, which he defined as "a fantasy, a rip off,"[11] and a Romantic discussion that was already obsolete by the end of the nineteenth century: "The opus of a great writer is never circumscribed to a country. Do you think that Neruda is not understood in Spain because he is not Spanish? That we Chileans don't understand Vallejo because he is Peruvian?"[12] This statements reveal the reasons Bolaño would not accept a description of his work as Chilean literature per se.

Most notably, as Nathan Scott McNamara points out, the Chilean author's success in the United States, after appearing in the prestigious magazine *The New Yorker*, being translated into English by Chris Andrews and Natasha Wimmer, and published first by New Directions and then by Farrar, Straus and Giroux, has transformed the way Latin American literature was conceived (thankfully away from stereotypical magical realist connotations), read, translated and published: "he opened publishing channels by drawing readers' attention to other writers in places like Chile, Mexico, and Argentina. He also helped turn English readers' attention away from the Latin American books of the 80s and 90s, and back in the direction of the modernists and realists of the 60s boom" (n.p.). Considering the dearth of literary translations in the United States, this is a welcome development for Latin American literature in general.

Overall, it is safe to say that a combination of all the factors mentioned above has turned Bolaño into the face of Latin American literature today, thankfully away from stereotypes about the omnipresence of Magical Realism or self-promotional literary manifestos. Whether the incessant publication of posthumous works may end up overexposing the writer or even damaging his literary reputation is still to be seen, as the content of most of the new texts is unknown to most of us. Be that as it may, at least his sudden inclusion into the so-called world literature or the World Republic of Letters has brought much-needed attention to contemporary Latin

American literature (as well as a revived interest in the Boom writers), thus increasing the potential translations in the United States and the rest of the world, as well as renewed critical attention to the works of younger authors, such as the ones included in this volume, as well as many other deserving ones. The impressive worldwide success of Bolaño's work has undoubtedly attracted renewed interest in the region's literature, which had been losing critical respect since the unprecedented success of the Boom writers. One cannot help but hope that some of the younger authors listed in this volume will follow in his footsteps, hopefully without becoming epigones of the Chilean master.

Notes

1. "Desde que está muerto, Roberto Bolaño no para de trabajar. . . . Uno se pregunta por qué los genios editan esos trabajos después de morir, si no lo hicieron cuando vivían. Quizá porque no lo hacen ellos, sino un ejército de agentes, editores, productores y herederos. Bolaño tiene un contrato de 500.000 euros y ha generado gordas peleas judiciales y mediáticas entre los administradores de su memoria. Pero no puede dar su opinión. ¿No deberíamos dejar que los artistas controlen su obra en vida, en vez de deformársela después de muertos?" (n.p.).

2. "El hecho de que Bolaño muriera joven y en la cima de su potencia creadora y su prestigio vedaba, supongo, cualquier otra posibilidad; la incurable propensión mitómana de nuestro medio literario, sumada a nuestra hipócrita e igualmente incurable propensión a hablar bien de los muertos—porque ya no molestan y pueden ser manipulados a placer, o quizá porque queremos compensarlos por lo mal que hablamos de ellos cuando estuvieron vivos—, ha hecho el resto" (n.p.).

3. Other authors, such as César Aira and Jorge Volpi, have also received impressive international recognition, but nonetheless not at the level of Bolaño's international critical acclaim.

4. "Como buen americano, soy un capitalista. El mercado tiene reglas y lo que dice sobre Bolaño es que las últimas obras han sido las más valiosas. Diría también que algunos de estos libros no deberían considerarse al mismo nivel literario que *Los detectives salvajes* o *2666*" (n.p.).

5. "Cuando un escritor es muy reconocido universalmente, como en el caso de Bolaño, los lectores agradecen que se publiquen hasta sus diarios o su correspondencia, así como ciertos documentos o textos (siempre que tengan valor literario) que hubieran podido quedar inéditos. Todo es publicable, pero siempre aplicando criterios. El principal: respetar escrupulosamente el texto dejado por el autor, así como contextualizarlo para que el lector tenga la información necesaria, e incorporarlo al conjunto de su obra sin que la desmerezca... Además de los criterios señalados, se ha trabajado con textos que en algún momento Roberto consideró finalizados; se ha realizado un riguroso estudio en el archivo del autor de toda la documentación vinculada al texto, garantizando un máximo de información y veracidad" (n.p.).

6. "Nosotros no podemos especular sobre si para Bolaño era un manuscrito terminado o no, publicable o no. El manuscrito está fechado y firmado, y son tres las libretas que lo contienen, en tres etapas de la escritura: notas, primer borrador y transcripción en limpio" (Sainz Borgo, n.p.).

7. "Que solo pasara al ordenador ese fragmento parecería indicar que Bolaño solo quiso rescatar esa historia, que puede leerse como un relato independiente, y dejó en manuscrito, pulcramente pasado a limpio, eso sí, el resto de una novela que posiblemente no le satisfacía" (n.p.).

8. "Novela de mierda" (n.p.).

9. "Si a él realmente le hubiera importado no publicar su obra inédita, hubiera dejado instrucciones explícitas a su viuda" (n.p.).

10. "Bolaño no era chileno, era un mexicano-catalán nacido en Chile. Eso se comprueba en sus decisiones léxicas y en su política literaria" (Morla n.p.).

11. "Una entelequia, una estafa."

12. "La obra de un gran escritor jamás está ceñida a un país. ¿Tú crees que a Neruda no lo entienden en España porque no es español? ¿Que a Vallejo no lo entendemos los chilenos porque es peruano?"

Works Cited

Birns, Nicholas. "The Part About the Critics: the World Reception of Roberto Bolaño." *Critical Insights: Roberto Bolaño.* Salem, 2015, pp. 50-64.

Birns, Nicholas, and Juan E. de Castro. *Roberto Bolaño as World Literature*. Bloomsbury, 2017.

Bolaño, Roberto. *2666*. Anagrama, 2008.

_____. *Amuleto*. Anagrama, 1999.

_____. *Cuentos. Llamadas telefónicas. Putas asesinas. El gaucho insufrible*. Anagrama, 2010.

_____. *Entre paréntesis. Ensayos, artículos y discursos (1998–2003)*. Ed.

_____. *Espíritu de la ciencia-ficción*. New York: Vintage Españl, una division de Penguin Random House LLC, 2017.

_____. *Los detectives salvajes*. Vintage Español, 1998.

_____. *Los sinsabores del verdadero policía*. Anagrama, 2011.

_____. *The Savage Detectives*. Translated by Natasha Wimmer. Farrar, 2007.

_____. *Woes of the True Policeman*. Farrar, 2012.

_____, and A. G. Porta. *Consejos de un discípulo de Morrison a un fanático de Joyce seguido de Diario de bar*. Barcelona: Acantilado, 2008. Print.

Cercas, Javier. "Print the legend!" *El País*, April 14, 2007.

Damrosch, David. "Introduction: All the World in the Time." *Teaching World Literature*. MLA, 2009, pp. 1-11.

_____. *What Is World Literature?* Princeton UP, 2003

Hevia, Elena. "La novela 'abominable' de Bolaño." *El Periódico. Ocio y Cultural*. Nov. 6, 2016. www.elperiodico.com/es/ocio-y-cultura/20161106/bolano-el-espiritu-de-la-ciencia-ficcion-inedito-postumo-5611731. Accessed Aug. 5, 2017.

House, Ricardo. *Roberto Bolaño: La batalla futura III*. Invercine, 2016.

Ignacio Echevarría. Barcelona: Anagrama, 2004. Print.

_____. *Espíritu de la ciencia-ficción*. New York: Vintage Español, una division de Penguin Random House LLC, 2017.

_____. *El gaucho insufrible*. Barcelona: Anagrama, 2003. Print.

_____. *La pista de hielo*. Barcelona: Seix Barral, 2003. Print.

_____. *El secreto del mal*. Barcelona: Anagrama, 2007. Print.

_____. *El Tercer Reich*. Barcelona: Anagrama, 2010. Print.

_____. *Una novelita lumpen*. Barcelona: Anagrama, 2009. Print.

Lemebel, Pedro. "Lemebel entrevista a Bolaño en Radio Tierra." *SoundCloud.com*. Nov. 1998. Web. 26 Sept. 2017. https://soundcloud. com/javier-sanfeli/lemebel-entrevista-a-bolano-en-radio-tierra.

Loy, Benjamin. "Mocking World Literature and Canon Parodies in Roberto Bolaño's Fiction." Edited by Nicholas Birns and Juan E. de Castro. *Roberto Bolaño as World Literature*. Bloomsbury, 2017, pp. 153-66.

Marcial Pérez, David. "No quiero sonar arrogante, pero no necesito consejos para elegir autor." *El País*, Nov. 29, 2016. www.elpais.com/ cultura/2016/11/29/actualidad/1480449397_609379.html. Accessed Aug. 9, 2017.

Massot, Josep. "La viuda del escritor, Carolina López: 'Roberto Bolaño tuvo tiempo de disfrutar el reconocimiento.'" *La vanguardia.com*, June 2011. www.lavanguardia.com/cultura/20101219/54091163845/ la-viuda-del-escritor-carolina-lopez-roberto-bolano-tuvo-tiempo-de-disfrutar-el-reconocimiento.html1. Accessed Aug. 8, 2017.

McNamara, Nathan Scott. "The Bolaño Effect: Latin American Literature in Translation on the Great and Steady Surge in Translated Titles." *Literary Hub*, Nov. 18, 2016. www.lithub.com/the-bolano-effect-latin-american-literature-in-translation. Accessed Aug. 1, 2017.

Morla, Jorge. "Carlos Labbé: 'En 75 años Chile se hundirá en el mar.'" *El País*, July 20, 2017. www.elpais.com/cultura/2017/07/20/ actualidad/1500571690_265047.html. Accessed Aug. 8, 2017.

Pollack, Sarah. "Latin America Translated (Again): Roberto Bolaño's *The Savage Detectives*." *Comparative Literature* 61.3, 2009, pp. 346–65.

Roncagliolo, Santiago. "Difuntos y rentables." Nov. 1, 2016. www.elpais. com/elpais/2016/11/01/estilo/1478008076_598301.html. Accessed Aug. 5, 2017.

Sáez Leal, Javier. "La guerra perpetua de Roberto Bolaño." *El País*, March 3, 2017.www.elpais.com/cultura/2017/03/03/ actualidad/1488558891_359759.html?id_externo_rsoc=FB_CC. Accessed Aug. 6, 2017.

Sainz Borgo, Karina. "Roberto Bolaño, el inmortal." *Gatopardo.com*. www.gatopardo.com/reportajes/roberto-bolano-inmortal. Accessed Aug. 1, 2017.

Scherson, Alicia, dir. *Il futuro*. Strand Releasing Home Video, 2013. DVD.

Zavala, Oswaldo. "The Repolitization of the Latin American Shore: Roberto Bolaño and the Dispersion of 'World Literature.'" Edited by Nicholas Birns and Juan E. de Castro. *Roberto Bolaño as World Literature*. Bloomsbury, 2017, pp. 79-97.

The "Coloniality of Power" in the Twenty-First-Century Peruvian Story "Rizoma" by Carlos Yushimito del Valle

Shigeko Mato

Introduction: The Twenty-First-Century Peruvian Gourmet Boom

"Insofar as Peruvian gastronomy is highly valued, people will be willing to pay more. The idea is that that money will go directly to traditional farmers and fishermen. We should include everyone,"[1] says Gastón Acurio, one of the Peru's most famous superstar entrepreneur-chefs ("Acurio" n.p.). Acurio's words highlight his enthusiasm for creating equal opportunities and social and economic equity for everyone through the boom of gourmet Peruvian cuisine.[2] He continues to show his dream of planting collective aspirations and successes in Peru through his "culinary revolution" (CREARSEPERÚ n.p.):[3] "Gastronomy and hunger are incompatible. . . . This moment demands that we leave all personal ambitions behind in order to move on to collective issues. We are aware of our role in promoting fair trade" ("Acurio" n.p.).[4] Because of his comments, promoting collective economic prosperity and social equality through Peruvian gastronomy, the name *Gastón* seems to connote the image of a generous, honest, responsible, and personable chef who sincerely cares about social change and justice.[5]

However, the recent leakage of "the Panama Papers,"[6] which reveals Acurio's offshore tax evasion practices, among many other wealthy people's practices in tax havens (Castilla n.p.), discredits and invalidates his declaration of collective "culinary revolution" for social change. His public response, defending his private and unshared tax practices by emphasizing the lawfulness of such practices in tax havens (Castillo n.p.), contradicts his philosophy of cooking that embraces the idea of collective and shared opportunities, benefits, success, and prosperity. Acurio's connection to the offshore tax havens, his initial vague answers to the digital investigation journal *ojo-publico.com* about his involvement in the tax havens, and his later response repeating the legality of his use of the tax havens are immoral and disappointing. But, what is more immoral and disappointing is that Acurio's inspirational words toward social change have been shown to have no connection to reality.

However, the disclosure of this unreality may not be surprising to some of the critics of the Peruvian gastronomic boom, such as Mario Zúñiga Lossio, Raúl Matta, and María Elena García, who had already foreseen the limits of Acurio's promise of social integration and equality for all, before the scandal of "the Panama Papers." Zúñiga Lossio perceives Acurio's discourse, despite his frequent declaration of "benefits for all," as a discourse of capitalist domination of an urban upper class elite that constructs a folkloric or exotic image of marginalized rural "Other" (indigenous food) or estheticizes the "Other," in order to "embrace" the "Other," "sophisticate" it, and ultimately sell the image of wonderful food made in Peru, the land of "harmonious" *mestizaje* and multiculturalism, in global capitalist markets (5, 10-14, 16, 18-19). Similarly, Matta claims that the recent national promotion of Peruvian cuisine, which fanatically values multicultural ethnicities, reflects the capitalist ideology of individualism and entrepreneurship shared by urban elites' "gastronomic techniques and discourses" ("Dismantling" 66). In the name of multiculturalism, the urban elite entrepreneurs associated with the country's political power decontextualize the traditional Andean and Amazonian indigenous knowledge of food, and gentrify the formerly marginalized tradition and food as a cosmopolitan and sophisticated cuisine that can compete with other high culinary canons in global markets (66). According to Matta, in this capitalist gastronomic fervor, the main purpose of promoting Peruvian cuisine is not to develop socioeconomic equity, but to "gain international visibility and economic capitalization," to "enhance the country's reputation and foster business," and finally to "compete in global markets" (66).[7]

García also reveals these other faces of gentrification and inequality hidden in the fervor of the "gastronomic revolution," by demonstrating a disconnect between the promises of APEGA, the

Peruvian Society of Gastronomy, which promotes culinary tourism and social equality from the perspective of urban elites, and the sentiments of marginalization, exclusion, and neglect brought by the gastronomic boom, as expressed by Chirapaq, the Center of Indigenous Cultures in Peru (an indigenous organization located in Lima) (510-18). García further goes on to point out another dark side of a gastronomic boom that invades the sovereignty of indigenous food knowledge and practices. The elite class running the promotion of Peruvian cuisine, reevaluating the value of indigenous food on their own terms, may install global models of industrial animal farming and agriculture that not only disrespect the indigenous animal and agricultural value system, but also physically and environmentally harm nonhuman bodies (518-20). Considering these dark consequences, García sees the repeated "coloniality of power"[8] in the Peruvian gastronomic boom and thus the impossibility of attaining social equality between "chefs and peasants" through the boom (507, 520-21).

"Rizoma": The Story of Andean Potatoes and the "Coloniality of Power"

Peruvian writer Carlos Yushimito del Valle's (1977-) short story "Rizoma" ("Rhizome," 2013) depicts the feverish climate of a gastronomic boom in Lima that takes the reader to an even darker consequence than that imagined in the above-mentioned scholars' critical observations of the current boom. In "Rizoma," the author portrays the decomposition of human society into a cynocephalic (dog-headed and human-bodied) dystopia. "Rizoma" can be read, therefore, as a science fiction story that foretells the gruesome outcome of the nonstop fetishization of gourmet food. It is a story in which newfangled dishes are constantly and tirelessly innovated and marketed through various media sources, satirizing gourmet magazines, TV cooking shows, and food festivals with celebrity chefs. In this food "culture industry,"[9] food products (foodstuffs) no longer hold the traditional, regional, and communal values and meanings of food, but only serve to entertain gourmet restaurant-goers' palate. Those who can afford gourmet cuisine, mostly the bourgeois upper and upper middle classes, are too occupied with being amused by brand-new cutting-edge dishes and services to be aware of sociopolitical and environmental issues related to food, such as the reality of world hunger and the unknown consequences of genetically engineered food. In this cultural environment that does nothing to stimulate their consciousness, people start losing their ability to think and turn into mindless and cannibalistic monstrous beings at the end.

The etymological root of the word *monster*, the Latin *monstrum*, means both 1) "divine portent" and "warning" and 2) "something marvelous or prodigious" (Hoad 299). Yushimito's monstrous, rabid beings, infested and infected human bodies, can be a portent or warning that signals a decadence of a human society degraded by brain-numbing entertainments and satisfactions. In this sense, the emergence of the monstrous beings implies the first etymological meaning, serving as a warning sign of the degradation of society caused by the incessant pursuit of entertainment and consumerism. However, what Yushimito warns of is not only the lack of consciousness of the masses and their constant desire to be amused but also, perhaps more importantly, the manipulation of the masses by a continuous global power system that Aníbal Quijano calls the "coloniality of power" ("Coloniality of Power" 533).

According to Quijano, "Eurocentered capitalism" was imposed by Europeans on their colonies during the colonial period, and remains predominant today over the entire globe ("Coloniality of Power" 533-35, 539, 541-42). In other words, "the model of power that is globally hegemonic today presupposes an element of coloniality" (533). In his essay "Coloniality and Modernity/Rationality," Quijano further indicates the continuance of an aspiration for cultural Westernization among the cultures of colonized populations:

> With respect to the colonial world . . . , history was conceived as a [sic] evolutionary continuum from the primitive to the civilized; from the traditional to the modern; from the savage to the rational; from pro- [sic] capitalism to capitalism, etc. And Europe thought of itself as the mirror of the future of all the other societies and cultures; as the advanced form of the history of the entire species. What does not

cease to surprise, however, is that Europe succeeded in imposing that "mirage" upon the practical totality of the cultures that it colonized; and much more, that this chimera *is still* so attractive to so many. (176; emphasis added)

Quijano's description of coloniality suggests internalized colonialism, the perpetuation of Western European colonial mentality in their former colonies, making people unconsciously accept the superiority and attractiveness of Europe.

The Limenian society that Yushimito creates in "Rizoma" is an example of such a society where upper and upper middle class people blindly and indifferently live with the "coloniality of power," stemming from internalized "Eurocentered colonialism," to borrow Quijano's term (168). Setting up this society of blindness and indifference, the author presents an ambitious entrepreneurial gourmet chef who exoticizes indigenous culture and food in order to discover "something marvelous" out of indigenous culture and food through his cutting-edge cooking techniques imported from Europe. His clients are also drawn to the exoticization of indigenous culture and food, always waiting for "something marvelous" to be presented on their plates. In the end, people's desire to discover "something marvelous" leads to their own conversion into rabid cannibalistic monsters that are equated with a mythical dog-headed and human-bodied monstrous being. The rabid infection is unstoppable, with the monsters taking over the society. In short, the end product of their search for "something marvelous" is the birth of the monsters. Going back, then, to the second etymological meaning of the word *monster*—"something marvelous and prodigious," Yushimito's monsters can be interpreted as an embodiment of the long-lasting repetition of colonial desire for finding "something marvelous" and the repeated destructive consequence of such colonial pursuit, fortifying the perpetuation of the "coloniality of power" in present-day Lima. Situating the birth of the monsters in the twenty-first-century "coloniality of power," Yushimito urges the reader to become aware of the possibility of the extinction of the human species when mindless masses, incapable of seeing a repeated "coloniality of power," passively accept it or allow it to continue to habituate in society.

The story opens with the ending scene in which the first-person narrator and protagonist, Gumersindo Mallea, a surviving human being on top of a Ferris wheel, observes the multitude of hungry cynocephalic beings attempting clumsily to crawl up to him. Then, the narrator, looking back over the past two months, recounts what has happened before he comes to face the monstrous beings.

The first flashback scene that comes to Gumersindo's mind is his meeting with his boss, Haroldo, director of a gourmet magazine, *Gourmet*, about his article series on "techno-gastronomy."[10] Gumersindo is a feature columnist for the magazine who reports on restaurant inauguration parties and food festivals, interviews chefs, and, once in a while, finds popular recipes to be published in another column without copyright permission. Although he goes along with the publisher's missions of attracting magazine readers' attention to new dishes and restaurants, and making them want to consume more and more, he is not disinterested in educating his readers regarding controversial issues, giving them information, and making them think. He has written an article about "molecular gastronomy," based on published research, and wants to continue to write serial articles dedicated to this topic. However, his boss dissuades Gumersindo from continuing his series because the theme is so controversial that some readers have complained about his article. His boss admits that Gumersindo's first article is well written and well researched, but claims that their readers prefer not to think:

> Our readers are loyal consumers, creatures with profound and noble emotions. . . . They like to feel in control of something that they incorporate into their organism and process automatically. . . .they are what I call reflex consumers. The kind of audience that does not want to chew with their brain, but with their teeth. . . . [O]ur readers are expecting a magazine like ours to be an extension of this automatic gesture that intensifies their existential idleness. Maybe you don't like to hear it, but we are creatures of habit. (78)[11]

In order to please their mindless readers-consumers, Gumersindo's series is canceled. But ironically, he is sent to cover a food festival on avant-garde cooking, the topic closely related to the "techno-gastronomy" of his cancelled series.

Gumersindo's flashback narration, then, takes the reader to the food festival, where an invited Catalan celebrity chef, Severí Mollà, gives a press conference. Mollà promotes the idea of "techno-cuisine" in Peru, and the way he talks about Peruvian cooking resonates with a paternalistic and colonial discourse: ". . . to talk about techno-cuisine in this country is to barely emit the original cry prior to the alphabet... to put the first stone in Machu Picchu, to make the first knot in a quipu. Pardon me, but I must say this to you: you are still eating a corpse..." (81-82).[12] Mollà continues:

> Of course, the gastronomy of this country, so beautiful and hospitable . . . is undoubtedly *one of the richest minerals of the continent. . . .* The only thing missing has been the machinery to extract it. Think about that rich and brilliant corpse resting in the quarries! Look at it and bring it to fruition! Turn it into that gold ring to be put on your finger!
>
> (Applause)
> (((Applause)))
> ((((((Applause)))))) (82)[13]

Mollà's attitude reflects the colonizer's mentality that imposes his Eurocentric ideas of enlightening on the "backward" and "ignorant" Peruvian population that does not know how to take advantage of rich natural food resources or how to develop and manage Peruvian food culture and industry in the global market.

What is more disturbing is the audience's passive attitude that accepts and almost worships Mollà's Eurocentric discourse of "progress." The majority of the audience are journalists, but they only ask him kind, favorable, and flattering questions. In the middle of enthusiastic applause and flattery, Gumersindo is the only one who tries to ask a provocative question about the origin of his style of "techno-cuisine," attributing it to a French chemist, Hervé This's "molecular gastronomy," but Mollà rejects the influence of "molecular gastronomy," insisting on a total detachment from it. Their question and answer session does not generate or stimulate any further discussions, not because of the discomfort the audience feels, but because of their indifference. Gumersindo reflects: "My question was an –ànticlímax, of course, from which the morning was no longer able to recover. It did not seem important to anyone. The journalists were moving their mouths, restless, anticipating what they would eat" (84).[14] This indifference exhibits not only a lack of critical thoughts among the journalists who only look for some entertainment for themselves and their readers but also a sense of disconnect from the past that encourages the audience to think only about future progress without reviewing how and why the "origin" of this "techno-cuisine" emerged in the past and has evolved thus far.

Althought Gumersindo's question does not serve to generate controversy with respect to Mollà's Eurocentric project of installing the same Catalan model of progress in Peru, it reveals the audience's blindness to the disassociation between the past and the present, and their inability to further critically analyze the possible harms to Peruvian food knowledge, practice, and culture that such a decontexualized understanding of Peruvian gastronomy can produce. This atmosphere in which the audience accepts and even admires Mollà's insensible suggestions recalls the perpetuation of "coloniality of power" articulated by Quijano (176). The "mirage" of a European style of cooking and food industry brought by Mollà from Catalonia is still seducing the contemporary audience of the former Spanish colony, fortifying the perpetuation of the model of global power structure that situates the European techniques of cooking over the indigenous/native food knowledge, culture, and values.

Among the people in the audience who are seduced by Mollà's speech is a local French chef, Federico Colobert, who actualizes Mollà's colonial discourse of extracting natural resources in the name of progress and economic prosperity, without recognizing the normalized colonial mentality. Colobert is so allured by Mollà's "techno-gastronomy" that he cannot see that his ideology and practice of cooking are a repetition of colonial domination over indigenous food and cooking traditions and knowledge. All he cares about is to invent an avant-garde plate out of the Peruvian native ingredients, such as potatoes, through cutting-edge cooking equipment and technology.

At the food festival, Colobert finds Gumersindo and, keeping his voice down, tells him about Colobert's deconstruction of *la causa rellena*:[15]

> [I] have managed to alter some flavors following the process of thermal immersion. And the Peruvian potatoes called *papa huayro*, for example: I have succeeded in deconstructing the dish, *causa rellena*, thanks to an enzyme, so that I can make the potatoes peel themselves, and in this way inside there is a natural puree! You cannot image such a divine flavor flowing from them. A flavor that seems to come from the beginning of time when there were no senses and everything was new. (86)[16]

In contrast to Colobert's excitement, Gumersindo's responds unenthusiastically: "I am not capable of imagining it" (86).[17] To this, Colobert responds, "Well, exactly. . . . My objective is that people do not have to imagine anything at all. In a few days, people will eat without the need to use their imagination" (86).[18] If Colobert's practice of transforming the indigenous food, *la papa huayro*, into an avant-garde style of cuisine following the European model shows his ambition for his individual success, fame, and prosperity, his unawareness of this appropriation of the indigenous culture and Mollà's and his own colonial mentality bring the danger of spreading and normalizing the absence of consciousness in society that impedes people from critically thinking—imagining—and thus recognizing the long-standing "coloniality of power," or the twenty-first-century internalized colonialism right in front of them.

Therefore, it is not surprising to learn that the name of Colobert's restaurant is Canibalia and that, at the door, there is an image of a beautiful indigenous woman eating her own arm next to the sign *Canibalia*. Colobert explains to Gumersindo, who is visiting the restaurant to write a report on it, that the name corresponds to "the voracity and self-sufficient refinement of contemporary society" (88).[19] Although he does not give any further explanations of the meaning of this phrase, we may presume that in his unconscious colonial mind the voracity of the society is somehow connected to the savagery or primitivism represented by the anthropophagic indigenous woman, and "the self-sufficient refinement" implies that this primitivism can (must) be refined at *his* restaurant through his "techno-gastronomy," which offers his clients a culinary tool by which to become "civilized." What is shown behind his unconscious colonial mind is not only the exoticization and commercialization of cannibalism without any specific contexts but also the abiding colonial binary classification of cannibalism/the primitive/the indigenous on one side and high French (European) cuisine/the civilized/French background chef and urban exclusive clients on the other. This colonial binary classification also indicates the superiority of the European and the inferiority of the indigenous.

Colobert's following words suggest such an Eurocentered colonial classification: "We have succeeded in adapting the technique of spherification *to a standard similar to the current European ones*, which, certainly, fills me with pride, because now chirimoya fruit can be transformed into gelatin and can look like the transparent small bits of eggs of caviar" (89; emphasis added).[20] His main intention is to show Gumersindo, visiting his restaurant, his successful transformation of chirimoya fruit into jellylike cubes through his "techno-gastronomic" techniques (spherification), but his words, whether intentionally or unintentionally, convey that "the darkness" of the indigenous fruit, chirimoya, must be "lightened" by a European method and technique, in order to be as refined (or gentrified) as the delicacy of caviar.

Despite this obvious presence of a colonial mentality, Gumersindo does not ask any critical questions, but instead keeps taking notes about the things that he sees without any reactions or doubts. He is not a journalist who lacks a critical mind, but simply conforms to his boss's policies. Thus, when he, reviewing his notes, writes an article about Canibalia, he first includes sentences that can raise readers' sociopolitical consciousness, but ends up erasing all the sentences he has written. For instance, he starts with "In the world, big things are happening,"[21] but he changes it to "big things could be happening" (89).[22] Then, he carefully inserts sociopolitical issues: "Universal education. Public health. The elimination of world hunger. However, those big things do not happen. Small things, instead of them, occur" (89-90).[23] He seems to avert his eyes from reality, but his insertion of these issues in his article insinuates his willingness to pronounce his concerns about them in a subtle and ambiguous way. Gumersindo's ambiguous message continues to appear in the next sentence: "For example, we devour with absolute creativity each element that God put on earth" (90).[24] This sentence, on the one hand, can stress that human creativity can affect "small things" on earth. On the other, it can also imply that if humans "devour" all the "small things," it can cause a destruction of earth against God's will and nature. In the end, however, the ambiguity in his sentences disappears, not because he decides to make his point clear but because he erases all the sentences, thinking about Haroldo's negative reactions. He ends up turning in to his boss an article entitled "Canibalia: Avant-garde of the palate for sophisticated appetites" (90),[25] which satisfies his boss.

Although Gumersindo complies with the journal's conservative policy, he still expresses his opinion to Haroldo:

> [P]erhaps, we are so obsessed with the preparation of dishes, with the nature of consumables, that we forget that we ourselves are a possible food. . . . We are like flies kissing all the foods . . . until the day when God's hand arrives and crushes us. (91)[26]

Though Haroldo responds "there are things that it is better to not to know" (91),[27] Gumersindo cannot ignore his concerns about the relentless human lust for constantly innovating new dishes and its negative effects on society.

Meanwhile, the news of a female customer biting off a waiter's nose at Canibalia is reported in a newspaper. After this first incident, similar biting attacks frequently occur, and more than eighty persons are hospitalized. It turns out that the first aggressor has carried an infectious virus called HH1 and has transmitted it to her victims, who eventually become aggressors and spread the virus. The Ministry of Public Health alerts people to stay calm, assuring that hospitals have been providing their maximum care in high alert, but does not offer residents any preparations for evacuations. Gumersindo, in the midst of the viral outbreak, unable to erase the image of the indigenous cannibalistic woman at Colobert's restaurant from his mind, goes to the municipal library to conduct archival research. The documents that he gathers seem sporadic and unrelated, but each roughly shows the theme of deaths, burials, or cannibalism, dated between Columbus's 1492 expedition, the conquest, and colonial time. For instance, there is an article that talks about a slave who poisoned plantation owners in Haiti slowly over the course of six years through food and was later burned alive. The plantation owners were buried with their mouths full of salt. The other articles contain the following information: three Spaniards in the Andes decapitated another Spaniard to eat because of hunger; two Spaniards killed in the indigenous rebellious movements, which are believed to be incited by pre-Columbian indigenous *huaca* (*wak'as*) spirits against Christianity and the Spanish conquest in the sixteenth century in Peru; a myth of the revival of the dead at a pre-Columbian tomb; Columbus's disappointment because he could not find dog-headed and human-bodied beings; his interpretation of two native people in a Caribbean island whose arms were missing as cannibal people; and Bartolomé de las Casas's account about a Spanish captain who ordered sticks to be put into the mouths of the people who were burned alive in order not to have to hear their screams and shrieks.

After gathering the information, Gumersindo goes to see Colobert at this restaurant and relates his speculation about how this infectious disease started at Colobert's restaurant. Gumersindo thinks that the enzymes from the potatoes produced in Ayacucho released something poisonous that the chef ignored or did not know how to control. He indicates,

> My suspicion is the following, Colobert. The enzymes of those potatoes that you ordered from Ayacucho released something. Something that you didn't know about or didn't know how to control. Something that maybe you desired, but didn't know. At the beginning,

I was sure that your desire was to see us all turning into cynocephalus and cannibals; I remembered the image of the indigenous woman who was eating her own arm and I thought I could see in her a small perverse gesture. But that would be so obvious… and you, in the end, are not a conspirator. I suppose that you are only naive. (98)[28]

Gumersindo concludes that the combination of Colobert's irresistible desire to create a cannibalistic atmosphere, coupled with his experiments with his cutting-edge techno-cooking at his restaurant, and his ignorance and irresponsibility are the principal causes of the outbreak. However, Gumersindo's conclusion does not end here; instead, he continues to insinuate that Colobert's desire can be a repeated desire inherited from the time of Columbus's exploration and encounter through colonial times:

As I think I have shown you, the desire behind that attribute, poorly domesticated till today, was latent all these centuries, circulating in the mind, in the hearts of many people. And finally, today it has been ingested by accident and it has used you, let me tell you, as a catalyst; you were the enzyme of this old desire. (98-99)[29]

Although it is not clear how Gumersindo comes to reach this conclusion through his archival research, it seems that he draws a connection between Colobert's desire and the colonial desire for cannibalism. Gumersindo sees Colobert's desire as the principal cause for the origin and propagation of the epidemic of the HH1 virus and the sequential breeding of something akin to a dog-headed human-bodied species, just as Columbus's search for that dog-headed species led to the conquest and colonization in Latin America. The narrator thus conflates high-tech culinary manipulation of native foods with the colonial destruction of the indigenous population, the slavery of Africans, torturous deaths, rebellions, and resistance movements with their ongoing violence and deaths.

A closer look at the theme of the burials of human bodies after being tortured and/or killed, shown in the archives, helps the reader see the connection that Gumersindo makes: between the soil contaminated by the unnaturally destroyed human bodies in the time of the conquest and colonization, and the potatoes grown in that soil of the Andes brought to Colobert's restaurant in the present day. Furthermore, if the reader goes back to a particular archive document with more careful attention, recording the 1570 incident in which two Spaniards were found dead in Huamanga, he or she may see another layer of connection between colonial times and the present. According to this document, the Andean indigenous divine spirits were awakened to possess the indigenous people and drive them to dance in order to expel the Christian God and restore the indigenous divine power:

> [H]uacas no longer possess stones, as in the times of the Incas, but men. That trembling that impels them toward the convulsion of dance, the expulsion of Christian God from the body, is known as Taki Onccoy, Disease of the Chant; and he has now . . . the tomb inside himself. (97)[30]

"That tremblin"[31] refers to an indigenous rebellion movement against Christianity and Spanish conquest, known as Taki Onccoy, "the sickness of the chant," or "dancing sickness" (Stern 124), or "disease of the dance" (Mumford 150), which started in Huamanga. Many historians agree, despite the differences in their interpretations of Taki Onccoy (Taki Onqoy), that this indigenous movement started in the 1560s and spread out to Cuzco, Lima, and La Paz (Mumford 151-55). Huamanga is a northern province of the Ayacucho region, and one can observe a curious parallel between the outbreak of the indigenous movement in this region in the past and the outbreak of the poisonous enzymes of the potatoes produced in this same region in the present. Besides these connections, there are at least two more: between the current virus outbreak spreading out throughout the country in the twenty-first century and the indigenous movement that extended to other cities in the sixteenth century; and between the name of this movement, "sickness of the chant" or "disease of the dance," and the actual virus epidemic.

After contemplating these connections between the European conquest and colonization and the present-day colonial desire and baggage, the reader can come to see a more complicated and

complete interpretation of Gumersindo's statement quoted above—
"the desire behind that attribute, poorly domesticated till today, was
latent all these centuries, circulating in the mind, in the hearts of
many people" (98).[32] "The desire . . . poorly domesticated" (98)[33]
refers not only to Colobert's desire for reproducing cannibalism
(the repetition of Columbus's and other conquerors' and colonizers'
desire), but also to the long-lasting desire of the colonized and
oppressed for resistance and liberation. Gumersindo's articulation
of this desire of both the colonizer and the colonized leads the
reader to recognize that the colonial desire and baggage latently and
persistently prevail in society.

Only if Gumersindo's findings through his archival research
were officially reported to the public to warn about the catastrophic
consequence of Colobert's colonial desire for cannibalism, the
society as a whole might be able to halt the total conversion of
the human species into cannibalistic monstrous beings. However,
Gumersindo's findings are only privately shared with Colobert, who
later commits suicide according to the news, and with Tominaga, an
unpretentious and artless Japanese chef who disregards the culinary
boom of "techno-cuisines" and stays with Gumersindo until they
are about to be attacked by the rabid horde. Unfortunately, the idea
of challenging his boss's order and the journal's policies, in order to
divulge his criticism against "techno-cuisine," does not occur to him
with any sense of urgency and crisis. In this sort of society where
people are always hungry for and constantly fed by the latest culinary
inventions and techniques without any sociopolitical consciousness
and where no one dares to disseminate critical opinions against some
kind of boom, people become their own bait for the entertainment
and consumerism of cannibalism without ever realizing it.

The story ends with a scene in which the last human survivors
in the city, Gumersindo and Tominaga, unable to escape from the
masses of hungry monstrous beings, do not have any other choice
but to accept their uncontrollable propagation and domination over
human society. The very last sentences may leave the reader with a
feeling of devastation facing the total destruction of humankind and

humanity, as well as a feeling of uncertainty, unable to envisage the future in which all the creatures buried underground are awakened:

> And in the darkness, I heard them getting confused. They were vague echoes that came from far below, from that place that is even lower than the world, and where all the creatures, except men, cover themselves with sheets, bury their eyes, and silently, are beginning to come to life. (104)[34]

This ending is not surprising, considering how easily Mollà, the Catalan chef, and Colobert, the French chef in Lima, have succeeded in seducing the upper and upper middle class consumers through, on the one hand, a colonial discourse on the Europeanization of the "primitive" Peruvian cooking and, on the other, through a colonial desire to recreate the ambience of cannibalism by cooking the indigenous food—potatoes from Ayacucho—with cutting-edge techniques. More specifically, Mollà's speech quoted above,[35] showing an analogy between a rich mineral and native Peruvian food, not only encourages the extraction of the mineral (the native food) by a European model of technological development, but also anticipates the same devastating consequences after the extraction of Peruvian food; consequences such as the destruction of indigenous populations, not to mention cultures and knowledge, lands, and natural resources.

Conclusion: Behind Gourmet Chefs' Beautiful Dishes

There is no evidence that these two ambitious chefs wanted to see the extinction of the human species in Lima and eventually in the globe, and Yushimito does not seem to blame the dark consequence of the gastronomic boom on anyone. However, his story draws attention to their Eurocentric attitude, which reflects a colonial mentality and suggests that the resilient "coloniality of power" can bring a devastation to human society, and, eventually perhaps, death to the human species if no one dares to recognize that "this chimera of ['coloniality of power'] is still so attractive to so many," borrowing again Quijano's words ("Coloniality and Modernity" 176).

This extreme transformation of human beings into cynocephalic zombies may only happen in a science-fiction dystopian fantastic world. However, there is an undeniable similarity between the mindless society of Lima depicted in Yushimito's fiction and the uncritical public that is attracted to "the chimera" of Gastón Acurio's beautifying of Peruvian food, despite his scandalous duplicity revealed in "the Panama Papers." It seems that the Peruvian press and public pay much more attention to Acurio's culinary activities and restaurant businesses than they do to his avoidance of paying taxes and the pompous lack of solidarity that avoidance implies. Meanwhile, more celebrity chefs who were trained in Europe and North America, such as Pedro Miguel Schiaffino, known as "the jungle chef," and Virgilio Martínez, "the Andes explorer," who tend to take some photos with local indigenous people from the communities that they visit (López-Carlos),[36] go to Amazonian and Andean communities in order to get native ingredients to aestheticize Peruvian food. Yushimito's "Rizoma", then, urges us to take a moment to observe the possible "coloniality of power" reflected in these chefs' beautiful dishes and photos.

Notes

1. "En la medida en que la gastronomía del Perú sea un bien preciado, la gente estará dispuesta a pagar mucho más. La idea es que ese dinero vaya directamente a los campesinos, a los pescadores artesanales. Se debe incluir a todos" (n.p.).

2. In his speech at the opening ceremony of the academic year of 2006, at La Universidad del Pacífico in Lima, Acurio attempted to inspire the young audience to create new concepts and brands special and peculiar to Peru, in order to establish a fresh and positive image of Peru's national identity and promote it at an international level. Acurio believes that the construction of a positive national identity of Peru that sparks collective aspirations and goals is the first indispensable step to discover and produce Peruvian concepts and brands, and that these concepts and brands, that Acurio calls "un poder de seducción," must come from the Peruvian culture and identity founded through its *mestizaje* (interracial and intercultural mixings). He states: "es en ese mestizaje donde los peruanos deben

encontrar la fuente de inspiración no solo para generar riqueza sino sobretodo para aceptarnos y querernos como nación y recién a partir de ahí poder encontrar hacia dentro todas aquellas ideas que luego saldrán transformadas en productos y en marcas a conquistar el planeta" (CREARSEPERÚ n.p.).

3. Acurio understands *mestizaje* simply as the harmonious blending of many different cultures and races that has enriched Peruvian culture and identity. Also, he seems to genuinely believe that a united Peru through new Peruvian concepts and brands stemming from its *mestizo* culture and identity can bring Peru economic prosperity and a sense of pride that *all* the Peruvians can enjoy. His message is that Peru will be a nation where "las oportunidades están basadas en una educación igual para todos, una justicia igual para todos y un Estado que, de la mano con sus ciudadanos, vigila e interviene enérgicamente frente a la arbitrariedad, el abuso y el rompimiento de las reglas de juego pactadas por todos" (CREARSEPEREÚ n.p.).

4. "La gastronomía y el hambre son incompatibles. . . . Este momento nos exige dejar de lado los afanes personales para pasar a temas colectivos. Somos conscientes de nuestro rol de promover el comercio justo" ("Acurio" n.p.).

5. In his essay, "El sueño del chef," in *El País*, a prominent Spanish newspaper, Mario Vargas Llosa praises not only Acurio's creativity, but more importantly his enthusiasm and efforts to include everyone and his generosity to offer opportunities to those who are motivated. Vargas Llosa expresses, "Esa generosidad y espíritu ancho no es frecuente entre los empresarios, ni en el Perú ni en ninguna otra parte. . . . Si hubiera un centenar de empresarios y creadores como Gastón Acurio, el Perú hubiera dejado atrás el subdesarrollo hacía rato" (n.p.).

6. "The Panama Papers" refer to the leaked documents (11.5 million files) from the Panama-based law firm Mossack Fonseca that reveal the immoral practices and tactics of tax avoidance and evasion in offshore tax havens of the most powerful and wealthy people in the world (Harding n.p.).

7. In another article, "República gastronómica y país de cocineros: comida, política, medios y una nueva idea de nación para el Perú," Matta continues to argue that this type of capitalist model, boosting Peru's reputation as a viable and safe country for internal and

external investments, depends on the spirit and efforts of individual entrepreneurs and investors, whose assets, profits, and benefits remain individual. Thus Matta concludes that the benefits of the "national" Peruvian cuisine campaign, ultimately, do not extend equally to all the participants (35-36).

8. García borrows Aníbal Quijano's term to show that the hierarchical power relations between the European colonizer/urban upper class elite and the colonized/rural indigenous other, which were created based on racial and racist social categorizations during the period of European colonial domination, are still reproduced and normalized even today in Latin American societies as well as on the globe.

9. I borrow Max Horkheimer and Theodor W. Adorno's term "culture industry," which appeared for the first time in their essay "The Culture Industry: Enlightenment as Mass Deception" (1944). They define "culture industry" as a capitalist and political system in which popular entertaining forms of culture are made and propagated by those in power to be sold to the masses. They argue that the commodification of culture, whose principal purpose is to sell it and profit from it, results in the mass (re)productions of standardized formulas (94-95, 98-100). What is harmful about this standardization, which Horkheimer and Adorno call "pseudoindividuality," is the illusion of individual autonomy through which capitalism manipulates the masses to become, consciously or unconsciously, passive, moldable, and compliant members of the capitalist system (124-25).

10. "Techno-gastronomy" can be also called "techno-emotional cuisine," a term preferred by a Catalan chef, Ferran Adrià (Domene-Danés 105), whose idea can be traced back to the "molecular gastronomy," coined by an Oxford physicist, Nicholas Kurti, and a French physical chemist, Hervé This (108). All these different names indicate the same idea: a physical and chemical transformation of familiar food to unfamiliar and experimental food produced through advanced and innovative cooking technology, techniques, methods, and equipment (108).

11. "Nuestros lectores son consumidores leales, animales con sentimientos profundos y nobles. . . . Les gusta sentirse dueños de algo que incorporan a su organismo y procesan automáticamente. . . . son lo que llamo consumidores reflejos. Esa clase de público que no quiere masticar con el cerebro, sino con los dientes. . . . [N]uestros lectores están esperando que una revista como la nuestra sea una extensión de

ese gesto automático que agudiza su ociosidad existencial. Tal vez no te guste oírlo, pero somos animales de costumbres" (78).

12. "... hablar de la tecno-cocina en este país es apenas emitir el grito germinal previo al alfabeto... poner la primera piedra en Machu Picchu, hacerle el nudo inicial a un quipu. Perdonadme, pero os debo decir algo: todavía estáis comiendo un cadáver..." (81-82). A quipu is a recording device made of rope knots used in the Andean regions in the pre-Hispanic time.

13. "Claro que la gastronomía de este país, tan hermoso y hospitalario... no deja de ser *uno de los minerales más ricos del continente*.... Tan solo ha faltado la maquinaria para extraerlo. ¡Pensad en ese rico y brillante cadáver que se aletarga en las canteras! ¡Miradlo y hacedlo florecer! ¡Convertidlo en ese dorado anillo que os calce en el dedo! (Aplausos) (((Aplausos))) ((((((Aplausos))))))" (82).

14. "Mi pregunta fue un anticlímax, por supuesto, del cual ya la mañana no consiguió recuperarse. A nadie pareció importarle. Los periodistas movían sus bocas, inquietos, adelantándose a lo que comerían" (84).

15. *Causa rellena* is a typical Peruvian terrine made of mashed yellow potato, usually filled with tuna or chicken.

16. "[H]e conseguido alterar algunos sabores siguiendo el proceso de inmersión termal. Y la papa huayro, por ejemplo: he logrado deconstruir la causa rellena, gracias a una enzima, de modo que logro hacer que se pelen solas y por dentro, ¡sean un puré natural! No se imagina usted el sabor tan divino que brota de ellas. Un sabor que parece venir del principio de los tiempos, cuando no había sentidos y todo era nuevo" (86).

17. "No soy capaz de imaginarlo" (86).

18. "Pues precisamente.... Mi objetivo es que la gente no tenga que imaginarse *absolutamente* nada. En unos días, la gente podrá comer sin necesidad de imaginar" (86).

19. "La voracidad y al refinamiento autosuficiente de la sociedad contemporánea" (88).

20. "Hemos conseguido adaptar la técnica de esferificación *en un estándar semejante a los europeos actuales*, lo cual, ciertamente, me llena de orgullo, porque ahora la chirimoya se puede convertir en gelatina y parecerse a los huevecillos transparentes del caviar" (89; emphasis added).

21. "En el mundo están sucediendo cosas grandes" (89).

22. "Podrían estar sucediendo cosas grandes" (89).

23. "La educación universal. La sanidad pública. La eliminación global del hambre. Sin embargo, esas cosas grandes no suceden. Ocurren, en su lugar, cosas pequeñas" (89-90).

24. "Por ejemplo, devoramos con absoluta creatividad cada elemento que puso Dios sobre la tierra" (90).

25. "Canibalia: Vanguardia en el paladar para apetitos sofisticados" (90).

26. "[T]al vez, estamos tan obsesionados con la preparación de los platos, con la naturaleza de los insumos, que se nos olvida que nosotros mismos somos un alimento posible. . . . Somos como las moscas que besan todos los alimentos . . . hasta el día en que la mano de Dios llega y nos aplasta" (91).

27. "Hay cosas que es mejor ignorar" (91).

28. "Mi sospecha es la siguiente, Colobert. Las enzimas de aquellas papas que mandó traer usted de Ayacucho liberaron algo. Algo que usted ignoraba o no supo controlar. Algo que tal vez deseaba, pero no sabía. Al principio, yo estaba seguro de que su deseo era vernos a todos convertidos en cinocéfalos y caníbales; recordaba la imagen de la mujer indígena que se comía el brazo y me parecía entrever en ella un pequeño gesto perverso. Pero eso sería tan evidente... y usted, al fin y al cabo, no es un conspirador. Supongo que usted es tan solo un ingenuo" (98).

29. "Como creo haberle mostrado, el deseo detrás de aquel atributo, mal domesticado hasta hoy, estuvo latente todo estos siglos, circulando en la mente, en los corazones de mucha gente. Y al fin, hoy se ha consumado por accidente y lo ha usado a usted, déjeme que le diga, como catalizador; usted fue la enzima de ese viejo deseo" (98-99).

30. "[L]as huacas ya no se apoderan de las piedras, como en los tiempos del Inca, sino de los hombres. Aquel temblor que los impulsa hacia la convulsión del baile, a la expulsión del dios cristiano del cuerpo, es llamado Taki Onccoy, Enfermedad del Canto; y él tiene ahora . . . a la huaca metida dentro" (97).

31. "Aquel temblor" (97).

32. "El deseo detrás de aquel atributo, mal domesticado hasta hoy, estuvo latente todo estos siglos, circulando en la mente, en los corazones de mucha gente" (98).

33. "El deseo . . . mal domesticado" (98).

34. "Y en la oscuridad, yo los oía confundirse. Eran apenas ecos que venían desde muy abajo, desde ese lugar que está incluso más abajo del mundo, y donde todas las criaturas, salvo los hombres, se cubren con las sábanas, entierran sus ojos, y sigilosamente, empiezan a nacer" (104).

35. See the seventh page of this study.

36. In his conference presentation, Jorge López-Canales explores how these chefs of European ethnic background from urban upper-class society search for "exotic" native ingredients from the interior regions of the Amazon and Andes and discusses how postcolonial hegemony is reproduced in the boom and globalization of Peruvian cuisine.

Works Cited

"Acurio, Gastón. 'La gastronomía y el hambre son incompatibles.'" *El Comercio*, Dec. 28, 2009. <archivo.elcomercio.pe/sociedad/lima/gaston-acurio-gastronomia-hambre-son-incompatibles-noticia-387132.> Accessed May 24, 2016.

Domene-Danés, Maria. "El Bulli: Contemporary Intersections between Food, Science, Art and Late Capitalism." *BRAC–Barcelona Research Art Creation* 1.1, 2013, pp. 100-26. <dialnet.unirioja.es/descarga/articulo/4863705.pdf.> Accessed June 17, 2016.

Castilla, Óscar C. "#PanamaPapers: Las compañías offshore de Gastón Acurio." *OjoPúblico*, April 4, 2016. <panamapapers.ojo-publico.com/articulo/los-paraisos-fiscales-de-gaston-acurio.> Accessed May 27, 2016.

CREARSEPERÚ (Centro Regional del Acción para la Responsabilidad Social en el Perú). "Discurso de Gastón Acurio en la Universidad del Pacífico Año 2006." Sept. 11, 2011. blog.pucp.edu.pe/blog/crearseperu. Accessed May 26, 2016.

García, María Elena. "The Taste of Conquest: Colonialism, Cosmopolitics, and the Dark Side of Peru's Gastronomic Boom." *The Journal of Latin American and Caribbean Anthropology* 18.3, 2013, pp. 505-24. <onlinelibrary.wiley.com/doi/10.1111/jlca.12044/full.> Accessed June 1, 2016.

Harding, Luke. "What are the Panama Papers?: A Guide to History's Biggest Data Leak." *The Guardian*, April 5, 2016. <www.theguardian. com/news/2016/apr/03/what-you-need-to-know-about-the-panama-papers.> Accessed Sept. 30, 2017.

Hoad, T. F. "Monster." *The Concise Oxford Dictionary of English Etymology*. Oxford UP, 1986, p. 299.

Horkheimer, Max, and Theodor W. Adorno. "The Culture Industry: Enlightenment as Mass Deception." *Dialectic of Enlightenment: Philosophical Fragments*. Edited by Gunzelin Schmid Noerr. Translated by Edmund Jephcott. Stanford UP, 2002, pp. 94-136.

López-Canales, Jorge. "Peru on a Plate: Postcolonial Legacy and the Quest for Culinary Authenticity." *Transforming Legacies, Association of Iberian and Latin American Studies of Australasia*, July 4, 2016, Massesy University, Albany, Auckland, NZ. Conference Presentation.

Matta, Raúl. "Dismantling the Boom of Peruvian Cuisine: From the Plate to Gastro-Politics." *ReVista: Harvard Review of Latin America*, Fall 2014, pp. 64-66. <revista.drclas.harvard.edu/book/dismantling-boom-peruvian-cuisine.> Accessed June 1, 2016.

_____. "República gastronómica y país de cocineros: comida, política, medios y una nueva idea de nación para el Perú." *Revista Colombiana de Antropología* 50.2, 2014, pp. 15-40. <www.scielo. org.co/pdf/rcan/v50n2/v50n2a02.pdf.> Accessed June 1, 2016.

Mumford, Jeremy. "The Taki Onqoy and the Andean Nation: Sources and Interpretations." *Latin American Research Review* 33.1, 1998, pp. 150-65. <www.jstor.org.ez.wul.waseda.ac.jp/stable/pdf/2503902.pd f?refreqid=excelsior%3A33c08cd31936435398a0893945fc2c0b.> Accessed July 28, 2016.

Quijano, Aníbal. "Coloniality and Modernity/Rationality." *Cultural Studies* 21.2-3, 2007, pp. 168-78. <www.tandfonline.com.ez.wul. waseda.ac.jp/doi/full/10.1080/09502380601164353.> Accessed April 27, 2017.

_____. "Coloniality of Power, Eurocentrism, and Latin America." *Nepantla: Views from the South* 1.3, 2000, pp. 533-80. <edisciplinas. usp.br/pluginfile.php/295861/mod_resource/content/1/Quijano%20 %282000%29%20Colinality%20of%20power.pdf.> Accessed June 6, 2016.

Stern, Steve J. "The Tragedy of Success." *The Peru Reader: History, Culture, Politics.* 2nd ed. Edited by Orin Starn, Carlos Iván Degregori, and Robin Kirk. Duke UP, 2005, pp. 124-48.

Vargas Llosa, Mario. "El sueño del 'chef.'" *El País*, March 22, 2009. <elpais.com/diario/2009/03/22/opinion/1237676414_850215.html.> Accessed May 26, 2016.

Yushimito, Carlos del Valle. "Rizoma." *Los bosques tienen sus propias puertas.* Peisa, 2013, pp. 73-104.

Zúñiga Lossio, Mario. "Límites y posibilidades de lo multiculutral e intercultural en el discurso del Chef peruano Gastón Acurio." *Revista Cultural Electrónica: Construyendo Nuestra Interculturalidad* 4, 2007, pp. 1-21. <www.yumpu.com/es/document/view/37127004/ limites-y-posibilidades-de-lo-multicultural-e-intercultural-en-el.> Accessed May 31, 2016.

Canal Dreams, Panama Separatists, Great-Power Politics, and the Making of Juan Gabriel Vásquez's *The Secret History of Costaguana*___

Gene H. Bell-Villada

At one point in Chekhov's play *Three Sisters* (1901), Lieutenant Colonel Vershinin muses thus: "The other day I was reading the diary of that French politician, the one who went to prison because of the Panama scandal . . . It was so moving the way he described the birds he could hear from his prison window . . ." (258). The casual allusion is to Charles Baïhaut, France's onetime Minister of Public Works, who in 1893 was imprisoned for bribes taken from investors in the ill-fated French canal effort in Panama, and who, following his release, published a diary in 1898. The passing comment from a remote Russia suggests the extent to which the tangle of events surrounding the fabled Isthmus and the French Canal catastrophe would reverberate in various corners of the world.

From mid-nineteenth century to the opening years of the twentieth, the idea of a canal traversing Panama (or, alternatively, Nicaragua) was a dream to be entertained by several countries and that would lead to some grand-scale developments, to wit: a massive construction project undertaken in Colombia's then-Department of Panama by a French enterprise in the 1880s; the eventual collapse of the entire venture, leading to scandal and disgrace in France in the 1890s; the continuous presence and the rise of (ever-latent) separatist sentiments in Panama; the diplomatic-political maneuvers and military intervention of the United States; the legendary rise of aggressive President Teddy Roosevelt; and, last but not least, Panamanian secession and, for the nation of Colombia (which offered next to no resistance), the loss of its northernmost territory. All of this, and much more, took place years before the US Canal opened for business in 1914. It serves as subject matter for *Historia secreta de Costaguana* (2007; trans. 2011), a masterful work of fiction by Colombian novelist Juan Gabriel Vásquez (1973-).

An Isthmus, Imbedded in History

Being a historical novel, Vásquez's book is inevitably dense with historical information. For clarity's sake, here follows a précis of that background. In doing so, I rely primarily on David McCullough's monumental volume *The Path between the Seas* (1977), credited as a key source by Vásquez himself in his concluding Author's Note to *The Secret History of Costaguana.*

The story begins with Ferdinand de Lesseps (1805-1894), a handsome, courtly viscount and a charismatic, inspiring figure. Flush from having headed the enterprise that had brought to completion the Suez Canal (1859-1869), he now saw in Panama an opportunity to replicate that engineering feat through the Société Internationale Interocéanique de Darien. For the preliminary investigations, de Lesseps appointed Lucien Napoléon-Bonaparte Wyse, a lieutenant in the French Navy. Wyse was the illegitimate offspring of Napoleon I's niece Princess Laetitia; his mother in turn was a daughter of the emperor's erratic brother Lucien. Laetitia, for her part, would marry an Irish diplomat called Sir Thomas Wyse. (Hence the international mix of names.)

In 1876, de Lesseps charged Wyse with organizing and leading seventeen French experts on an exploratory journey through Darien. All contracted malaria; three of them perished. On his return, a battered Wyse felt discouraged, but de Lesseps forged ahead and sent him on a scouting trip and diplomatic mission to Colombia, which resulted in the Wyse Concession, guaranteeing ninety-nine years' Canal privileges to France.

By 1880, de Lesseps was raising shares for the canal venture. Large-scale excavation works began in 1882. Unfortunately, the viscount had seriously misjudged the physical conditions for "his" new canal, he expecting to build yet another sea-level waterway. Back at Suez, the terrain had been mostly flat, desert, and sandy, and the climate dry. Panama, by contrast, featured mountains, jungles, rivers, along with humidity and heavy rains to contend with—plus mosquitoes. At that time there were no known cures for malaria or yellow fever. Once the massive project was underway, a minimum of 20,000 people from all walks of life (European professionals as well as Caribbean laborers) were to die, mostly from disease, before the French quit in 1888.

Meanwhile, internal divisions, both Colombian and Panamanian, had been on the rise. According to Enrique Santos Molano's polemical history, *1903. Adiós Panamá* (another source listed by the novelist), there were four separatist attempts on the Isthmus in the nineteenth century, one as early as 1830 (a time in which Venezuela and Ecuador, let us recall, were also in the process of seceding from Bogotá). In one such incident, when, in 1855, a group of Panamanian artisans attempted to found a separate republic, the national Congress conceded in response that the Isthmus was a special entity within Nueva Granada (as the country was then known) but with military, monetary, and citizenship affairs remaining in the hands of the central government (Santos Molano 107). The latter reversed themselves in 1886, repealing a more liberal 1863 Constitution and reducing the nation's divers states to departments. The English-language Panamanian daily *The Star & Herald* already saw this move as grounds for separation, employing the word *patriots* for those Isthmians opposed to the demotion.

Around this time, Colombia found itself bled and weakened by its succession of civil wars. One such conflict in the 1880s virtually destroyed the Panamanian city of Colón (first founded by Americans in 1850, as the Atlantic Coast depot for the trans-Isthmian railroad); the town was also bombarded by US warships. The notorious War of a Thousand Days, 1899-1902 (famously fictionalized by Gabriel García Márquez), included pitched battles on the Isthmus even after hostilities on the mainland had ended.

Major Colombia-United States relations went back to the 1846 Bidlack Treaty, which guaranteed train traffic across Panama and granted to the United States the responsibility of protecting railroad operations, with American gunboats posted regularly offshore near both Colón and Panama City. Following the French debacle, in the US press and Congress, and from assorted lobbyists and then-Assistant Secretary of the Navy Theodore Roosevelt, there was open discussion about the possibility of an American-built Canal somewhere on the larger Isthmus. Hence, throughout the 1890s and into the turn of the century, lengthy, snail's-pace deliberations took place between Bogotá and Washington. In 1902 alone, two different Colombian ambassadors, Carlos Martínez Silva and José Vicente Concha, tried to work out a deal, to the detriment of their health.

The high point of these negotiations was the Hay-Herrán Treaty (January 22, 1903), worked out between Secretary of State John Hay and Dr. Tomás Herrán, Colombia's chargé d'affaires in Washington DC. It allowed the French company to sell its entire rights and properties to the United States and gave the latter full control over a six-mile-wide Canal area over a 100-year period. A payment of $10 million in gold and a yearly rent of $250,000 were also guaranteed to Colombia. On August 12, however, the Colombian Senate unanimously rejected Hay-Herrán, objecting to Colombia's being excluded from receiving any portion of the $40 million that the United States was slated to disburse to the French syndicate for its concession. In reaction, now-President Roosevelt wrote angrily to Hay, complaining about "those contemptible little creatures in Bogotá" and its "lot of jack-rabbits."

From all this back-and-forth, there emerged a series of secret three-way talks and long-range maneuvers involving Panamanian notables, New York City lobbyists, and Washington politicos, with a view to separating the Isthmus from Colombia. The Isthmian contingent included Dr. Manuel Amador, chief physician of the Panama Railroad (and future President of the new nation); José Agustín Arango, a senator from Panama; and J. Gabriel Duque, originally from Cuba, owner of the *Star & Herald* along with other enterprises, and head of the local firefighters. Another well-known, long-active French operative, now an American ally, Philippe Bunau-Varilla, provided them military instructions and the reassurances of protection by the US armed forces. There was even a design for a Panamanian flag (later replaced).

Late in October that year, Dr. Amador arrived in Colón. There he made contact with, among others, G. Herbert Prescott, manager of the Panama Railroad, and Colonel James Shaler, the railway superintendent (their employer possessed the sole means of transport between the two coasts), as well as with city police chief Porfirio

Meléndez (who signed on as a leader of a separatist uprising on the Atlantic littoral). For military backing, Colombian General Esteban Huertas was approached; his contingent of National troops had gone unpaid for months; he was thus inclined to secession. Huertas's efforts would earn him $65,000, with $50 each for his soldiers. In time, the US battleship *Nashville* was posted offshore near Colón.

Colombian loyalist Generals Juan Tovar and Ramón Amaya now arrived in Colón for immediate stationing in Panama City, with an army battalion under their command. Colonel Shaler persuaded the officers to take a train equipped with a single car to the Pacific, their troops presumably to be transported on the next train, when sufficient cars would be available. Weapons and ammo would be stocked in a rear car (which, the secret plan had it, would then be detached and left behind in the jungle). The foot soldiers were temporarily assigned to one Colonel Eliseo Torres.

The plot succeeded beyond expectations. Just hours after their arrival in Panama City, Generals Torres and Amaya were placed under arrest by a surrogate officer named Salazar and his army company. The military pair were marched in public to Cathedral Plaza before a throng of thousands, who shouted "¡Viva Huertas! ¡Viva Amador! ¡Viva Panamá libre!" Later that evening, the Colombian gunship *Bogotá* lobbed a half-dozen missiles into the town, killing a Chinese merchant and a donkey—the sole instance of actual, armed combat in the entire operation.

Back in Colón, Colonel Torres, unaware of what had transpired on the Pacific side, was informed by Colonel Shaler that, due to orders received from the US Navy, the railway would not be transporting Colombian troops to Panama City. The *Nashville* meanwhile pointed its guns at the wharf and at the Colombian ship *Cartagena*—initially stationed offshore but that now retreated into the distance. In time, Shaler and Chief Meléndez offered Colonel Torres $8,000 to depart with his troops for the mainland on a Royal Mail Steamer called the *Orinoco*. In Panama City, Dr. Amador convinced Generals Tovar and Amaya to surrender; they were soon put on a train to Colón, where they eventually embarked on a ship headed for the port of Cartagena. Shortly thereafter, 400 US Marines landed on the Atlantic littoral.

On November 3, 1903 (coincidentally, Election Day in the United States), Chief Meléndez stood before a cheering multitude and read aloud the declaration of Panama's independence from Colombia. Dr. Amador went on to assume power as the first president. Three days later, Washington recognized the new sovereign nation. Within a week, a total of nine US warships were deployed to near Colón and Panama City harbors, under orders to block any landing by Colombian troops. Resistance from Bogotá was nil.

President Theodore Roosevelt achieved special prominence in the wake of this operation. Surprisingly in retrospect, for years following the events, much of the US press and of Congress was rather critical of the entire affair. Roosevelt, for his part, in a speech given to an open-air crowd in Berkeley in March 1911, made his most notorious statement: "I took the Isthmus, started the Canal, and then left Congress... to debate me." Or, in a better-known version relayed from private conversation, "I took Panama" (McCullough 384).

One Novel, Three Plots

Some acquaintance with the foregoing is helpful for gaining a thorough grasp of Vásquez's *Costaguana*. Indeed, his novel includes most of that background (proper names and all). Its true-life materials are as seamlessly worked into its narrative texture as the documented United Fruit Company facts are woven into the middle chapters of *One Hundred Years of Solitude*.

Vásquez's relatively brief yet complex novel is made up of three fully developed, equally weighted plotlines.

One of these plots is the Panamanian-Colombian history summarized above.

A second, more foregrounded plot tells of the procreation, the life and development, and the subsequent London exile of the book's first-person narrator, José Altamirano. José's father, Miguel, had accidentally engendered him with a Colombian lady, Antonia de Narváez, in an adulterous amour aboard an English steamer on the

Magdalena River in 1854. After a couple of summarily recounted, nondescript decades on the mainland, José shows up at Colón, there meeting his prodigal progenitor, who has since grown into a journalist of sorts—a publicist for the Panama Railroad and next for the prospective French Canal. In time, the mammoth French venture takes over, and high-ranking engineer Gustave Madinier dies tragically of yellow fever, in the wake of which José marries the Frenchman's widow, Charlotte; together, they beget and raise a daughter, Eloísa. Following the collapse of the French effort, father Miguel pays a nostalgic visit to some abandoned excavation machines amid the jungle, where, for undisclosed reasons, he drops dead. The War of a Thousand Days next ravages the Isthmus, and among its indirect casualties is Charlotte, shot in panic at her home by a wayward deserter named Anatolio Calderón. Despondent, a bereaved José leaves behind his adolescent female offspring and heads for London.

The third plot, intertwined with the second, and anticipated in the book's title, both opens and closes—frames—Vásquez's narrative. It gives us select glimpses into the life and the death of Joseph Conrad, with whom José is to experience two dramatic encounters. Conrad's own projected novel *Nostromo* (1904), let us recall, is set in a fictional South American country called *Costaguana*, and arguably has as its general inspiration the Colombian-Panamanian intrigues (with some Colombian and Venezuelan place names retained to boot). Well, on a working trip to England in late 1903 that becomes exile, José meets with Joseph (the parallel in names is presumably deliberate) at the London home of (real-life) Colombian politician and writer Santiago Pérez Triana, where he, José, pours out to the famous Anglo-Polish author the woeful history of his homeland.

From London, José next hears about and informs us in close detail about the secession ("I, evangelist of the crucifixion of Colombia"—287). Then, in his melancholy exile he will happen upon the initial installment of *Nostromo* in a weekly magazine, and he painfully realizes that Conrad has pilfered his entire story while omitting José's role therein. Confronting Conrad in his living room, the injured Colombian demands an explanation, to which the lofty

Pole replies, "I owe you nothing" and "This, my dear sir, is a novel" (297). The dialogue continues along such lines until a downcast José slips out into the London chill. Vásquez's novel in turn ends with the pointed, punning, polyvalent words, "the unfortunate history of Costaguana" (301).

How Metafictional Is This *Secret History?*

At *Secret History*'s inner core is the tortuous matter of Colombia-cum-Isthmus that comprises plot one. In much of these pages, Altamirano *père* emerges as a kind of local prime mover through what narrator José dubs his "refraction journalism." An anticlerical Mason and post-Enlightenment believer in technological progress, Miguel will morph into a mouthpiece and virtual stand-in for de Lesseps himself, parroting the man's opinions, minimizing the construction death figures, and generally drawing a deceitfully rosy picture of the Panamanian situation. Regarding the viscount, son José quotes father Miguel, "He's the man I would have liked to be" (130)—and in a sense is what he becomes.

The historical portions of *Costaguana*, by contrast, are true to events as recounted in the standard histories (notably McCullough's). Personalities, treaties, and ships are all retained by name. At the same time, Vásquez humanizes this past, captures the feeling of ordinary, everyday life surrounding the Panamanian-French affair. In so doing, he gives flesh to the suffering of fictional participants such as the engineer Madinier and his young son Julien, whose absurd deaths are due not only to the foolhardy enterprise but also to the promotional skills of de Lesseps, via publicist Altamirano. Much the same can be said about the grief of widow Charlotte and her victimization by an AWOL Colombian soldier, himself a casualty of the Thousand Days' War. Ariel González Rodríguez brings out this trait when he mentions "the insistence with which [Vásquez] aims to have the stories of characters lacking in historical importance coincide with large-scale events" (57, my translation). Or, as Ricardo Carpio Franco notes, the function of such episodes is to "bring us close to the historical facts" (14, my translation).

Given the partial, subjective way in which *Secret History* is told, the temptation is to see it as an instance of postmodern "historiographical metafiction," a genre that, in Linda Hutcheon's words, "problematize[s] the entire notion of subjectivity," she particularly singling out those works that feature "an overtly controlling narrator" in whom we readers fail "to find a subject confident of his/her ability to know the past with any certainty" (117). José himself notes that, in writing of his father's elaborate untruths, he is a "witness to a witness" (122). The added presences of Conrad, "Costaguana," and *Nostromo* within his text make it a narrative about a narrative, with a fictional narrator telling us about two other fiction-spinning narrators. It is thus all the more tempting to view José as an "unreliable narrator" in this novel of Nabokovian sorts of artifice. (The recurring apostrophic phrase, "readers of the jury," seems in conscious echo of Humbert Humbert addressing "members of the jury" via the prolix defense brief that is *Lolita*.)

Still, what is more striking about Vásquez's book is its broad adherence to the known facts about Colombia-Panama-French Canal-US interventionist history, albeit as experienced through and colored by José's prose lens. The *meta* in this fiction does not question the "historiography." José in fact qualifies as something unique: he is, as it were, an *omniscient* first-person narrator who happens even to know things that he normally couldn't have witnessed, that logically he could not know. In two of the more dramatic instances, he knows about father Miguel's solo, fatal trek in the jungle; he knows the personal background and trajectory of Anatolio Calderón, knows how he accidentally murdered Charlotte. Strangely enough, José's very existence in some ways goes unexplained: we never find out what he does for a living or to sustain himself, nor how he has learned English, which he employs freely. And while he is quite reliable in reporting his father's lies and as chronicler of Panama, he is an unreliable father, abandoning his adolescent daughter Eloísa even as a he sets sail for London, later directing his 300-page report and apology to her as a prime "reader of the jury."

Indeed, *Historia secreta de Costaguana* can ultimately be seen as a true history, a "deep" history of (as Carpio Franco initially notes) nineteenth-century Colombia. The book comes brim-filled with key dates and landmark events from that past. Father figure Miguel Altamirano (no coincidence) is born in 1820, the year in which Bolívar entered Bogotá and which serves as the standard, textbook date for Spanish-American Independence. Miguel's own anticlerical, unnamed father in turn had fought the Spaniards, and was downed by a pro-Catholic bayonet. There is a long paragraph on the life and deeds Bolívar shared with lover Manuela, suggesting parallels with the Miguel-Antonia affair (both women had had English husbands, just for starters). Railroad construction on the Isthmus (that iconic instance of nineteenth-century "progress"); the building of the frontier town and port of Colón ("Aspinwall" for the Americans, "Christophe Colombe" for the French) and its tangled, violent growth; the constant civil strife; the Canal issue; the treaties; the secession—all are packed between the book's two covers. Toward the end, José will realize that his daughter is Panamanian, not Colombian—a moment of symbolic, almost allegorical recognition. Father and child have mutually seceded, so to speak.

Vásquez's is not the first Latin American work of fiction to take on the Canal as subject matter. Catalina Quesada Gómez lists a half-dozen such novels published between 1913 and 1955 by authors Ricardo Miró, Joaquín Bileño, Demetrio Aguilera Malta, and Renato Ozores. Not being acquainted with these writings, I can only take it on Quesada's word when she adjudges them as "exposé literature, with very weak aesthetic demands."[1]

Secret History functions differently. Rather than *dénonciation* as its focus, it depicts the secession of Panama not in polemical terms but rather as the overdetermined consequence of multiple factors and human blunders, ranging from the poor judgment of de Lesseps and of the French enterprise to the dysfunction of the Colombian State, the civil wars, the US meddling, and the cruel indifference of nature. If anything, it portrays the history of Colombia as, in González Rodríguez's words, "a compendium of errors, poorly beaten paths, and irreparable losses" (56, my translation). Given its narrative and interpretive complexity, to label *Historia secreta* as a critique of US imperialism or a novel "about colonialism" would be a gross simplification. On the other hand, by concentrating the entire story within the vision of José Altamirano—"the only true character in the novel" (Carpio Franco, 17; my translation)—that past is rendered subjective, personal. The ample, impersonal forces of Colombia et al. are breathed life into via the account of an illegitimate, disaffected, uprooted, nineteenth-century Colombian.

The Weight of the Past, and Present Anxieties

There are two major works of fiction with which Vásquez's novel bears a relationship of a kind famously signaled by critic Harold Bloom in *The Anxiety of Influence*: namely, Conrad's *Nostromo* and García Márquez's *One Hundred Years of Solitude*. Regarding the former, Vásquez in many ways rectifies the portrait of "Costaguana" and of the breakaway region of "Sulaco," which serve as setting for the English novel. Vásquez the Latin American artificer now restores for readers the concrete textures and social components of a country dreamt up by the Anglo-Polish imaginer, placing more emphasis on real-life, local figures than on assorted fictive, European personages. Significantly, in 2007 (the same year of the appearance in print of *Historia secreta*), Vásquez published a short biography of Conrad— the first such in Spanish—wherein he cites contemporary reviews of *Nostromo* that thought the book "too difficult, somewhat confusing and . . . not apt for the general reader" (77, my re-translation from the Spanish). (I must confess that, in re-reading *Nostromo* for this essay, I found myself disappointed in its long, implausible speeches; its proliferation of overblown characters; and its subtle condescension toward its Hispanic actors. At the risk of falling into 1980s canon-bashing, I would like to suggest that *Historia secreta de Costaguana* is much the better book than *Nostromo*.)

The other novel with which Vásquez wrestles is, inevitably, *One Hundred Years of Solitude*. Early on in *Costaguana*, José directly addresses daughter Eloísa, saying, "this is not one of those books where the dead speak, or where beautiful women ascend to the sky, or priests rise above the ground after drinking a steaming potion" (15). The anachronistic disclaimer makes clear to all us readers that this story is *not* magical realism. And yet, in a 2010 interview with Jorge Ruffinelli, the author grants, "When I began writing *The Secret History* . . . I realized I was writing a book about the Colombian Caribbean and the nineteenth century. And this is basically [García Márquez's] territory... So of all the ways of doing this I think I chose the most difficult way, which was to write a fiction that wouldn't run away from García Márquez but would try to use some of the same tools to just get in the ring with him and fight a little bit" (161-62).[3]

A few years before that, in his key essay, "El arte de la distorsión," Vásquez urges readers to approach *One Hundred Years* as a historical novel. In this respect, he singles out the episodes of the banana strike and military repression, which he praises as "one of the best chapters in [the novel]." His praise, moreover, has to do not with the magic but with its historical accuracy, "the ways … the passages in which the historical facts are reproduced with the faithfulness of a documentarian" (41, my translation).[2] As has become somewhat notorious, García Márquez is too often reduced to magic, while his fidelity to Colombian history is seldom remarked upon. Significantly, his novel is sometimes used as supplementary reading in Latin American history and political science courses in the United States and Europe.

It is worth noting that both these Colombians have written novels with major episodes involving Colombia as a target of US imperialism—the banana company in one work, the loss of Panama in the other. Both authors relate these stories with subtlety and sans didactic or propagandistic intent. In the end, Vásquez's is a work not so much about those events as about the *history* of such events– "history" in the double sense of *what happened* in the past and also *how one tells*, the *telling of*, those past happenings. As he himself observed in a 2010 interview with Rita de Maeseneer and Jasper Verkaeke, "In *Costaguana*, the grand object of reflection is History with a capital 'H.' That novel brings back in a much more literal way the same debates about the similarities and differences between the narrative we receive and the truth of the facts, about how the construct we know as history as no more than one possible version" (10, my translation). At the same time, there is in Vásquez's writing an agenda both political—and deeply personal: "We write because reality strikes us as imperfect, problematical, incomprehensible" (11, my translation).

In a presumably unintended echo of Unamuno, of whom it was often said, "le duele España" (an untranslatable idiom, signifying, roughly, "his Spain hurts"), Vásquez in that same interview describes Colombia as "a dark territory whose society and history I do not understand, and it hurts/pains me" (11, my translation). Fittingly, the novelist's stated concluding words to Maesseneer and Verkaeke are, in Spanish, "Colombia es mi obsesión" (12).

Notes

1. "Littérature de dénonciation, avec de très faibles exigences esthétiques" (83, my translation).

2. Incidentally, I examine this very topic in my own article, "Banana Strike and Military Massacre: *One Hundred Years of Solitude* and What Happened in 1928."

3. For further elaboration of this three-way relationship between Vásquez, Conrad, and García Márquez, see Semilla Durán, pp. 554-55.

Works Cited

Bell-Villada, Gene H. "Banana Strike and Military Massacre: *One Hundred Years of Solitude* and What Happened in 1928." *Gabriel García Márquez's* One Hundred Years of Solitude: *A Casebook*. Edited by Gene H. Bell-Villada. Oxford UP, 2001, pp. 127-38.

Bloom, Harold. *The Anxiety of Influence: A Theory of Poetry*. Oxford UP, 1973.

Chekhov, Anton. *Three Sisters*. In *The Plays of Anton Chekhov*. Translated by Paul Schmidt. HarperCollins, 1997, pp. 257-322.

Carpio Franco, Ricardo. "Espejos, simulacros y distorsiones: Hacia una tipología de la 'metaficción historiográfica' en *Historia secreta de Costaguana*, de Juan Gabriel Vásquez." *Espéculo. Revista de Estudios Literatraios* 44, 2010. https://pendientedemigracion. ucm.es/info/especulo/numero44/espesimu.html. Date accessed: 26 September 2017.

Conrad, Joseph. *Nostromo*. 1904. New American Library, 1960.

García Márquez, Gabriel. *One Hundred Years of Solitude*. Trans. Gregory Rabassa. Harper & Row, 1970.

González Rodríguez, Ariel. *Cuatro novelistas colombianos*. Editorial Universidad Autónoma de Colombia, 2015.

Hutcheon, Linda. *A Poetics of Postmodernism: History, Theory, Fiction*. Routledge, 1988.

De Maeseneer, Rita, and Jasper Verkaeke. "Escribimos porque la realidad nos parece imperfecta."' (Interview with Juan Gabriel Vásquez.) *Ciberletras* 2010. http://www.lehman.cuny.edu/ciberletras/v23/demaeseneer.html. Date accessed: 26 September 2017.

McCullough, David. *The Path between the Seas: The Creation of the Panama Canal, 1875-1914*. Simon and Schuster, 1977.

Nabokov, Vladimir. *Lolita*. Putnam, 1958.

Quesada Gómez, Catalina. "Vacillements. Poétique de déséquilibre dans l'oeuvre de Juan Gabriel Vásquez." *Les espaces des écritures hispaniques et hispano-américaines au XXI siècle*. Edited by Eduardo Ramos-Izquierdo and Marie-Alexandra Barataud. Presses Universitaires de Limoges, 2012, pp. 75-85.

Ruffinelli, Jorge. "Juan Gabriel Vásquez: History, Memory, and the Novel." (Interview with the author.) *Nuevo Texto Crítico* 26-27.49-50, 2013-2014, pp. 151-63.

Santos Molano, Enrique. *1903. Adiós Panamá. Colombia ante el Destino Manifiesto*. Villegas Editores, 2004.

Semilla Durán, María Angélica. "Le récit cannibale: *Historia secreta de Costaguana* de Juan Gabriel Vásquez." *Hommage à Milagros Ezquerdo: Théorie et fiction*. Edited by Michèle Ramond, Eduardo Ramos-Izquierdo, and Julien Roger. Adehl, 2011 pp. 545-61.

Vásquez, Juan Gabriel. "El arte de la distorsión." *El arte de la distorsión*. Alfaguara, 2009, pp. 29-43.

_____. *Historia secreta de Costaguana*. Alfaguara, 2007.

_____. *Joseph Conrad: El hombre de ninguna parte*. Norma, 2007.

_____. *The Secret History of Costaguana*. Translated by Anne McLean. Riverhead, 2011.

CRITICAL
READINGS

Anacristina Rossi and the Uses of Literature in Costa Rica

Rudyard J. Alcocer

"So you're the little woman who wrote the book that started this great war."

(Abraham Lincoln, upon meeting Harriet Beecher Stowe, 1862)

The fiction of Anacristina Rossi (Costa Rica, 1952-) encompasses many of the virtues and tensions associated with modern Latin American literature; as such, though relatively unknown in the United States, it deserves careful reading and assessment. Rossi's fiction can be both new and old, current and dated, conventional and cutting edge. While registering the cultural diversity, cosmopolitanism, and bilingualism of her native Costa Rica—indeed, this country's many complexities—her fiction simultaneously traffics perilously close to caricatured racial and gender roles. Her treatment of these topics, on its own, might have yielded at most very specialized, scattered acclaim. When, however, she merged these topics with her passion for particular political concerns—concerns that found an eager audience in Costa Rica—the results were transformative. This was the case with *La loca de Gandoca* (*The Madwoman of Gandoca,* 1992), a novel that attained rare success in bringing about political change in her country. That stated, we shall see that *La loca de Gandoca* does not stand alone among Rossi's fictional works in testing and transgressing social boundaries. One could argue, in fact, that Rossi is masterful and courageous in identifying delicate social topics within Costa Rica and then pushing the boundaries of those topics to their breaking point; in so doing, at times she has found a broad readership but occasionally her experiments in pushing the boundaries have been met with resistance and criticism. Ultimately, while Rossi's oeuvre speaks to many issues characteristic of Latin America and its literature, it is at heart an oeuvre that must be read in light of Costa Rica's national debates.

Rossi's fiction registers, in the first instance, the variable functions literary texts can have: variations often informed by regional and cultural elements. Counterintuitively, perhaps, literary texts remain capable of wielding societal power in Latin America in ways that seem to have been lost elsewhere. In the United States, for example, gone are the days when a novel like Harriet Beecher Stowe's *Uncle Tom's Cabin* (1852) could help start a war. The reasons for such a shift in the United States are undoubtedly highly complex and perhaps even impossible to ascertain with any precision, but they could involve the rise (and competition from) other media, the atomization of society, and so on. In addition, as Rita Felski (2008) has argued, in the North American academy, literary studies have become characterized by a "hermeneutics of suspicion" hesitant to ascribe meaning to literary texts, let alone any societal impact. In contrast, literary texts in Costa Rica enjoy comparatively lower levels of internal competition from the other media, not to mention lower levels of competition from other literary texts.[1] One could argue further that—through a number of factors—literary texts are better positioned to make their mark in a Costa Rican society that is relatively small in population, relatively homogenous in demographic terms (more on this below), and relatively literate (97 percent compared to 86 percent in the United States).[2] As concerns Rossi's fiction in its broad relations to Costa Rican society, make its mark it very much has.

Lest we forget, Rossi too deserves plenty of credit for the success of her fiction. Generally speaking, Rossi's Costa Rican readership is simultaneously able to recognize itself in her fiction *while* also seeing the country's societal flaws and contradictions. It is, perhaps, this distinctive double maneuver that helps explain her success. In the pages ahead, I shall examine three of Rossi's four novels to date while paying close attention in two of these novels, especially *La loca de Gandoca,* to several features of Costa Rican society that surface and resurface in varying ways across her fiction. These societal features include the country's gender relations, racial and class divisions, governmental corruption, and grassroots environmentalism. In this panorama of Rossi's fiction, my aim will be evenhandedness, recognizing both its strengths and its weaknesses.

María la noche: A New Voice Emerges

Rossi studied in London, Paris (a degree in translation and interpretation), and The Hague (a degree in women's issues and development). This experience abroad undoubtedly inspired her first novel, *María la noche* (Maria the Night, 1985), which was awarded her country's Aquileo J. Echeverría Prize for best novel in 1985. Although the focus of this chapter will lie in her later novels, we can nonetheless detect in *María la noche* many of the features that would reappear later, including shifting narrative perspectives, an emphasis on gender relations and issues of sensuality, eroticism, and mutual incomprehension between men and women: features that would also characterize her collection of short stories *Situaciones conyugales* (Conjugal Situations, 1993). One might, additionally, describe *María la noche* as Rossi's bohemian novel, set primarily in the smoke-filled pubs and damp libraries of London, and in which characters compete to assert and flaunt their cultural capital. In this respect, one could argue that despite some commonalities, there is a fundamental break between *María la noche* and her later novels because these are set in and explore a Costa Rican cultural context, whereas the former explores, in broad terms, the Hispanic *émigré* experience in a non-Hispanic region of the world.

As is the case in her later fiction, *María la noche* experiments with shifting narrative perspectives: Antonio, the initial narrator in the novel and a student at the London School of Economics, is seeking to mix a bit of pleasure into his regimented academic existence. One night, at a pub, he admires from a distance a young woman named Mariestela. Shortly thereafter, the narrative transitions to her perspective. The dialogue between these two characters is interspersed with English phrases, which is, in effect, a preview of the bilingualism of Rossi's later fiction, given its emphasis on the Caribbean coast of Costa Rica, where English is spoken along with Spanish. The dialogue, moreover, and the perspectival shifts, reveal the difficulties these two characters have in communicating, in understanding the other, and in being understood by the other. These difficulties in communication are rooted in gender differences. Mariestela, for instance, critiques Antonio's manner of touching her: "It's not anyone's fault, you simply don't know how to touch a woman. Maybe that's because for a man to learn how to touch a woman involves discovering his own feminine side."[3] Knowledge of others—of the opposite gender, at least—requires, according to Mariestela, an unusual and profound knowledge of oneself in all the facets a given self may have.

La loca de Gandoca: Environmentalism and "Development"

Rossi's masterpiece may be *La loca de Gandoca,* a slim novel published in 1992 and written urgently during a four-month span stemming from the author's involvement in environmental activism (Kearns 1). While *La loca de Gandoca* may be more plot-driven and politically engaged than *María la noche,* it maintains nonetheless an interest in processes of self-discovery. The title speaks volumes: *La loca* here means a madwoman, rather than a flamboyant homosexual, which is occasionally how the word is understood in the Spanish-speaking world. Daniela Zermat is the passionate protagonist. It remains to be seen, however, in what way we are to understand her supposed madness; after all, madness can be understood in relative terms. In other words, who considers her mad and for what reasons? Perhaps others are mad and she is sane (i.e., only "mad" in a figurative sense). Meanwhile, the word *Gandoca* in the title is more straightforward: it is the name of a nature reserve on the Caribbean coast of Costa Rica; more precisely, the Gandoca-Manzanillo Wildlife Refuge, in a region long inhabited by the country's indigenous and Afro-Costa Rican populations. This reserve, as the story commences, has long been neglected because it is not on the country's Pacific coast, which—as Zermat herself recognizes—has bluer water, a sunnier climate, and is more frequently visited by foreign tourists. Gandoca does, however, possess spectacular biodiversity; in addition, because it has been relatively neglected, it is pristine. Now, the foreign developers and corrupt elements of the Costa Rican government want to carve up Gandoca for their own gain by turning it not only into a tourist resort but also into a veritable tourist town, as has already occurred on the Pacific coast of the country. Can Zermat stop them?

La loca de Gandoca is often considered part of Latin America's tradition of testimonial literature inasmuch as it details many real-life events in which the author took part and about which—through thinly veiled changes to personal names—she furnishes testimony. Such testimonial literature stands in contrast to an understanding of literature as mere entertainment or escapism; testimonial literature is understood through its political commitment (as in the French notion of *littérature engagée*), a commitment capable of effecting real change in a given society. As Sofia Kearns outlines in her introduction to the English translation of the novel, many of the events in the storyline actually occurred: Ecodólares, the predatory foreign developer in the novel, for example, was in reality a firm named the Eurocaribeña Hotel Company (Kearns 6). The novel's corresponding impact on Costa Rican political discourses was similarly extraordinary: Rossi herself was the author of a formal complaint against the Costa Rican government's dubious measures to compromise the reserve, and although faced with death threats (Kearns 6), she succeeded in bringing about governmental legislation designed to truly protect the reserve.

In other respects, however, *La loca de Gandoca* is fictional rather than testimonial. Let us begin with a look at the narrative, which is bifurcated in structure: on the one hand, it details Zermat's efforts to stop the ravaging of Gandoca. These efforts expose the Orwellian nature of Costa Rican government: a labyrinth structured to protect the interests of the ruling classes; just when Zermat thinks she is in the correct government bureau in order to file a complaint regarding abuses to Gandoca, she is told she is in the wrong bureau, or that she needs to present a new environmental impact study because the first one is outdated. In an aside reminiscent of Orwellian doublespeak, Zermat laments, "Latin America is a land of tyrants. The tyrants characteristically say, for instance, that a green object is blue and that anyone who doesn't see the color gets punished" (40).[4] She falls victim to governmental obfuscation repeatedly: the many obstacles she encounters and her many frustrations bestow on the narrative the quick pace of a thriller; eventually she goes so far as to dress like a man ("big-nosed, moustached, and bespectacled" 86)[5] in order to overhear high-level conversations involving the nature reserve. Who knew that an environmentalist novel could be such a page-turner! Through her actions, moreover, Zermat (and Rossi, by extension) holds a very unflattering mirror up to Costa Rican society, a society, led by corrupt officials, willing to disregard or misinterpret existing environmental regulations in order to sell its natural bounty for a quick profit. Rossi admits that she too, in real life, had to resort to wearing a disguise in her battles against corruption: a disguise she still owns! (Polsgrove n.p.)

On the other hand, the novel is a love story: Zermat's love interest is a murky, shadowy man named Carlos Manuel, who says very little when he is present in the narrative, and then exits the narrative abruptly. *La loca de Gandoca,* however, can in many ways be described as lyrical because the narrative in general and certainly several discrete portions of it are addressed toward a largely absent Carlos Manuel: by all accounts a brilliant man, presumably from the Costa Rican central valley, who went to the country's Caribbean region to conduct anthropological fieldwork. Although Zermat and Carlos Manuel tried to make a life together in Gandoca, he succumbed to despair and alcoholism. Because of this, one could argue, Zermat's mission to save Gandoca is informed by a more intimate narrative characterized by personal tragedy.

One could ask, with plenty of justification, whether or not the dual political and personal dimensions of the novel comprise a coherent narrative. Are there, in effect, two disparate narrative threads in search of a novel? In response to this question, I point to a moment in the narrative where we see the clearest expression of why the novel could be seen as unified precisely in the way that Zermat's sadness over Carlos Manuel's death led to clear political convictions, particularly as the so-called development or destruction of Gandoca shifted to a higher gear, despite her prayers to the gods of the African pantheon: "Then my sadness turned to rage, I stopped thinking about Carlos Manuel's death, and instead of complaining

---

to Oxum, I decided to complain to the Wildlife Office" (61).[6] As such, the message of the novel comes into focus: Zermat's zeal is not only political and environmental, but also involves significant personal sacrifice. In addition, far from being solely a nature reserve for the protection of animal and marine life, Gandoca is also a place where people have led full lives for generations, with all the joy and suffering that full lives entail.

Meanwhile, there are other elements in the narrative that reflect Zermat's own eclecticism and that could, in the presence of an unsympathetic reader, truly call her sanity into question. As a white Costa Rican, Zermat is predictably Roman Catholic; in the novel there are several allusions to Catholicism, not the least of which is the mention of her preparations for her son's First Communion (61). In addition, Zermat, as we saw above, not only prays to African gods but is also in veritable dialogue with them: it is the goddess Yemanyá, for instance, who instructs Zermat to speak to Oxum (58). Eventually, Catholicism and Santeria yield in the novel to a different kind of force: if Zermat requires reassurance in her risky political convictions, there is an appeal within *La loca de Gandoca* to magical realism, a narrative technique often associated with Latin American exceptionalism. We see this appeal during a tranquil moment before the novel approaches its climax: Zermat has gone into the woods to contemplate and to try to find peace in the midst of the political scandal she is stoking; as she stands near a lagoon, an unusual flying insect approaches her and eventually reassures her by saying, in plain Spanish, that she has allies in the natural world in her battles against the forces of governmental corruption. The insect does so, however, only after asking her to make clear to her readers "that I am neither a metaphor nor a stylistic device, nor is this an instance of magical realism. My presence is authentic" (78).[7] Against allies like that, not to speak of Zermat's inherent pluck, the Costa Rican government and its foreign backers never stood a chance. Given that Rossi claims that the novel is 99.9 percent reality (Polsgrove n.p.), the talking insect—one would presume—inhabits the solitary tenth of one percent that is completely invented.

Ultimately, *La loca de Gandoca* amounts to a referendum on the essence of the Costa Rican national project. Is Costa Rica going to remain, for instance, a country whose government "only remembers that the blacks exist when it wants either their votes or their lands" (49-50).[8] If the government's treatment of its black population seems bad enough, according to Zermat (and Rossi, one can assume), its attitude toward indigenous groups is actually worse: "It's even worse with the indians: since they don't vote or understand Spanish, the government doesn't even have to bother to lie to them" (50).[9] Similarly, is it a country that will blindly follow foreign models of development, indeed, foreign models pertaining to the all-important distinction within Latin America between civilization and barbarism? After all, who is Zermat to try to stop a French developer who threatens to build a discotheque in the middle of Gandoca while affirming: "I built them in Nice, a civilized place, and you're going to tell me that I can't build them here!" (67).[10] To Zermat's (and Rossi's) great credit, an eco-friendly and democratic vision of civilization and development prevails in Costa Rica within the fiction of *La loca de Gandoca,* as well as, many would argue, in the real Costa Rica, a country that is widely seen as a regional *and* world leader in its environmentalism. Meanwhile, in other respects one could question the novel's manner of contesting social and political boundaries. It is often considered politically transgressive, for example, to articulate issues that affect marginalized minority populations, as *La loca de Gandoca* does in the case of the indigenous and, especially, Afro-Costa Rican populations. The novel, however, describes ways in which corrupt politicians mischievously turn these populations against Zermat; in despair, she pleads with the "Mother [or Goddess] of the Sea": "Don't abandon me to the onslaught of the European destroyer and of the fickle black" (72).[11] Are there limits to how one can fictionalize minority populations to which one does not belong? This question brings us Rossi's next novel.

Limón Blues: Afro-Costa Ricans and the National Project

How would Rossi follow up the tremendous impact she made in *La loca de Gandoca*? If in *La loca de Gandoca* Rossi made the

Caribbean region of Costa Rica and its inhabitants an important part of the backdrop in the midst of broader issues of an environmental and political nature, in the prize-winning *Limón Blues* (2002), Rossi places this region (including its principal city, Limón), and its inhabitants front and center in the concerns of the narrative, not unlike the case of its sequel, *Limón Reggae* (2008). Similarly, while *La loca de Gandoca* suggested the important role the United States—among other potentially predatory nations—has played in Costa Rican affairs, in *Limón Blues* we are witness firsthand to the often brutal control the United States exerted over the Central American country around the turn of the previous century. Generally speaking, in creating a more nuanced portrait of Caribbean Costa Rican society, she reasserts the role of the region into the Costa Rican national project. As she explains in the novel's epilogue, this region, which she first visited as a child during the 1950s, was for several decades dating back to the end of the nineteenth century a splendorous West Indian enclave separated from the rest of Costa Rica. According to the author, it might as well have been a separate country given the eight-hour train ride from the capital to the Caribbean coast, not to mention the linguistic and ethnic barriers between residents of the Caribbean region and *la meseta central* (the central valley), home of the traditional population centers of the nation. While in the latter the residents are traditionally Spanish-speaking, Roman Catholic, and Spanish American in their cultural practices and outlook, residents of the Caribbean region are traditionally English-speaking, Protestant, and more recently arrived (from the British West Indies) into Costa Rica than their fellow countrymen. Although descendants of enslaved Africans brought to the West Indies, by the late nineteenth and early twentieth centuries (the timeframe for *Limón Blues*), they saw themselves—at least within the context of the novel's opening chapters—primarily and functionally as subjects of the British Empire, as opposed to Costa Rican nationals or descendants of Africans; in other words, black West Indians as opposed to Afro-Costa Ricans. The latter term would not surface for several decades (blacks obtained Costa Rican citizenship in 1949).

Limón Blues, to a significant extent (and despite its flaws), recounts the quest for dignity and respect by the Caribbean region's Afro-Costa Ricans vis-à-vis their conationals. This desire to reconstruct and narrate a particular group's history that is usually not seen as belonging to the main collective narrative of a nation is labeled by Britton Newman (who in turn borrows the concept from Alison Landsberg) as a "prosthetic" memory (Newman 53-55); in effect, as potentially useful and potentially awkward as a prosthetic limb may be to a body. Furthermore, if in *La loca de Gandoca* the Afro-Costa Rican population was in many ways Other to the protagonist, in *Limón Blues* Rossi attempts to challenge and, to a significant extent, blur the distinction between black and white Costa Ricans.

The novel's hero is Orlandus Robinson, a young man from Jamaica newly arrived in Costa Rica with the purpose of sending money back home to his impoverished homeland. Despite a narrative perspective that shifts repeatedly and, occasionally, too abruptly, Orlandus is at once the focal point of the narrative, its most developed character, and at times the sexual object of female characters. The last of these characteristics underscores one of the novel's problematic features: one of the primary social taboos Rossi explores in the novel is the one that exists in Costa Rica as concerns romance between black West Indians and so-called *pañas,* which is the term they use to designate their Spanish-speaking conationals. During the historical period in which the novel is set, that is, the first couple of decades of the twentieth century, such interracial romance would have been very rare and very difficult to acknowledge openly, especially if it involved a black man and a white woman; sexual relations involving black women and white men, meanwhile—given Costa Rica's hypocritical attitudes toward gender relations—were more readily tolerated even if not given official sanction. Black West Indians, moreover, were during that time restricted from entering the central valley where the national capital, San José, is located. Along these lines, *Limón Blues,* which was meticulously researched by the author, is part fiction and part historical snapshot, and it references several verifiable events in the country's historical record.

These include the nefarious activities of the US-based United Fruit Company and the collective efforts (featuring Marcus Garvey) to counter those activities and to protect West Indians in Costa Rican territory.

One could, however, flag some of the novel's rhetorical steps, all of which seem taken in an effort to describe and ultimately transgress Costa Rica's taboo on romantic relations between black West Indians and *pañas*. Early in the novel, Orlandus and a *pañawoman* named Leonor Jiménez stumble upon each other on the streets of Limón. Despite the presence of many others during this encounter, including several *paña* dignitaries, Orlandus and Leonor make very apparent to one another their mutual physical attraction. She, however, must prove capable of breaking her commitment to a marriage that is, in effect, a farce, given that her *paña* husband, a member of the Cósta Rican oligarchy, has sexual encounters seemingly with all women save for his wife. In a revealing moment of introspection, Leonor decides to throw caution to the wind and pursue the attractive young black man (Orlandus) she saw in Limón. She maintains certain doubts, however: "She knew nothing about the black man. Leave nothing to chance. Before moving forward, find out: if he's clean, if he has a woman, if he frequents prostitutes."[12] We have at this moment, then, through Leonor's perspective, an elaborate account of certain stereotypes *pañawomen* held about black West Indians. Interestingly, despite the fact that Orlandus is the novel's protagonist, any stereotypes black West Indians hold about the *pañas* lack the same degree of detail and intimacy. Could this be because black West Indians are kinder people than the *pañas* and less prone to stereotyping others? It is possible. Another reason, however, could be that despite the best authorial efforts to perceive reality in the manner of black West Indians, Rossi is ultimately unable to do so. In an interview, Rossi has affirmed that she and her writings about black West Indians have been criticized on this very score: besides short stays on Costa Rica's Caribbean coast when she was a youth, she has never spent significant periods of time there during adulthood, a surprising fact given her advocacy of issues pertinent to the residents of that region (Polsgrove n.p.);

in addition, she has been criticized for dramatizing romantic and sexual relations between Afro-Costa Rican men and white women from the country's central valley, effectively objectifying the former while suggesting—unintentionally, no doubt—that Afro-Costa Rican *women* are somehow undesirable to men of their own ethnicity (Polsgrove n.p.).

Later in the story, after Orlandus and Leonor have become lovers, he serves as her Virgil (as well as, one could argue, the readers' Virgil) through the layers of black West Indian society in Costa Rica. There came so many discoveries on Leonor's part thanks entirely to Orlandus's guidance; so many sectors of this society that had been unknown to her, so many secret organizations and ceremonies that had hitherto been hiding in plain sight. Such is her mindset on a visit to one such ceremony: "She thought, 'Where did they come from?', and then she was ashamed: they had always been there but she had never seen them because she saw through the Master's eyes, which looked right through servants and the poor."[13] In a fascinating reversal, the protagonist in the novel is not necessarily the character learning the most about the complexities of Costa Rican society; instead, the character learning the most is the one who most resembles the author. In an effort to give voice to and better understand the Other within a Costa Rican cultural context, Rossi, in effect, tries but ultimately fails in *Limón Blues* to speak *for* or *as* the Other. Despite this shortcoming, the novel is of sufficient quality as to merit a personal assessment from its readers. It also bears mentioning that my assessment of this novel, that is, an assessment issued by a scholar working within the ideological norms of the North American academy, is not necessarily shared by some Costa Rican (even Afro-Costa Rican) intellectuals. For example, Quince Duncan, perhaps the premier Afro-Costa Rican author, has praised *Limón Blues* for the way in which Rossi (a relative outsider to Afro-Costa Rican culture) has sought to internalize the struggles of a group to which she does not belong (Manzari 88).

By way of conclusion, in her fiction Rossi has consistently sought to expose and challenge her country's social norms. These norms (or contradictions) have varied in substance and focus, ranging from issues of gender, environmentalism, and political corruption, to ones of race and ethnicity. Oftentimes, her fiction is able to syncretize several of these issues simultaneously. While challenging both societal norms as well as narrative conventions, her novels never lack courage and occasionally unlock pronounced and rare societal responses that have led to practical changes in how Costa Rica is governed. Particular critical assessments notwithstanding (the ones expressed here, for example), Rossi and her fiction deserve our attention and interest.

Notes

1. According to UNESCO figures, in 2003—the most recent year for which there is data—there were approximately 1,315 total books published in Costa Rica, of which literary texts were presumably a fraction. In the United States (albeit more recently: 2013), there were more than 300,000 books published in a single year, that is, more than 200 times the rate of publication in Costa Rica.

2. Costa Rica literacy figures based on UNESCO estimates; US figures based on US census. Interestingly, Rossi herself characterizes Costa Rica as a nation largely uninterested in reading and literature (Polsgrove n.p.).

3. "No es culpa de nadie, simplemente no sabés tocar a una mujer. Tal vez porque para un hombre aprender a tocar a una mujer es descubrir su propia parte femenina" (36). All translations are my own unless otherwise indicated.

4. "América Latina es tierra de tiranos. Los tiranos se caracterizan por decir, ante un objeto que es por ejemplo verde, que el objeto es azul. Castigo al que no lo vea de color azul" (38).

5. "Un hombre narigón, bigotudo y con anteojos" (84).

6. "Entonces la tristeza se me mudó en rabia, dejé de pensar en la muerte de Carlos Manuel y en lugar de reclamarle a Oxum decidí reclamarle a la Oficina de Vida Silvestre" (58).

7. "Que yo no soy una metáfora ni un recurso de estilo. Que esto no es realismo mágico. Mi presencia es verdad" (75).

8. "Sólo se acuerda de que los negros existen cuando quieren sus votos o sus tierras?" (48).

9. "Con los indios es peor, como ni siquiera votan ni entienden español no tienen que molestarse en mentirles" (48).

10. "¡Las puse in Niza, un lugar civilizado, y va usted a decirme que no las puedo poner aquí!" (64).

11. "No me abandonés ahora ante el embate del europeo destructor y del negro voluble" (68).

12. "No sabía nada del negro. No dejarlo a la suerte. Antes de proceder, averiguar: si era limpio, si tenía mujer, si frecuentaba a las prostitutas" (43).

13. "Pensó: ¿de dónde salieron?, y luego se avergonzó: siempre habían estado allí pero no los había visto porque ella tenía los ojos del amo, que pasaban a través de sirvientes y pobres" (60).

Works Cited

Felski, Rita. *Uses of Literature*. Blackwell, 2008.

Kearns, Sofia. "Introduction." *La loca de Gandoca / The Madwoman of Gandoca*. Anacristina Rossi. Translated by Terry J. Martin. Edwin Mellen, 2006, pp. 1-10.

Manzari, H. J. "Rompiendo el silencio: Entrevista con el escritor costarricence Quince Duncan." *Afro-Hispanic Review*. Vol. 23, No. 2, Fall 2004, pp. 87-90.

Newman, Britton. "The Politics of Prosthetic Memory in Anacristina Rossi's *Limón Blues*. *Latin American Literary Review*, Vol. 40, No. 80, July-December 2012, pp. 52-66.

Polsgrove, Carol. "Carol Polsgrove on Writers' Lives: Anacristina Rossi." Interview.,www.carolpolsgrove.com/interviewanacristina-rossi. Accessed March 18, 2017.

Rossi, Anacristina. *María la noche*, 3rd ed. Editorial Costa Rica, 2011 (1985)

_____. *La loca de Gandoca*, 2nd ed. Editorial Legado, 2009 (1992).

_____. *La loca de Gandoca / The Madwoman of Gandoca*. Translated by Terry J. Martin. Edwin Mellen, 2006.

_____. *Limón Blues*. Alfaguara, 2002.

_____. *Limón Reggae*. Alcalá La Real Jaén: Alcalá Grupo Editorial, 2008. Print.

_____. *Situaciones conyugales*. San Jose, CR: REI Centroamérica, 1993. Print.

UNESCO y Centro regional para el fomento del libro en América Latina y el Caribe (CERLALC). "Producción y comercio internacional del libro en Centro América, República Dominicana y Cuba, 2003." CERLALC, 2005.

Archiving Diaspora in Daína Chaviano's
Mainstream Fantasy————————————————

Los cubanos somos los marcianos de la Tierra.

(Chaviano, *El hombre* 23)

In *La ficción Fidel* (The Fidel Fiction, 2008), Paris-based Cuban exile writer Zoé Valdés observes that Fidel Castro is like Frankenstein: a nearly fictitious character whose recognition is part of everyday life and parlance. She is uncertain, she adds, whether Cubans or Americans have contributed more to the marketing of the fiction or the "product" Fidel Castro, but this uncertainty does not nullify Castro's own role in his own branding: "above all he created himself; he is own doctor Frankenstein, he himself sewed the monster."[1] There is a sense of familiarity in Valdés's irreverent, enraged, and incredulous tone; it reminds us of other prominent Cuban exile writers, such as Reinaldo Arenas and Guillermo Cabrera Infante. Yet Castro's depiction as a monstrous creature also transports us to another less familiar literary terrain: Cuba as a pertinent location for the production of science fiction, fantasy, and related genres.

According to Andrea L. Bell and Yolanda Molina-Gavilán, editors of *Cosmos Latinos: An Anthology of Science Fiction from Latin America and Spain*, following the triumph of the Revolution in 1959, Cuba experienced "a great increase in production" in the genre of science fiction (8). Representative books include Ángel Arango's *¿Adónde van los cefalomos?* (Where do Cephalomes Go? 1964), *El planeta negro* (The Black Planet, 1966) and *Robotomaquia* (Robotomachy, 1967), as well as Miguel Collazo's *El libro fantástico de Oaj* (The Fantastic Book of Oaj, 1967) and *El viaje* (The Voyage, 1968). This "creative energy" came to a halt in the following decade, as a result of the severe repression and censorship that enveloped writers and intellectuals during a period critics denominate *quinquenio gris* (gray five years). Nevertheless, the work of pioneers Arango and Collazo helped train, according to Bell and Molina-Gavilán, younger sci-fi writers in the late seventies and throughout the eighties (9). From this younger generation, Daína Chaviano (1957-) is, without a doubt, the most popular writer. Already in 1979, Chaviano gained recognition as she received the first Premio David de Ciencia Ficción for her short story collection *Los mundos que amo* (The Worlds I Love). Thereafter, her fiction was consistently praised. Among them, *Historias de hadas para adultos* (Fairy Tales for Adults, 1986) was a bestseller in Cuba, while her *Fábulas de una abuela extraterrestre* (Fables of an Extraterrestrial Grandmother, 1988) received the Anna Seghers Award of the Berlin Academy of Arts in 1990.

After a prolific career on the island not only as a fiction writer but also as a television and radio host and scriptwriter, Chaviano migrated to the United States in 1991. From then on, she has moved away from sci-fi, but her commitment to fantasy remains, as evident in her tetralogy "La Habana oculta" (Occult Havana): *El hombre, la hembra y el hambre* (Man, Woman, and Hunger, 1998), which is set in the early 1990s, *Casa de juegos* (House of Games, 1999) and *Gata encerrada* (Locked up Cat, 2001), both of which take place in the second half of the 1980s, and *La isla de los amores infinitos* (*The Island of Eternal Love*, 2006), which is set in the late 1990s yet has a broader time frame that encompasses more than a century. In these novels, spiritualism, fantasy and—to varying degrees— erotic encounters function as vehicles to escape from the repression and suffering in post-revolutionary Cuba, the "obligada miseria" (mandatory misery), as put by one character (*El hombre* 43).

If throughout the 1980s Chaviano was a cult writer, it is fair to say that at present, after the commercial success of *La isla de los amores infinitos* (hereafter *La isla*), she has secured a spot in the literary mainstream. Some may consider the writings she has produced outside of Cuba too saturated with fantasy clichés and soap operalike twists for a serious critical analysis. In fact, *El hombre, la hembra y el hambre* begins by evoking a soap opera: "She doesn't know it, but her life is about to change, like in those soap operas where coincidences seem to conspire against the protagonist."[2] Entering the mainstream often excludes writers from academic criticism. But this general exclusion from academic circles would have preceded Chaviano since it is also commonly experienced by sci-fi and fantasy fiction writers, with the notable exception of Ursula Le Guin and Margaret Atwood, whose works have thrived even in the entertainment and media market. After revealing his secret addiction to sci-fi, critic Frederick Luis Aldama comments on the predicaments of another market: "if graduate students were inclined to write on SciFi alone, faculty would likely encourage the student to mix up his or her dissertation with other storytelling modes—for job placement marketability" (xvii). This, in part, explains why in comparison to the fervent reception *La isla* has enjoyed internationally, relatively few scholars have examined it.[3] But again, the diminished academic attention it has received is mostly due to the fact that it is a novel directed to a mainstream audience.

In more than one sense, *La isla* is a global novel. Apart from divulging the historical trajectories of the African, Chinese, and Spanish in Cuba, as well as of Cubans in the diaspora, it has been translated to twenty-seven languages to date, making Chaviano the most translated Cuban novelist in history. Most recently, the Russian edition was published in 2017. While the fantasy genre and the promise of a love story hinted at by the novel's title may have accelerated Chaviano's worldwide success, I focus on the novel's suitability in another—more intimate—setting: the classroom. While in my conclusion I insert insights from my experience teaching *La isla* in a college-level seminar on Cuban literature, my broader objective here is to present Chaviano as a "teacherly writer." With this, I do not merely mean that her novels are teachable; I rather borrow the expression "teacherly" from critic Elena Machado Sáez in her study of Caribbean novelists in the diaspora who strive to maintain a pedagogical ethical imperative as they are "both facilitated by and in tension with the market demands placed upon diasporic fiction" (1). In the midst of the mixed blessings of an increasingly multiculturalist market, these writers choose to develop a pedagogical relationship with the reader, at times even incorporating scenes of teaching: "By educating their readers, diasporic writers highlight the ethical lessons that can be drawn from Caribbean history" (82). In what follows, I explore how through a strategic pedagogical structure, *La isla* also makes the experiences of marginal groups from Cuba (namely women, ethnic minorities, political dissidents, and exiles) accessible to a wide-ranging audience. But before examining *La isla*, for the sake of contrast and to contextualize Chaviano's acute awareness of what sells in a global market, I will briefly turn to *El hombre, la hembra y el hambre* (from now on *El hombre*), Chaviano's first novel as a diasporic writer.

Being chronologically the third novel of the "La Habana oculta" series, *El hombre* exposes the demoralization faced by a group of recent university graduates who struggle to find jobs and a sense of purpose during the economic crisis that hit Cuba after the dissolution of the Soviet Union in 1991, a period euphemistically called "Special Period in Times of Peace." Beyond the shortage of soap and other basic commodities, the characters are desperate for food. An economist-turned-butcher, for example, finds ways to smuggle some meat and feed his family. Invoking alien forces, he says: "No, brother, I'm not leaving this position before I die . . . unless a miracle happens and aliens come to take me elsewhere."[4] Hunger, which is evoked with changing descriptors—"millennial hunger," "Painful and sharp hunger. Inextinguishable. Sadistic"[5]—acquires a spiritual quality. The protagonist Claudia, a recently graduated art historian, is visited by three spirits: an African slave who serves as her guide, a mute spirit called El Indio who appears to warn her of imminent risks, and a Chinese mulatto who malevolently rouses her sexual appetite. Soon enough, Claudia's hunger turns sexual. While at the beginning of the novel she laments how the crisis has affected the people—"the island is on sale . . . Not only its labor, but also its soul"[6]—toward the end she is an accomplice. Claudia ends up prostituting herself in exchange for a handful of dollars: "The entire island had turned into a brothel where its pupils were engineers and doctors."[7]

In addition to the travails of younger Cubans who cannot identify with the goals of the Revolution, the novel reflects on

Cuba's place in the world market through a critique of the tourism industry, which was heightened during the "Special Period." Critic Esther Whitfield describes the novel as a sort of guidebook of Cuba's history, a handbook for the foreign tourist: "The reader is a visitor, and the novel takes him or her by the hand, making the country's linguistic and sociopolitical landscape both comprehensible and inviting" (194). Being like Claudia and her friends, who are experts of the inner workings of Havana's thriving black market, after leaving Cuba in 1991, Chaviano would become herself (whether intentionally or not) a cultural informant of life inside the island.

El hombre received the prestigious Spanish Azorín Prize and launched Chaviano's career within a large transnational Spanish-language audience. Unlike *La isla*, however, *El hombre* has not prospered in translations. In part, this may be the result of an inherent untranslatability: while in English already the title would lose its original playful, poetic, and symbolic resonance (Man, Woman, Hunger), in the German and Czech editions (the only published translations to date of *El hombre*), the title was changed to *Havana Blues*. Nevertheless, being the subject of several scholarly articles and doctoral dissertations, *El hombre* has been embraced within academic circles. This, as mentioned earlier, is not the case with bestseller *La isla*.

Despite the numerous characters and a time frame that spans from 1850 to 1998, the plot of *La isla* is fairly easy to follow. Cecilia, a Cuban journalist living in the United States for four years, is writing an article about a ghost house that has appeared throughout Miami. While carrying out her research, Cecilia makes regular visits to a bar where an old Cuban woman named Amalia tells her fragmented and yet accessibly packaged stories of a Cuban family of African, Spanish, and Chinese descent. As the title of the novel suggests, there are various romantic relationships. The protagonists of the prominent love story are a young Amalia, who is a descendant of an African slave and a Spanish family, and Pag Li or Pablo, the son of Chinese immigrants in Havana. Another imminent love story is presented at the end when Cecilia meets Miguel, Amalia's grandson and a character who is paratextually introduced from the beginning and throughout the novel, in the form of epigraphs under the title "De los apuntes de Miguel" (From Miguel's Notes). These epigraphs are popular Cuban expressions, such as "There's a Chinaman behind me" (60) or "Not even the Chinese doctor can save him" (164), and they are followed by a commentary of what they mean. As such, they effectively verify the place the Chinese hold in the Cuban imaginary.

To further facilitate the reading of the novel, the family trees of Amalia and Pablo are presented at the beginning, with the names and birth dates of all characters whose lives are narrated. The titles of the fairly short chapters come from popular boleros, which highlight the romantic tone and subplots of the novel, while the six sections into which the novel is divided carry titles that direct the readers' attention to the multiracial origins of this family saga. The first section, for example, is explicitly titled "The Three Origins." This is a technique that is avoided in Cuban exile writer Severo Sarduy's novel *De donde son los cantantes* (*From Cuba with a Song*, 1967), which we could call a precursor to *La isla* as it also engages with Cuban popular music (suffice it to say the title of his novel alludes to a famous song by Trío Matamoros) and the three racial components in Cuban society: "Three cultures, at least, have been superimposed to constitute the Cuban—Spanish, African, and Chinese—; three fictions alluding to them constitute this book" (154). Echoing Sarduy, Chaviano reveals that she wrote *La isla*, among other reasons, due to her "desire to tell a story that would re-create the symbolic union of the three ethnicities that make up the Cuban nation, especially the Chinese, whose sociological impact on the island is greater than what many people suppose" (318). Yet what distinguishes *La isla* is not the appearance of Chinese characters (a long list of literary works other than Sarduy's precedes her in that regard),[8] but the fact that these stories are narrated from the points of view of female characters: "it is women who speak for their long-lost ancestors, rewriting both their family histories and the nation's and revealing the complexity and fluidity of Cuban identity" (Fuentes 1).

Despite intending to give voice to women and pay homage to Cuba's multiracial heritage, at times the narrator of *La isla* has a rather reductive lens: the female protagonist becomes hysterical without a male lover, while Cubans of African and Chinese descent are exoticized. For example, after some dates with a Cuban American man named Roberto, Cecilia's "romantic problems" are resolved: "She felt completely happy" (189). As this relationship ends she suffers depression; she is overtaken by a "mysterious, isolated fever" (211), for which she visits a doctor who simply recommends her to rest. In regard to the representation of the African and Chinese in Cuba, we find occasional exoticizations that promote what Ignacio López-Calvo calls "benevolent Orientalism" (67). During a santería ritual, for example, a toothless santera's voice is described as "ancestral," with "a sensual, agitated rhythm, like the galloping of a beast" (106). When Cecilia meets Miguel, the embodiment of Cuba's three origins, she thinks: "his features were so exotic that they struck her as almost otherworldly" (309). The word Chaviano uses for "otherworldly" in the Spanish original is "extraterrestres" (extraterrestrial, alien).[9]

It could well be said that Chaviano's fiction responds too much to mainstream demands for love tales between exotic people in strange environments. But these criticisms, it should be noted, are also commonly targeted to Latin American women novelists who gain success in the global literary market, such as Isabel Allende and Julia Álvarez. Hence, to what extent do market demands precede and haunt these women, regardless of what they write? How much do they consciously give in to those demands?

Helping us address these questions, Machado Sáez examines how various Caribbean diasporic novelists who write in English experience the anxiety of becoming agents of commodification of their respective nation's culture and history. As such, they offer narratives of the past that readers can follow, yet cannot simply consume in a passive manner. According to Machado Sáez, some achieve this through the implementation of pedagogical models, such as Paulo Freire's critical "problem-solving" pedagogy. In contrast to the "banking" model of education, which is a content-driven method based, for instance, on lecture or memorization, Freire's problem-solving model aims at student participation and collaboration. Hence, the ethical imperative of narrating the past is shifted to the readers, as they are incited to take on the challenge of reflecting not only on the content but also on the way in which a novel's components are presented. Readers become researchers.[10]

At first glance, one could consider that in *La isla*, Chaviano seeks to educate her readers, guide them through 150 years of Cuban history, by employing the banking pedagogical model. Structurally, there is an older "teacher" (Amalia) and a curious "student" (Cecilia), with whom the reader can follow the stories being told. Unlike *El hombre*, which invites the reader to decipher or feel alienated from the complex and playful jargon of the "Special Period," *La isla*, with its overly romantic language and its multiple but easy-to-follow storylines, presents events and characters in an orderly manner—in consumable fragments. While *El hombre* constantly has the reader guessing who the plural narrative voices belong to, *La isla* provides not only the visual aid of a family tree at the beginning of the novel but also explicit hints in each chapter, leaving, thereby, little "research" to her readers.

A few mysteries are left open (at least initially), such as the intangible house and Cecilia's continued sense of alienation in Miami. But even these are resolved for the reader. Toward the middle of the novel, Cecilia discovers a pattern of the days of the house's apparitions: July 26 alludes to the attack of the Moncada barracks in 1953 led by Fidel Castro; January 1 is the day when the Cuban Revolution triumphed; August 13 is the day Fidel Castro was born, and so forth. They are, according to Cecilia, "*bad* national holidays" or "unlucky days for Cuba" (130-31). All enigmas are spelled out for the reader. Toward the end, as Cecilia learns from Miguel that Amalia has been dead for over a year, the narrator explains Cecilia's connection to the phantom house: "She had *no further doubts*; she, too, was a visionary, someone who could talk to spirits. That's why she carried within her a house inhabited by the souls of her loved ones" (313; my emphasis). Given the tone of certainty, there is little room for the reader to interpret details like these otherwise. While *El hombre* has an open ending in which Claudia envisions an "esperanza de botecito" (hope in the shape of a little boat, 312), which readers may or may not interpret as an escape from the dystopian island, in *La isla* everything is rationalized. We are told, in that respect, that Miguel had decided to visit the bar in Miami, where he meets Cecilia and brings the main plot full circle, following the advice of his grandmother Amalia, who had appeared to him in a dream.

La isla fits the definition of what Tzvetan Todorov calls "fantastic-uncanny." In this subgenre of the fantastic, "events that seem supernatural throughout a story receive a rational explanation at its end. If these events have long led the character and the reader alike to believe in an intervention of the supernatural, it is because they have an unaccustomed character" (44). Explanations within this genre, which may be summarized according to Todorov as "the supernatural explained," include coincidences, dreams, and prearranged apparitions—all of which we find in *La isla*. Yet in Chaviano's novel, there is more than the plot. Amidst the drama and the supernatural, Chaviano inscribes a plethora of silenced voices throughout history, as well as censored attitudes she would have witnessed in the eighties and early nineties. Although employing a top-down narrative approach, she summons the reader to delve into the ways Cuban history unfolds into the present.

La isla has a decidedly archival and intertextual style. For example, through an annoying parrot, Chaviano playfully inscribes a series of chants that a reader may not notice. The parrot screams: "Throw them out, throw them out" (77), "Viva Fidel! Traitors go to hell!" (78), "Down with the scum!" (243), "Fidel! Give the Yankees hell! Fidel, thief! You've stolen all our beef!" (243).[11] They are chants that were articulated on the streets of Havana during the Mariel boatlift in 1980 and the *balseros* crisis in the 1990s. In defense of the bird, its owner Delfina comments: "She's one of the Lord's creatures . . . I forgive her because she knows not what she does" (244). The Cuban people's prolonged support for Castro's regime is rationalized as being caused by a sort of programmed ignorance. Nevertheless, Delfina's rationalization is not really original; she is quoting Christ at the Cross. This way, the writer questions not only the jaded pro-Fidel claims, but also—quite subtly—those against Fidel.

Miguel's "apuntes" (notes) are another example of sonic references, which not only give the book an air of authenticity but also alert the reader to Cuba's oral histories that are often difficult to find in writing. Having said this, the popular expressions archived by Miguel remind us of Afro-Chinese Cuban historian Antonio Chuffat Latour's *Apunte histórico de los chinos en Cuba* (Historical Notes on the Chinese in Cuba, 1927), which incorporates the origins of some of the sayings and characterizations of the Chinese in Cuba, such as that of the "médico chino" (Chinese physician,34-35). Likewise, the mention that Pablo's great-great-grandfather had worked in Cuba for several years, twelve hours a day, "bound by a contract he had signed, unaware of its weight" (19), directs us to the infamous contract that Chinese coolies signed before being sent to the island, a contract that, according to historian Evelyn Hu-DeHart, was mistranslated. While in Spanish the heading of the contract was "Emigración China para Cuba" (Chinese Emigration to Cuba), in Chinese it read "Labor Employment Contract"—that is, it made "no allusion to immigration, but, rather, to work" (42). Considering that Pablo's great-grandfather had been a *mambí*, "as the Cubans called the rebels who fought against the Spanish army" (70) and that Pablo then urges his daughter to visit a monument with the inscription "There never was a Chinese Cuban deserter; there never was a Chinese Cuban traitor" (284), further alerts the reader about the participation of the Chinese in Cuba's independence struggles throughout the nineteenth century. Lastly, Pablo's struggles when he is jailed for suspected counterrevolutionary activities echo the personal experience of real-life Chinese Cuban Napoleón Seuc, whose partially testimonial study *La colonia china de Cuba 1930-1960* (The Chinese Community in Cuba 1930-1960,1998) is mentioned by Chaviano as one of her key sources for the writing of the novel (*La isla* 381).

While in Miami, Chaviano would have been able to experience not only a spiritual reconnection with Havana but also a desire to investigate her nation's history. Hence, in an interview from 2009, she reveals how she could come into contact with Cuban textually: "the amount of information I was able to recover or acquire about my country in Miami is something that I would have never achieved living on the island."[12] Along those lines, it is crucial to consider that *El hombre* was largely inspired by the work of the historian Manuel Moreno Fraginals. At the beginning of the novel, Chaviano thanks him for giving her the impulse to "explore the *occult* history of Cuba, that history that they never taught us at school" (my emphasis).[13] We thus realize that the word "oculta" in the title of the novel cycle "La Habana oculta" refers not only to a spiritual and magic side to Havana but also to its often-buried histories. The term "oculta," in Spanish, bears the meanings "occult" and "hidden." In this respect, it is worthwhile to turn to Moreno Fraginals's seminal essay "La historia como arma" (History as a Weapon,1966), which urges historians to write history based on the unearthing of "the rich world of untouched and never mentioned things."[14] Like a historian, who—Moreno Fraginals further argues—must not be afraid to discover new ways of constructing the distant past or to study the history of the recent past, Chaviano manages to narrativize Cuba's "Special Period" alongside the histories of those who were marginalized throughout history. This way, the writer reminds us how the past does not cease to shape the future of its people. As put by Pedro Pablo Porbén in his analysis of Chaviano's sci-fi novel *Los mundos que amo*, "History has the potentiality of taking different return routes, since the past may or may not be the direct cause of the present (in the end, everything is speculation)."[15]

Lastly, in terms of intertextuality it is worth mentioning that many characters from "Occult Havana" reappear in *La isla* to guide Cecilia as she searches for a sense of self in Miami. Gaia, whom Cecilia meets in order to resolve the mystery of the phantom house, is the protagonist of *Casa de juegos*. Through her, Cecilia finds out that the origins of the house lie in Havana. Melisa, the protagonist of *Gata encerrada*, is a friend of a friend of Cecilia's and when they meet for the first time, she enigmatically urges Cecilia to take care of herself before it is too late. Lastly, Claudia, from *El hombre*, makes two brief appearances hinting at Cecilia that she is capable of communicating with the dead. In order to rationalize the attitudes of these characters toward Cecilia, the reader is invited to peruse (and perhaps purchase) Chaviano's earlier novels. Intertextuality functions as a marketing-minded strategy, yet it is also a tactic of cult writers. In the end, these textual connections extend further back to Chaviano's early sci-fi writings. Although as a diasporic writer Chaviano would have felt the pressure to adopt a more mainstream style for a larger audience that craves to read about life in Cuba, her commitment to sci-fi can surely be found between the lines in her recent novels. After all, according to Claudia, from *El hombre*, "We, Cubans, are the Martians of Earth and only an alien can understand what happens to another alien."[16] With this observation, we could reinterpret Cecilia's unusual first impression of Miguel's exotic features as "extraterrestrial" not as an Orientalist gesture but rather as an inside joke for Chaviano's faithful readers, that is, the readers of her earlier sci-fi, as well as a strategic manner to assure that the Chinese have contributed to the imaginary of the Cuban people. Although the history behind the presence of the Chinese in Cuba remains unknown to some, like parallel extraterrestrial worlds and beings, it is there even before one becomes aware of it. Fantasy further facilitated Chaviano's ability to embrace her diasporic identity. According to Matthew David Goodwin, "Science fiction and fantasy are uniquely able to deal with the experiences of migration in that they are generally dependent on the existence of at least two worlds, and it is migration that puts these worlds in contact" (xii). Even though Chaviano's audience has evolved, her writing has constantly and devotedly reflected on diaspora.

La isla makes Cuba's irremediable diasporic condition accessible to mainstream readers. While the novel may be considered a light reading, it should be noted that this is not necessarily the case for those for whom Spanish is a second language. This is what I realized after assigning the novel in a Cuban literature class for a two-week period.[17] While most of my students were relieved that they could follow the plot-driven text—unlike in the case of Sarduy's *De donde son los cantantes*, which they had read before—a few found the length of Chaviano's novel (around 380 pages) excessive. Not all were enthusiastic about Cecilia's relentless sentimentality or the eroticization of feminine bare legs on the book cover. One student expressed her utter disappointment with the novel's ending, while another one insisted that there had to be more to the ghost house than the explanation provided so explicitly by the narrator. All in all, Chaviano excels at counterpointing the complex histories of Cuba's diasporic subjects, as well as at placing contemporary Spanish-language fantasy on the map. Whether read in an airport in a Russian translation or in the Spanish original in a classroom in Connecticut, the invitation to learn so much of the history of peoples whose spirits and monsters follow them wherever they go surpasses the diverging opinions of what makes a good or bad story.

Notes

1. "Sobre todo se creó a sí mismo; él es su propio doctor Frankenstein, él mismo cosió al monstruo" (9).

2. "Ella no lo sabe, pero su vida está a punto de cambiar, como en esas telenovelas donde las casualidades parecen confabularse contra la protagonista" (11).

3. See Wooley Martín, Rosales Figueroa, and Fuentes. A few other scholarly papers on *La isla* can be found in the author's website, www.dainachaviano.com.

4. "No, mi hermano, yo no dejo este puesto ni muerto... a no ser que ocurra un milagro y vengan los extraterrestres para llevarme a otro sitio" (87).

5. "Hambre milenaria" (41); "hambre dolorosa y punzante. Inextinguible. Sádica" (137).

6. "Esta isla se vende . . . No solo su mano de obra, sino también su alma" (23).

7. "La isla entera se había convertido en un burdel donde sus pupilas eran ingenieras y doctoras" (292).

8. For a thorough examination of the Chinese in Cuban literature, see López-Calvo, especially his readings of Cristina García's *Monkey Hunting* (2003) and Zoé Valdés's *La eternidad del instante* (2004), which in many respects prefigure the content and style of Chaviano's bestseller.

9. The original Spanish reads as follows: "sus rasgos eran tan exóticos que casi se le antojaron extraterrestres" (373).

10. As an example, Machado Sáez refers to a collaborative online annotation project of *The Brief and Wondrous Life of Oscar Wao* (2007), launched by Junot Díaz's fans (198-203).

11. The translator of *La isla*, Andrea G. Labinger, modifies the content of some of the protest chants in order to recreate rhyme patterns lost in English translation. The original quotes in the Spanish version are: "Que se vayan, que se vayan," "Pin pon fuera... Abajo la gusanera" (101), "¡Abajo la escoria!" (298), "¡Fidel, seguro, a los yanquis dale duro! ¡Fidel, ladrón, nos dejaste sin jamón!" (299).

12. "La cantidad de información que pude recuperar o adquirir sobre mi país en Miami es algo que jamás hubiera logrado viviendo en la isla" (Chaviano, Interview by Fernández and Trimberger, n. p.).

13. "Explorar la historia oculta de Cuba, esa que nunca nos enseñaron en la escuela" (9). To learn about Chaviano's personal acquaintance with Moreno Fraginals, consult the Interview by Fernández and Trimberger.

14. "El riquísimo mundo de cosas intocadas y nunca comentadas" (20).

15. "La historia tiene la potencialidad de tomar diferentes rutas de retorno, pues el pasado puede que sí o puede que no sea la causa directa del presente (al final, es todo especulación)" (232).

16. "Los cubanos somos los marcianos de la Tierra, y sólo un extraterrestre puede entender lo que le pasa a otro" (23).

17. I would like to thank my students for helping me appreciate Chaviano's fiction in ways I did not predict. I particularly thank Juanita Álvarez, Devon Feuer, Rachel Guetta, Karen Jiménez, Eva Moskowitz, and Martin Rubin for their insightful comments.

Works Cited

Aldama, Frederick Luis. "Confessions from a Latin@ Sojourner in SciFilandia." *Latin@ Rising: An Anthology of Latin@ Science Fiction and Fantasy*. Wings, 2017, pp. xv-xx.

Bell, Andrea L., and Yolanda Molina-Gavilán, editors. *Cosmos Latinos: An Anthology of Science Fiction from Latin America and Spain*. Wesleyan UP, 2003.

Chaviano, Daína. *El hombre, la hembra y el hambre*. Planeta, 1998.

_____. *Havana Blues*. Translated by Alena Jurionová. Mladá Fronta, 2001.

_____. *Havana Blues*. Translated by Yasmin Bohrmann. Lichtenberg, 1999.

_____. *La isla de los amores infinitos*. Grijalbo, 2006.

_____. Interview by Manual Fernández and Michael Trimberger. "Ecos de un pasado que se niega a morir." *Caribe: Revista de Cultura y Literatura* 12. 1, 2009, pp 71-80. www.dainachaviano.com/interview.php?item=19#.WX4xgNPyveQ. Accessed May 26, 2017.

_____. *The Island of Eternal Love*. Translated by Andrea G. Labinger. Riverhead, 2008.

Chuffat Latour, Antonio. *Apunte histórico de los chinos en Cuba*. Molina, 1927.

Fuentes, Ivette. "The Three Origins: The Cuban Ajiaco and Chinese Cuban Voices in the Narratives of Mayra Montero and Daína Chaviano." *Anthurium: A Caribbean Studies Journal* 7. 1, 2010, pp. 1-11. Accessed June 1, 2017.

Goodwin, Matthew David. Foreword. *Latin@ Rising: An Anthology of Latin@ Science Fiction and Fantasy*. Wings, 2017, pp. ix-xiii.

Hu-DeHart, Evelyn. "Chinese Coolie Labor in the Nineteenth Century: Free Labor or Neoslavery?" *Contributions in Black Studies: A Journal of African and Afro-American Studies* 12, 1994, pp. 38-54.

López-Calvo, Ignacio. *Imaging the Chinese in Cuban Literature and Culture*. UP of Florida, 2008.

Machado Sáez, Elena. *Market Aesthetics: The Purchase of the Past in Caribbean Diasporic Fiction*. U of Virginia P, 2015.

Moreno Fraginals, Manuel. *La historia como arma y otros estudios sobre esclavos, ingenio y plantaciones*. Crítica, 1983.

Porbén, Pedro Pablo. "Fotonovela, ciencia-ficción y revolución en *Los mundos que amo*, de Daína Chaviano." *Revista Iberoamericana* 78. 238-39, 2012, pp. 225-43.

Rosales Figueroa, Ileana. "La mente como espacio de poder en Daína Chaviano: negociando e imaginando el régimen castrista de La Habana." *L'Érudit Franco-Espagnol* 4, 2013, pp. 50-64.

Sarduy, Severo. *From Cuba with a Song*. Translated by Suzanne Jill Levine. Sun & Moon, 1994.

Todorov, Tzvetan. *The Fantastic*. Translated by Richard Howard. Cornell UP, 1975.

Valdés, Zoe. *La ficción Fidel*. Planeta, 2008.

Whitfield, Esther. "The Novel as Cuban Lexicon: Bargaining Bilingualism in Daína Chaviano's *El hombre, la hembra y el hambre.*" *Bilingual Games: Some Literary Investigations*. Edited by Doris Sommer. Palgrave Macmillan, 2003, pp. 193-201.

Wooley Martín, Karen. "Dynamics of Encounter: Sino-Cuban Memory and Migrations in *La isla de los amores infinitos.*" *Orientalismos: Oriente y Occidente en la literatura y las artes de España e Hispanoamérica*. Edited by Joan Torres-Pou. PPU, 2010, pp. 119-27.

Claudia Piñeiro: In the Matter of the Feminist Novelizing of Recent Argentine Social History___

David William Foster

Y teniendo tacho con tapa para nuestra basura, nos quedamos tranquilos. (We're fine as long as our garbage cans have lids.)

(Piñeiro, *Viudas*, 229)

Introduction

Claudia Piñeiro (Buenos Aires, Argentina, 1960-) is recognized as one of the most interesting and perceptive novelists of contemporary Argentina.[1] Her work is very much associated with the trends in Argentine social life that have become prominent since that country's return to constitutional democracy following almost a decade of neofascist military rule (1976-1983). During the period customarily called the Years of Lead, although officially touted as the Process of National Reorganization, it became exceptionally difficult to engage in critical cultural production. Narrative prose, filmmaking, and theater that questioned the military regime's interpretation of historical and political life was banned or severely restricted, against a backdrop of diverse forms of persecution, censorship, intimidation, extrajudicial arrest, torture, and assassination (euphemized as *disappearance*). Three social groups were perceived to be particularly vulnerable across the board: women who questioned the traditional Marian role as defined by the tyranny (we can conveniently call them feminists, although this is a denomination that is vigorously contested in Argentine society, being viewed as a privileged, white, middle class, Europeanizing/Americanizing commitment); Jews (the Christ-killers of the regime's ultrareactionary religious vision, but typically Jews who were oppositional intellectuals and activists); and so-called homosexuals (on the basis of their perceived threat to the paradigmatic machismo of the military, but also in the context of Argentina's perennially critical birth rate). Many cultural producers spanned one, two, or all three categories, and it is not uncommon to find postdictatorship writing marked by something like a grace note associated with such affiliations.

This grace note phenomenon is especially true in the case of women writers. Women's writing has always been a strong component of Argentine culture, with all due recognition of the deprivations of social and cultural sexism. Yet cultural production signed by women has, in addition to the prominence it may enjoy in postmodern Western cultural in general, a feminist component that has been remarkably present in Argentine culture since the mid-1980s and during and the transition from dictatorship to democracy. There are many superficial ways of calibrating this situation, from the number of women producing culture (typically, publishing fiction), a noticeable influence in certain cultural genres (e.g., women as investigative reporters), or the tendency of national and international critical institutions to highlight women's voices. While it is true that dynamics of marginalization and nonacknowledgment continue to occur, it is now impossible to discuss contemporary cultural production in Argentina without giving a proper accounting of the original contributions of artists like Claudia Piñeiro.[2]

Flawed Neoliberal Refuges

Piñeiro, who enjoys a lifetime vocation as a writer and who has, in addition to stories for children, made important contributions to dramatic writing, began publishing novels in the early twenty-first century, and her first work of fiction, *Las viudas de los jueves* (*Thursday Night Widows*; 2005), remains perhaps her most recognized and influential novel; it won the prestigious Premio Clarín and was made into a successful feature film in 2009 by noted director Marcelo Piñeyro.

Viudas focuses on one of the most important, if for many depressing, sociocultural realities of the return to constitutional democracy and the ensuing artificial economic boom the government promoted as part of an effort to instill a new sense of triumphant destiny on a society acutely depressed by the six and a half years of draconian military rule. That reality is the emergence of a mostly commercial and professional middle class able and willing to affirm its economic status through residence in one of the many gated residential communities that sprang up in the urban periphery surrounding a Buenos Aires that very much showed the wear and tear of recent military rule and socioeconomic stagnation.[3] By breaking with the challenges of urban life and seeking refuge in homogenous communities (at least aspirationally), this societal component both broke with a past that was burdensome as much psychologically as materially, and sought to create new social configurations based on a variety of affinities, the most important of which was making it big in the New Argentina of the mid-1980s.[4] At least until the violent bursting of the artificial bubble of prosperity and the descent of the country into several years of consequent and multifaceted chaos.[5]

Written from the differing points of view of the women who inhabit the fictional community of the novel, most of whose husbands represent the paradigmatic male go-getters promoted by the fevered pitch of the operations, deals, and no-holds-barred opportunities of the period, Piñeiro's novel is cast as an ethnographic report on the mores that accompany the practice of daily life represented by moving from the particularly intense rhythms of downtown Buenos Aires residential existence to the idyllic and edenic charms of the privileged realm of the gated community. All of these delights are concomitantly inflected a tone of awe by narrative voices that seek to convince the reader of the importance of such newfound housekeeping, which is described with the promotional enthusiasm of a sales brochure. As a consequence, many critics have underscored how, in the face of the many social problems of Argentina whose analysis has been favored by contemporary writers (intersecting the philosophic tendencies of so many male writers), Piñeiro asks the reader to invest in an interest in what ethically can only be contemplated with a certain morbid fascination: the contemplation of the lives of, if not the rich and famous, at least those who feel that they are being given the opportunity to transcend the grim quotidian realities of mean streets of urban spaces they have left behind. Such a differentiation is particularly evident in the tendency to contrast the problems of continuing to inhabit such spaces and how the *country* (the prevalent term in Argentine Spanish for the gated community) stands in beneficent relief to those spaces.

Yet, to read *Viudas* only as a fictionalized ethnography of a new sociodomestic opportunity for a privileged class in metropolitan Argentina is to miss the sinister tone that infiltrates that account, with its sense of implacable foreboding of the failure of what had been envisioned as a viable democratic alternative, driven by economic boom, to the military dictatorship. Referencing the as-yet not immediately evident twilight of the economic farce, Piñeiro's account introduces, often in a seemingly casual way (e.g., "that happened around the time power broker X committed suicide;" "that was right before the suspicious violent accident of the President's son"), an array of social, political, and cultural references that index both the impending doom of the economic model that permits the *country* way of life and the inevitable momentous societal disruption that its demise will generate. In this sense, Piñeiro's novel is, indeed, alluding to larger historical events that as much enable the players of the *country* way of life (touted as a new social model) as those events make these players unaware social agents in a perverted (because so deleteriously false) social drama.

One particularly telling example of this social drama involves the incursion from surrounding Latin American countries of individuals seeking employment in the *country* establishments and the other sorts of enterprises they represent. Where historically in Argentina cheap labor derives either from immigrant arrivals or provincials (so-called *cabecitas negras*—literally, "blackheads," individuals of Native American descent) who find their way to Buenos Aires seeking generally unskilled employment, both are characterized by their linguistic traits, whether the reputedly harsh accents of untutored peasants or the jumbled expressive ineptness of foreign arrivals (historically—and, therefore, no longer the case—immigrants from Spain were lumped in with the Argentine provincials). This continues to be a source of cheap labor today. But beginning in the early 1990s, with the economic bubble, Spanish-speaking immigrants (and Portuguese-speaking ones from Brazil) began to flood the city: the dollarized Argentine economy (the so-called one-to-one parity) was exceptionally advantageous to them. In the case of domestic servants, who are provided live-in accommodations, dollarized salaries were particularly attractive as remittances to their needy families left behind, and overnight it seemed that positions as maids, building supervisors, restaurant personnel, and the like were suddenly all Peruvian, Paraguayan, Chilean, and the like. One of the narrators of *Viudas* comments on this as a significant sociolinguistic detail: the familiar registers of Argentine Spanish—whether urban or provincial—seem in a rapid transformation to have become the solicitous, dulcet colloquial ones of, in the commentary at issue, young Peruvian girls that filled the area, for example, of the *country*'s playgrounds and the like. Subsequent to the 2001 crash, these non-Argentine "South American" registers will disappear, as such help returns to their own country, to be replaced by traditional servant stock and even by a privileged middle class that has rapidly become proletarian.

Piñeiro's novel is written as a flashback. It starts with the events of a late spring night in which, while their wives who serve as the novel's narrative perspective do not yet know it, a group of men who are accustomed to socialize together on Thursday evenings (hence, their wives, in a first instance, are "widows" of those homosocial gatherings), feign a collective fatal accident (electrocution in the pool of one of them while swimming) in order for their wives to collect on their insurance policies in advance of the economic disaster they have discovered is coming. Now literally widows, these women become something like modern-day Argentine furies who are forced to bear witness to the folly of economic models with which they have (mostly) unwittingly been enthusiastic collaborators.

From a feminist point of view, Piñeiro not only designs her novel as the view from women's lives of the sociopolitical policies forged and enforced by a male-dominated society that is unwaveringly sexist on multiple levels; it is also, by contrast to the many best-selling novels by male writers who are praised for taking on the so-called big picture of Argentine social life, a view from the ground level of a grinding day-to-day existence (no matter how ameliorated by imported wines that cost almost a month's salary of Peruvian maids and by pride of children enrolled in the best English-language schools in area) whose gilded trappings are about to rust away very quickly. The phenomena Piñeiro describes are to be found elsewhere in Latin America, from Mexico to Chile to Brazil, but the Argentines always get the bonus points, even when it comes to desperate face-saving suicide.

Betibú (*Betty Boo*; 2011) is also set in a suburban Buenos Aires gated community. Within this even more hermetically sealed environment than in *Viudas*, the machinations of the agents of political and economic power in contemporary Argentina are shrouded in the idyllic landscape of this hyperprivileged community, named, ironically La Maravillosa (The Marvelous [Place], a name that in equivalent English-language real estate hype might be something like Marvel Gardens). A mysterious violent death (it turns out to be the fifth in a series of such deaths) of one of the most privileged of the privileged in the community not only alters the idyllic balance of that universe, but also demonstrates the multiple secrets and cover-ups that are integral to the exercise of socioeconomic power at the highest levels of Argentine society. The otherness of this universe is only brought into more vivid relief when the novel moves in a track parallel to the efforts of investigative reporters from an important newspaper to resolve a case the police are unable—or unwilling—to deal with effectively. The fact that the murder resists solving parallels in turn a reality of the social narrative in Argentina: violent crime is the common coinage of power, and it is irrelevant that everyday individuals (such as the readers of the newspapers) can never know really how that power is exercised.

The Traps of Matrimony

One of the more sobering ideologemes of matrimony is that profound crises may either tear a union apart irreparably or, if the marriage is working as it is supposed to ("until death do us part"), the working through of critical situations like the death of a child, financial disaster, or a partner's infidelity will eventually reaffirm emphatically the bonds of the sociosexual partnership. Tradition has in mind heterosexist arrangements, but there is no reason to doubt the same popular wisdom applies to that institution of gay marriage that reproduces patriarchal heteronormativity, as both view as a common threat conjugal arrangements that are "open," "noncommitted in absolutist terms," or, in a word, "modern." The degree to which such so-called traditional marriage may exist is irrelevant to its evocation as a societal ideal propounded and even enforced (when fortuitously possible) by vigilant traditionalism. Piñeiro's *Tuya* (*All Yours*; 2005) is an acidic critique of this ideological imaginary.

Inés, who has been ignored sexually of late by her businessman husband, nevertheless labors on valiantly as a model stay-at-home middle class wife (such as there may be any left in urban Buenos Aires), ever attentive to her husband's creatural needs and to the rigors of dealing with a teenage daughter who inhabits her family world in perpetual anger, oedipally being adored by her father, whom she manipulates mercilessly, and being the victim of the vengeful manipulations of the mother whom she categorizes as among the worst. Into this world comes Inés's realization that her husband is cheating on her with a silly goose of a woman who signs her love letters "Tuya" (yours, with supine accents) and, among other fetishes, gifts him with romantically dedicated boxes of condoms. Inés becomes so busily engaged in dealing with Ernesto's infidelity that she does not have time to even perceive the crisis of unwanted pregnancy her daughter is experiencing, compounded by her abandonment by the child's father at the behest of the latter's mother, who tells her that it's her problem and she needs to deal with it on her own. What makes *Tuya* quite interesting is a comedy of errors over the identity of Ernesto's lover and the way in which Inés, complying unknowingly with her daughter's never-to-be mother-in-law's injunction, sets out to "deal with" the situation of her husband's cheating ways. Always recalling how her mother was abruptly abandoned by her husband, who was never to be seen again, Inés is acutely conscious of and focused with exemplary discipline, on keeping her man. This is a source of her daughter's contempt when the latter discovers her father's caddishness and the way in which the mother seems to accept it, but it becomes a major principle of social ideology in the execution of the plot in *Tuya*: the need to preserve, at all costs and despite the grounding in any manner of hypocritical behavior, the institution of traditional matrimony. Inés is apparently less concerned with Ernesto's caddishness than she is in how dumb he appears to be, both in his domination by what ends up being multiple lovers and in his incompetence in executing the details of his daily life. But just as Inés has always been there, the faithful helpmate who keeps his socks in order, she sees herself called to sort things out in the name of protecting the family unit. Even if this means abetting homicide and, ultimately, putting her hand to it as well.

Tuya has been likened to a detective novel, both in the way in which Inés must engage in carefully reason-based sleuthing in order to disentangle her husband's extramarital involvements and in the way in which forensic and other documentary-type material is included as part, directly and obliquely, of Inés's pursuit of criminal solutions in the name of matrimonial solidarity.[6] Not even when Ernesto decides to resolve his problems on his own by making Inés a scapegoat does she appear to give up her commitment to the ideal of protecting Ernesto in order to keep him conjugally bound to her. And yet, and yet…

Ambiguity filters in in the final segment of the novel, because we cannot be entirely sure that Inés has not decided to, finally, dump Ernesto and, like her father, just disappear. Such ambiguity derives from the fact that Piñeiro has constructed her novel around the figure of the unreliable narrator. Inés is not the only narrator of the novel, but it is her voice that predominates, and there emerges a proportionate relationship between the degree to which we grasp her unquestioned commitment to the absolutist rigors of traditional matrimony and the way in which the external narrator is able to plumb the depths of Inés's unfettered silliness. Thus, the feminist work being done in this novel to cue the reader's perception of how clueless about the lived experience of matrimony Inés is on the one hand and the unfettered cynicism she is willing to adopt in order to hold on to Ernesto. Ernesto's lack of moral fiber (to cast the matter in the traditional framework of Inés's thinking) and their daughter's boundless rage, which leads her, in another dimension of ambiguity in the novel, to put herself at the mercy of possible sex traffickers, are the collateral damage of the protagonist's radical inability to engage in a sociosexual critical (i.e., feminist, in American terms) analysis of the structure and hypocrisies of matrimony (which Piñeiro, through her external narrator is, in fact, doing for the reader). The inability of Inés to see matrimonial life in any way approaching what one might call a critical mode is, therefore, in the end, the most murderous conduct of the novel. In the end, the one who is the most dangerous "yours truly" is Inés, and not her husband's lovers.

In *Las grietas de Jara* (*A Crack in the Wall*; 2009), the architect Pablo Simó asks his teenage daughter what she thinks of him. She replies frankly, although not without some measure of affection, that she finds him pathetic; he is too afraid to pose the same question to his wife of twenty years. In this, Piñeiro's fourth novel, she turns for the first time to the universe of contemporary urban middle class Buenos Aires professionals. Although Simó is not just a masculine counterpoint of the women who dominate Piñeiro's fiction, he stands in fully developed counterpart to the men who are in the background in her other fiction and who are the customary disaffected interlocutors of her female characters across the pronounced gender divide that continues to sustain the hegemonic heterosexist society Piñeiro represents in her novels.[7]

There is the recurring motif in the novel of the architectural project to which Simó wishes to devote himself but cannot in the humdrum enterprise in which he has spent his entire professional life. If in the end he is able to break free from the tedium of that establishment and from his dead-end marriage with some hope for the realization of the architectural project of his dreams, it is only because he comes to accept the cynical dynamics of survival in his sector of Argentine society, a dynamics of hypocritical values and unrelenting exploitation of the other that makes the system work. Thus, while the novel foregrounds the tedium of Pablo's lifeless routine, there is nevertheless the growing sense of how the only way out for him is to play by the rules of the system and perhaps to better them.

Toward this end, Piñeiro sketches the trajectory of Pablo's epiphanic realization of what he must do to survive emotionally in the society in which he lives. His at first halting then decisive actions taken toward meeting his new goals are cast against the backstory of the criminal chicanery that drives the system. Once Pablo ceases to be a decent *homme moyen* and taps into the inner workings of the system of chicanery that sustains the vast urban landscape of Buenos Aires, he is able to have some sense of being in control of his own destiny. Far removed from US feel-good narratives about breaking free, starting over again, and gaining control over one's own life, toward transcendent spiritual and emotional fulfillment,[8] *Las grietas de Jara* is only coherent as a narrative project if we understand that it is the descent into skullduggery and immorality that "saves" the main character from the existence of the walking dead.

The title of the novel refers to the cluster of criminal acts of which Pablo becomes an unwilling participant but which decenter his dreary—pathetic—existence. A scam run on architects by one Jara—unquestionably a token for the immense wealth of scam artists Buenos Aires boasts—constitutes the backstory of the novel. Jara claims that a project of the architecture studio for which Pablo works has caused a serious crack in the wall of his apartment. This is not an unusual occurrence, and Pablo is charged in these cases with arranging to have the damage taken care of. The difference here is that Jara does not only want the crack repaired, but he also demands an outrageous monetary settlement. If the studio does not agree to his demands, he will tie the construction up in delays that can derive from complaints over violations of the building code. Since construction projects can only make a profit by violating construction codes, the scam artist's ace in the hole is that they will pay up rather than face potentially disastrous complaints and ensuing delays. But in this case Jara has overplayed his hand, and Pablo becomes complicitous in murdering him to get him out of the way. But when Pablo subsequently discovers by accident that the crack in Jara's wall was engineered by the latter and was not the consequence of work on the neighboring construction site, there begins a process by which Pablo understands that resigning from his job and running his own scam against his former boss and other studios is his ticket to personal fulfillment. Thus the noble dream of the Master Builder to execute the architectural project he has long held secret can only come at the price of an unfettered investment in the corrupt system that both makes dreams possible and taints them with intractable corruption.

An interesting dimension of Piñeiro's brutal novel is the presence of the city of Buenos Aires, and *Grietas* is the only one of her novels that actually figures the texture of the city in the narrative plot. Of course, since the main character is an architect, he is attuned to the enormous array of architectural accomplishments Buenos Aires has on display, although in the end we understand that the same sort of system of corruption in which he is involved today must have prevailed throughout the historical trajectory of the building of the city, just as it has in all aspects of the Buenos Aires urban project. One detail that is particularly interesting is Pablo's refusal to take a direct transportation route by bus from his home to his office. Rather, he prefers a cumbersome indirect route via subway that has him changing trains twice, as though the protracted journey through the underground tunnels of Buenos Aires were the best way to experience the infectious chemistry of the city.

Women Surviving Moral Dilemmas

Marilé Lauría, the protagonist of *Una suerte pequeña* (*A Small Piece of Luck*; 2015), is a respectable stay-at-home mom who lives in the venerable bedroom community of Temperley, south of Buenos Aires. One afternoon, she invites her six-year-old son and a classmate to go to the movies. Running late, she comes to a railroad crossing, where the guard barrier has suddenly descended as though a train were coming, although none appears after ten minutes; the entire neighborhood knows that the guard barrier is notorious for not working right. When the car in front of her decides to advance and circumvent the barrier, Marilé does too. At that moment, her car stalls on the tracks and the train can be seeing roaring into view. While she is able to get herself and her son out in time, the other child is paralyzed with fright and actually hinders her attempt to rescue him. A few moments later, he and the crushed car have been propelled down the tracks, and Marilé's life, as the cliché goes, changes forever.

Unable to stand the coldshouldering of her son, the hateful accusations of the other parents and neighbors (e.g., that she thought only of saving her own child), and the nasty response of her husband who expects her to take it so he doesn't have to change his son's private school (he owns a prosperous medical clinic in the neighborhood), Marilé decides to simply disappear, availing herself of money her husband keeps in the house and her credit card. She ends up in Boston, having immediately met on the plane a kind stranger who gets her a job teaching Spanish at the private school where he works. Robert, the kind stranger, dies suddenly of cancer, and Marilé finds herself tapped to evaluate a tony school that wishes to become an affiliate of the Boston institution where she teaches. The school is in Temperley, where her son (whom she has had no contact with for twenty years) continued with his life after her disappearance. Moreover, once back in Argentina (her first trip back since her departure), she learns that he has recently been contracted as a history teacher, and that she will be interviewing him as part of the vetting process of the potential new affiliate.

While the novel abounds in this chain of coincidences and sudden turns of bad fortune and good fortune (hence the ironic title of the novel), there are many plot details that get left out, such as whether or not Marilé must go through a judicial process of the death of her son's classmate, or how she manages to travel to the United States at the last moment without any mention of the trials of obtaining a visa, or how she becomes a Spanish teacher at the Boston school without any university training, and how she manages the hurdle of no work papers.

The return to Buenos Aires provokes the text that we read—that is, she maintains a record of her experience, with appropriate flashbacks to events that led her to leave the country. And it tells the story of her reencounter with her son, who does not acknowledge her, although he seems to recognize the birthmark on one of her hands. In the end, her son travels with his family to Boston to sign, in the name of the Temperley school, the accord with the Boston institution, and the novel ends with their reunion at Logan International: it is an ending that is promising, yet open enough for disaster to occur.

I have focused so much on plot here because it is the unusualness of the narrative logic, as much as the chain of *pequeñas suertes*, that makes the novel interesting. If it weren't for the psychological profundity of the representation of Marilé as complex review and interpretations of what she has experienced, how she responded to it, and the impact on those around her, one might dismiss the novel as a popular potboiler based on romance novel commonplaces, especially her meeting with her benefactor upon her arrival in the United States or the (mis)recognition that initially occurs with her son. Yet, the novel is precisely interesting and an example of highly creative fiction to the degree that Piñeiro defies the narrative expectations of romance novels and the way in which the strategically heightened turns of plot allow for the psychological probing of awareness, motivation, and response whose depth of exploration transcends any reader's superficial rush to dismiss it as based on a series of implausible circumstances. In this, it is probably Piñero's most classically feminist novel in its focus on the dystopian life of a woman in a still very sexist Argentine society.

There are two essentially universal themes of women's lives that come together—in the end, rather jarringly—in Piñeiro's novel *Elena sabe* (*Elena Knows*; 2007), one of only two short novels Piñeiro has published. In Argentina, these two themes have a particular inflection that relates to recent social history in that country, as constituents of profound unresolved issues since the return to constitutional democracy in 1983. Indeed, the period of neofascist tyranny (1976-1983) is deeply imbricated in these two issues.

One is the question of motherhood. Argentina, like Latin America in general, adheres to an extensively romanticized version of motherhood (*Madre hay una sola* = You only have one mother), although there are significant exceptions in cultural production to that romanticized version. Where there is a particular Argentine resonance is in the activist agenda of groups of mothers (and, by extension, grandmothers) that stretch back to the beginning of the dictatorship inaugurated in 1976, demanding information in public about the whereabouts of their "disappeared" children and grandchildren. Since the neofascist tyranny had a concerted program involving the extrajudicial elimination of its opponents, even after the return to democracy, many disappearances remain unresolved for complex reasons, part of which involve the inability/unwillingness of subsequent democratic governments to deal fully with the disappearances. The result is that the mothers and grandmothers remain a vocal contestational presence in Argentine social and political life. Piñeiro plays off of this situation in its description of the ageing and Parkinson's disease-afflicted Elena of the title's attempts to find out who is responsible for her daughter's death by hanging, even when both the police and her neighbors are convinced that she died by her own hand. The assertion that constitutes the title of the novel (= Elena knows), which recurs over a dozen times as a leitmotif of the narrative, and the degree to which the reader is willing to accept the implicit proposition that Elena really does know that her daughter's death was not by suicide and that it is reasonable for her to seek answers on her own is a coefficient of the extent of a popular mythology, especially enhanced in Argentina because of the aforementioned activist movement, that mothers possess special powers that include privileged intuitive knowledge and special rights out of deference to their enhanced maternal role in Argentina since the mid-1970s.

The other topic of women's lives is abortion, which in an Argentina that has been a model for all of Latin America in terms of personal sexual rights and the absolute right of individuals to administer their own bodies (see the reference to Leonor's attitude in *Las grietas de Jara* mentioned above), remains virtually the only nontransgressable taboo. One can debate various reasons for this, from the political power of the Catholic Church (in a country with a weak tradition of religious commitments) to questions of demography (Latin America's second largest country in size is its least populous), but the fact remains that abortion is illegal—which in turn only means that illegal abortions are rampant.[9]

In Piñeiro's novel, Elena has believed that, for twenty years, a young woman who seeks an illegal abortion in a clandestine clinic near the former's house, is grateful to her and her daughter for having "saved" her from the procedure, forcing her to return to her husband's house, content in the belief that they have prevented the woman from committing a moral fault that would haunt her for the rest of her life. When in her despair over the unresolved circumstances of her daughter's death, Elena turns to the woman she helped to keep from having an abortion to recruit her assistance in investigating at whose hands her daughter really died, she discovers an ugly truth. The woman whom they effectively obliged to be a mother by returning her to her husband's arms has wished fervently for twenty years for her supposed savior's death. Indeed, she would have killed her herself if she could. Far from being grateful to Elena for her daughter's violent right to life-style intervention, she vilifies the two women and describes in detail the inferno of motherhood to which they subjected her: in her mind their intervention was as much of a rape of her human dignity as was the rape at the hands of her husband that left her with an unwanted pregnancy. In the process, she forces Elena to understand that her own daughter's death was, indeed, an act of suicide, and the older woman must now continue to live, as best she can with her seriously degenerative disease, with two intertwined strands of awareness that she could never have thought, in her maternal wisdom, she would have to come to "know."[10]

There is a certain measure of implausibility about aspects of Piñeiro's plot. But as in the case of *Una suerte pequeña*, this dimension does not derive from deficient storytelling, but rather from the postmodern principle whereby a narrative is not a balanced representation of quotidian experience, but a semiotic algorithm whereby an interpretation of lived human experience takes precedence over transparent verisimilitude, even when, superficially, the narrative appears to be dealing with the verisimilar.

The Autobiographical Turn

Piñeiro's latest novel is also one of her only two short novels. *Un comunista en calzoncillos* (*A Communist in Underpants*; 2013) is also her most autobiographical novel, being apparently a memoir of her father and her reconstruction of his impact on her ideological formation. Set in 1976, the year in which the military assumed political power in the context of an overtly neofascist program of grim national reconstruction, the narrator recalls how, as a teenager she had to deal with growing reactionary attitudes in Argentina that became increasingly and openly hostile toward the left-wing political commitments of individuals like her father. While he did not himself become a victim of the campaign of extermination that took hold in the early years of the military government, he is for her a constant and privileged spokesperson for resistance to the tyranny.

Comunista is structured around a systematic opposition between the private and basically protective realm of the domestic household and the increasingly strident public world outside the home, iconized specifically by the narrator in terms of her problems at school as a consequence of her father's political affiliations. Whereas external rhetoric casts the latter as a menace to Western Civilization (this is literally the sort of language used by the propaganda of tyranny in Argentina at the time), the domestic portrait of the father is that of someone who is idiosyncratic but lovable, and the narrator portrays the family as suffering with indulgence the man's political positions and consequences such as losing his job and being shunned by his neighbors. The title of the novel underscores the domestic banality of politics, despite its murderous consequences at the hands of the oppressors. The figure "a communist in his underpants" is a trope on a cultural reference from the 1960s, when popular urban culture held considerable sway. By contrast to the stuffy social demands for social conformity, the image of *Buenos Aires en camiseta* (= Buenos Aires in its undershirt) alluded to popular resistance to authority. Such resistance would experience a more serious channeling than sartorial preferences in the array of left-wing contestations in response to the turn to the right following the populist Peronista administration and the military regime that overthrew it in 1955.

Piñeiro's most recent novel (as of this writing in late 2016), then, provides an overarching context for her narrative fiction: the political backgrounds and their repercussions on a personal level that still color daily life in Argentina.[11] Piñeiro's main characters and her narrators reference a society still in the grips of its hegemonic hypocritical social and political ideologies and the deadening effects on still marginalized social subjects such as women who, despite all the vaunted advances in gender equality in that country, are often barely able to perceive the social dynamic affecting them, much less to be in a position to contest its course. Even when some of her characters manifest signs of resistance, they are portrayed as either reinscribed in the social dynamic (such as the artist in *Grietas*) or the hapless elderly woman of *Elena*. The strong eloquence with which Piñeiro writes efficiently engages the reader in her narrative universe, but it is only to allow her to confirm that much more emphatically the bleakness of her fictional interpretations of contemporary Argentina. While so much contemporary Argentine fiction focuses on the working class and other elements of the lumpen, Piñeiro's characters are drawn predominately from the professional class and its satellites. But it is this class that sees itself as privileged keepers of the Argentine success story, when Piñeiro shows them, rather, as unconsciously efficacious guardians of enabling national hypocrisies.

Notes

1. Yet one must take note of how a recent monograph like Héctor Hoyos's, with the exception of the Chilean novelist Diamela Eltit, finds absolutely no room to include women writers in what is seen, essentially, as still a masculinist literary world, and one where there is evidently not even the need to explain why this is so.

2. Laura Elina Raso analyzes the phenomenon of gated residential communities in Latin America. Jeremy Lehnen references *Viudas* in his examination of the relationship of walled communities to urban violence.

3. The extent to which such a project is a cruel chimera and the ways in which the structural violence of Argentine society cannot help but follow these "refugees" from the larger social reality into their

protective cocoon are examined by Mariana Heredia in general terms and by Carolina Rocha with specific reference to *Viudas*. Speaking of a powerful "immunity imaginary," Scorer, with direct reference to *Viudas*, discusses the negative role of gated communities in restructuring concepts of community in contemporary Buenos Aires.

4. James K. Griesse discusses the backdrop in *Viudas* of the Argentine neoliberal project of the 1990s. Hortiguera speaks of the film version of *Viudas* as an example of the end of globalization in regard to the Argentine neoliberal project.

5. Piñeiro is mentioned by Cynthia Schmidt-Cruz in her examination of noir writing in Argentina.

6. I am avoiding the direct use of *feminist* because of its contested—and often repudiated—status in Argentine culture.

7. A distinctive feature of *Las grietas de Jara* is the quite negative image portrayed of women of Pablo's own generation: his wife is mostly seen given over to hysterics, and his colleague Marta, while a competent professional, is also a skilled gold digger. By contrast, the two young women in the novel, daughter Francisca (experimenting with her polymorphous sexuality) and aspirational lover Leonor (an impressively self-possessed graphic arts student) are portrayed sympathetically.

8. Regrettably, Spanish translations of facile US self-help literature sell immeasurably better in Buenos Aires than Piñeiro's novels do.

9. It is worth noting that in Spanish, the verb *abortar* includes the meaning of both spontaneous and induced abortion, and it is necessary to used lexicalized phrases to distinguish the two meanings.

10. Mónica Flórez provides a very interesting interpretation of *Elena sabe* in terms of postmodern detective fiction, in which the detective, much more important than the solution of the crime, achieves a moment of metaphysical anagnorisis.

11. I speak of how this quality of Argentine sociopolitical life becomes an issue in the scholarship on Argentine culture.

Works Cited

Drucaroff, Elsa. *Los prisioneros de la torre: política, relatos y jóvenes en la postdictadura*. Emecé, 2011.

Flórez, Mónica. "*Elena sabe* y los enigmas de la novela policiaca metafísica." *Lingüística y literatura* 58, 2010, pp. 39-50.

Foster, David William. "Lo contemporáneo como inmersión: sobre el ser argentino." *Cronopio* 55, 2014. https://www.academia.edu/9117284/ Lo_contemporaneo_como_inmersion. Accessed October 2, 2017.

Griesse, James K. "Economic Crisis and Identity in Neoliberal Argentina: Claudia Piñeiro's *Las viudas de los jueves*." *The Latin Americanist*, 2013, pp. 57-71.

Heredia, Mariana. "Ricos estructurales y nuevos ricos en Buenos Aires: primeras pistas sobre la reproducción y la recomposición de las clases altas." *Estudios sociológicos* 85, 2011, pp. 61-97.

Hortiguera, Hugo. "Después de la globalización: la destrucción de lo social en dos filmes argentinos. *Las viudas del jueves y Carancho*." *Letras hispanas: revista de de lieratura y cultura* 8.1 (Spring 2012): 111-27.

Hoyos, Héctor. *Beyond Bolaño: The Global Latin American Novel.* Columbia UP, 2015.

Lehnen, Jeremy. "Disjunctive Urbanisms: Walls, Violence and Marginality in Rodrigo Plá's *La zona* (2007)." *Mexican Studies/Estudios mexicanos* 28.1, 2012, pp. 163-82.

Piñeiro, Claudia. *All Yours.* Translated by Miranda France. Bitter Lemon Press, 2011.

_____. *Betibú.* Anagrama, 2011.

_____. *Betty Boo.* Translated by Miranda France. Bitter Lemon Press, 2016.

_____. *Un comunista en calzoncillos.* Alfaguara, 2013.

_____. *Elena sabe.* Alfaguara, 2007.

_____. *Las grietas de Jara.* Alfaguara, 2009.

_____. *A Crack in the Wall.* Translated by Miranda France. Bitter Lemon Press, 2013.

_____. *Thursday Night Widows.* Translated by Miranda France. Bitter Lemon Press, 2009.

_____. *Tuya.* Colihue, 2006, and Alfaguara, 2008.

_____. *Una suerte pequeña.* Buenos Aires: Alfaguara, 2015.

_____. *Las viudas del jueves.* Alfaguara, 2005, 2011, and 2012.

Raso, Laura Elina. "El edén cercado. Segregación espacial y construcción de identidades en las urbanizaciones privadas." *Tópicos del seminario* (Benemérita Universidad Autónoma de Puebla) 24, 2010, pp. 25-39.

Rocha, Carolina. "Systematic Violence in Claudia Piñeiro's *Las viudad de los jueves.*" *Arizona Journal of Hispanic Cultural Studies* 15.1, 2011, pp. 123-29.

Schmidt-Cruz, Cynthia. "The Argentine 'novela negra' critiques the 1990s in 'El vuelo de la reina' by Tomás Eloy Martínez and 'El mundo indiscreto" by Rubén Correa." *Chasqui: revista de literatura latinoamericana* 39.2, 2010, pp. 174-91. *Las viudas del jueves.* Directed by Marcelo Piñeyro. Castafiore Films, Haddock Films, et al., 2009.

Milton Hatoum: Interweaving the Local and the Global_____

Antonio Luciano Tosta

Milton Assi Hatoum (1952-) is one of Brazil's most prominent contemporary writers. His literary career includes four novels, one short story collection, and a volume of *crônicas*. His work has been published in fourteen countries and translated into twelve languages. Brazilian giant *Companhia das Letras*, publisher of major Brazilian authors such as Machado de Assis and Jorge Amado, as well as of international stars such as José Saramago, Jorge Luis Borges, Roberto Bolaño, and Alejo Carpentier, has published all of Hatoum's work. Altogether, he has sold more than three hundred thousand copies. Some of his short stories have appeared in magazines and anthologies in the United States, Mexico, and Europe, and he has published literary essays in academic journals and magazines in Brazil and Europe.

Born in Manaus, the capital of the state of Amazonas, on August 19, 1952, Hatoum made his debut in the Brazilian literary scene with great success. His first novel, *Relato de um Certo Oriente*, published in 1989 (*The Tree of the Seventh Heaven*, 1994), won the 1990 Prêmio Jabuti for best novel, one of Brazil's most prestigious literary awards. Hatoum's three other novels were also awarded the Prêmio Jabuti, which was evidence that his first win was far from being beginner's luck. *Dois Irmãos* (*The Brothers*, 2002) was published in 2000, and was translated into eight foreign languages. *Cinzas do Norte*, published in 2005 (*Ashes of the Amazon*, 2009), was also the recipient of the Bravo! APCA, and the Portugal Telecom Awards (now known as *Prêmio Oceanos*), this last one being considered by some as the Portuguese-language version of the British Booker Prize. Besides receiving the Jabuti, his novella *Órfãos do Eldorado*, published in 2008 (*Orphans of the Eldorado*, 2010), was shortlisted in the 2009 São Paulo Prize for Literature as best book of the year.

Hatoum received the stamp of approval from the Brazilian literary community already with *Relato de um Certo Oriente*. The novel was immediately acclaimed by the critics and the public. It is the story of a woman who returns to Manaus, where she spent her childhood, after about twenty years. She is looking for Emilie, her adoptive mother, and the matriarch of a Lebanese-Brazilian family. She contrasts the house she finds to the house of her childhood, present in her memories. The main narrator, whose name remains untold, arrives there the day before Emilie's death. She initially intends to put together an account for her brother, who lives in Barcelona, and she ends up adding the others' memories to her own in order to reconstruct her past. The memories they tell are the result of their own personal experience, as well as retellings of stories that they have heard from others. They also come from a variety of sources, such as letters and photographs.

Hatoum creates a sophisticated web of storytelling, which is a mark of the Lebanese oral tradition. Although the different accounts that cross the eight chapters of the novel stand independently, they complete one another, which at once underscores the multiplicity of perspectives that necessarily comprise "what happened" and, as a result, accentuate the fact that any representation of the past will necessarily always be incomplete. Such interweaving of stories is an important characteristic of *Relato*, as it mirrors the oral traditions of the "Orient," reminding readers, for instance, of the structure of the tales in *The Arabian Nights: Tales from a Thousand and One Nights*, in which one story contains others. It is not surprising that *The Arabian Nights* is one of the intertexts of Hatoum's novel, connecting his narrative to such tradition. Orality, in fact, is a trait of the Arab and Amerindian cultures, both representative of the Amazon region, as the novel shows. The main narrator, therefore, plays the role of organizer, although she claims to have difficulty in accomplishing that task: "I was incapable of organizing anything."[1] Nevertheless, in a metafictional passage, the unnamed narrator confirms her role in the novel, which is to make her voice fly "like a giant and fragile bird above the other voices,"[2] that is, to give coherence to the multiplicity of voices contained in the novel.

Hatoum pays close attention to detail in his narrative. Images evoke memories, and memories are filled with images in *Relato*. His descriptions are meticulous, exploring smells, colors, sounds, sizes, and actions with great care. The Manaus the main narrator encounters seems very different to her recollection. Twenty years later, it is a strange place. Despite being perceived as decaying, the city is also her home, and she comes to terms with it by the end of the novel. It is depicted as a multicultural city, a hybrid place where languages, religions, and customs live side by side and interact with each other. Among them, Hatoum pays particular attention to his Lebanese heritage. W. H. Auden's epigraph right before the first chapter is evidence of the novel's autobiographical character. It affirms the author's memorialist intent, and the novel's role as an instrument to preserve community history and identity: "Shall memory restore the steps and the shore, the face and the meeting place" (*Relato* 7).

The title of the novel also makes an important statement. His narrative is about an ethnic group that has managed to keep many of its original cultural traditions, but by the same token has changed and acquired its own traits, as its history now incorporates the experience of immigration and participation in a new society that has become their own. The expression "a certain orient"[3] in the title reiterates the group's ethnic nature and heritage, while calling attention to its difference. Rather than only emphasizing their otherness, however, *Relato* also underscores the family's Brazilianness, highlighting the multicultural nature of Brazilian society. Although the matriarch Emilie is very Catholic and it is her husband, the "father," who is a Muslim, she is the one who, paradoxically, becomes a symbol of the family and of their origins. As we follow her story from the main narrator's childhood until Emilie's death, we learn the family's history, its secrets, and conflicts. The effort to remember her is analogous to the act of not forgetting their roots, one of the messages of the novel.

Manaus is also the background for *Dois Irmãos*, a novel that explores the family and its complications as well. Hatoum's second novel achieved great popularity, leading to a theatrical production in 2008, and a miniseries for Globo TV, Brazil's major network, in 2017. The Amazonian city welcomed foreign immigrants at the beginning of the twentieth century. Again, Hatoum focuses on the Syrian-Lebanese community and its interaction with other groups in the Amazon region, such as the Amerindians. That amalgam of cultures is what Manaus—and, by extension, Brazil—are all about. Characters who come from all walks of life, from fish sellers to poets, have room in the novel.

The city's spaces and history are portrayed as we learn about the twin brothers Yakub and Omar and their family. The novel traverses Manaus's booming phase right after the rubber cycle, and follows the implementation of the free trade zone in the 1970s. The subsequent decay of the city coincides with the decline of the family in the narrative. National and international historical events, such as the military dictatorship and World War II, are also prominent on the pages of *Dois Irmãos*. The narrative is critical of the military regime. An example is the passage when Antenor Laval, Omar's teacher, is beaten up by the military police immediately after the 1964 coup d'état. He turns up dead afterward, suggesting that it was the work of the military regime. As in *Relato*, this integration of private and public events shows that the local and the global are always interconnected. Local history, the novel shows, is, to a greater or lesser extent, always affected by national and international affairs.

The plot centers on the story of the two brothers, their disputes, and their relationship with their parents and their sister. The twins have a difficult relationship and are very competitive, particularly in relation to women. Their personalities are different, as is their end in the story. While Yakub is reserved, conservative, and shy, Omar is ill-mannered and a freethinker. Yakub finishes his studies in São Paulo, becomes an engineer, and marries Lívia, who had been disputed by the brothers in the past. Omar gets infuriated when he discovers the marriage and runs away to the United States with his brother's money and passport. Later, Omar beats up his brother so harshly that he needs to be hospitalized. Yakub sues Omar, who is arrested and sentenced to two years and seven months of imprisonment. One cannot fail to link the plot to biblical tales, such as the stories of Cain and Abel and Jacob and Esau, as well as to Joaquim Maria Machado de Assis's famous characters Pedro and Paulo in his novel *Esaú e Jacó* (*Esau and Jacob*, 1904). The family plights and the biblical reference reveal that Hatoum's narrative, often read as regionalist, has a sound universal aspect. Passions, rivalry, revenge, incest, and prejudice are some of the other general themes in *Dois Irmãos*.

The family's house is also an important location in the novel. It is the stage for family as well as for various social conflicts, especially concerning the presence of the maid Domingas, an Amerindian, and her son Nael. As is still common in Brazilian households, servants live in the same house as the family they work for. The story, however, is more complex. Nael is the one who narrates the novel in first person, but the reader does not know this in the beginning. His father is one of the twins, but we are unsure of which one. He investigates their story in order to find out who his father is, but ends up telling a story of exploitation and abuse. As in *Relato*, Nael's stories are not only the result of events that he witnessed, but also of what he has heard from others. The search for his father symbolizes a search for his origins. Identity, therefore, is a major theme in *Dois Irmãos*. The confrontation between the two brothers, who look alike physically but have totally different personalities, also epitomizes the always challenging relationship between *the self* and *the other*.

As in *Relato*, the narrative explores memories and attempts at reconstructing the past. Nael's narrative encompasses about thirty years of the family history. There are other similarities with Hatoum's first novel. This is the story of a Lebanese family, which in Hatoum's case always points to an autobiographical element. Like Emilie in *Relato*, Zana, the mother of the twins, dies at the beginning of the story. Moreover, Yakub is returning home from a trip to Lebanon, as the main narrator in *Relato*, who also returns home at the beginning of the story.

Cinzas do Norte, Hatoum's third novel, introduces the readers to two friends and their families. Ramundo, known as Mundo, is the son of a powerful wealthy businessman from Manaus. Olavo, whose nickname is Lavo, is the narrator of the novel. He is an orphan, but was raised by his poor aunt, who is a seamstress, and her freeloader but passionate brother. With the help of letters written by characters such as Mundo and Lavo's uncle Ranulfo, Lavo tells Mundo's—and everyone else's—story. We follow these characters from their childhood in the 1950s to adult age. Mundo is a creative, artistic person, which is a source of conflict with his father, who dislikes his son's career choice. Trajano, Mundo's father, wanted his heir to be involved in the family's business. Although Mundo's family is wealthy, he is frustrated because the father's rigid rules and values make it challenging for him to achieve his artistic potential. Mundo rebels against his father's ruling, his hometown's parochialism, and later against the military dictatorship. He disagrees, for instance, with his father's exploitation of his Amerindian workers. There is, therefore, a parallel between his father's strictness and the military oppression.

The two characters, as the twin brothers in *Dois Irmãos*, can be interpreted as symbolizing the relationship between the self and the other. In this case, however, the characters are friends and not antagonistic to each other. Nevertheless, there is some level of jealousy between them. Mundo wished to be an orphan like Lavo, because his father shatters his dreams, and Lavo, who is too complacent, would like to be as bold and determined as his friend. He becomes a lawyer because Trajano takes him under his wing. Lavo's not very successful career is one more element that helps to compose his botched profile. After all, Mundo, rather than Lavo, is the protagonist of the story. The two friends are, therefore, completely different.

The story takes place in Manaus, but it expands to Rio de Janeiro, Berlin, and London. The Amazonian capital is a stage for class conflicts, as evidenced by the disparate socioeconomic levels of Mundo's and Lavo's families. There are several noticeable contrasts in the narrative. Child prostitutes and poverty-stricken Amerindians compose the human geography of the city, serving as tools to emphasize its many social problems. In one scene, for instance, Lavo sees an Amerindian family picking up from the floor the coins that Mundo had thrown to them (38). In *Cinzas do Norte*, the family's misfortunes accompany the tragedies in the Amazon

Forest, as well as the abandonment in the periphery of Manaus. The title points to such decay, as the "ashes" represent the destruction that crosses this story filled with pessimism, culminating with the death of Mundo, its protagonist.

The novel has a strong political tone, as it depicts the military dictatorship, a historical event to which Hatoum often returns in his writing, in greater detail than ever before. It is certainly one of Hatoum's most explicitly historical novels, as one gets a clear picture of the atmosphere in the region and the country from the 1960s to the '80s. The novel portrays the 1964 military coup d'état, the harsh *anos de chumbo* (leather years) of the military regime, Brazil's "economic miracle" from 1969 to 1973, and the *abertura* (opening), the period that started with Ernesto Geisel's presidency in 1974 and lasted until João Baptista Figueiredo's government in 1985, marking the end of the dictatorship. Besides its regional and historical elements, the plot brings several other elements that make it appealing to the reader: friendship, love, passion, jealousy, greed, obsessions, loyalty, betrayal, secrets, and revelations. There are also obscurities in the story of the two families. Ramira, Lavo's aunt, used to be in love with Trajano, Mundo's aristocratic father. Ranulfo, Lavo's uncle, used to date Alicia, Mundo's mother. She left Ranulfo for Jano, of Portuguese descent, because of the latter's better economic situation. Alicia is a mestiza from the Amazon. Like Nael in *Dois Irmãos*, she does not know who her father is. The narrative suggests that it might be a French traveler, again calling attention to the region's multicultural makeup. Mundo, however, is not Jano's child; his father, the reader learns later, is Arana, a local artist. Art, in fact, and its role, are important themes in this novel. Paternity is another one, which is a sign of Hatoum's fascination with themes such as origins, belonging, and identity.

The epigraph of Konstantinos *Kavafis* 1910 *A Cidade* (*The City*) alerts the reader of *Orfãos do Eldorado* that the novel is about a city. It comes as no surprise for Hatoum's readers that once again the Amazonian author has decided to write about his hometown. As the epigraph suggests, the city will follow the author and, as a result, his writings: "The city will go with you. You will walk aimlessly through the same streets."[4] If the setting of Hatoum's fourth novel has not changed, the time has. He alludes to the myth of the Eldorado in the title because he is now writing about a phase of great progress in the Amazonian capital, between World War I and World War II. It was a time when the region attracted travelers from all over the world: "People from many countries and from all the corners of the world arrived there."[5] Its inhabitants also left for other cities, characterizing Manaus as a city with great human flow: "young men who were going to study in Recife, in Salvador, and in Rio de Janeiro."[6] A good part of the action also takes place in Belém and especially in the fictional Vila Bela, a city that resembles Parantins, now the second largest city in the state, and where the Cordovil family resides.

The author explores Manaus's metropolitan side, its urban characteristics, which is relevant because the Amazon region usually inhabits our imagination as a jungle. Like every metropolis, Manaus has its share of social problems, and the narratives exposes them: "The problem were the poor people, the government did not know what to do with them;" "At dawn one could see the families who slept on old newspapers on the squares."[7] The novel highlights the coexistence of indigenous and foreign cultures in multicultural Manaus. Hatoum's depiction of indigenous cultures is also worthy of note, as there are references to aboriginal languages and especially many indigenous legends. Arminto, the protagonist and narrator of the novel, was raised by Florita, an Amerindian woman who introduces him to the indigenous reality in the region, their folk and fantastical tales. Florita later becomes his lover. Arminto also falls in love with Dinaura, an orphan Amerindian who breaks his heart by disappearing.

As is common in Hatoum's novels, the family is again at the center of the narrative. This is the story of three generations: the grandfather Edílio, the son Armando, and the grandson Arminto. As in *Cinzas do Norte*, there is a conflict between father and son in *Orfãos do Eldorado*. Arminto and his father Armando do not get along. Part of the tension takes place because Arminto thinks that his father blames him for the death of his mother at childbirth. Origins and identity, therefore, are important themes in this text. Even after Armando's death, which takes place at the beginning of the novel, the father and the tensions between the two remain ever-present. As Armando's only heir, Arminto inherits the empire his father built during the rubber cycle after his death. Due to his incompetence and lack of interest as an administrator, however, he loses everything. His economic loss is parallel to the Amazonian region's economic decline. The Eldorado in the title is also the name of a ship that goes shipwrecked, symbolizing the deterioration of the family and the region, which is also a microcosm for the country. The novel was adapted into a film in 2015.

Hatoum published *A Cidade Ilhada* (*The Island City*) in 2009. The volume explores universal themes such as love, the pursuit of dreams, machismo, poverty, discrimination, betrayal, aging, and death. The fourteen short stories in his collection offer the readers a peek into the author's experiences around Brazil and the world. Although Hatoum has been known for his portrayal of his hometown Manaus, in *A Cidade Ilhada* the scenery also changes to Brasília, São Paulo, Paris, Palo Alto, Bangkok, and cities like Berkeley and Barcelona, where the author resided for some time. Manaus was only one of the places where he lived in Brazil. He left his hometown in 1967 to live in Brasília, where he stayed until 1970. He studied at the University of Brasília's Colégio de Aplicação. He then moved to São Paulo, and received a BA in architecture from the Universidade de São Paulo. He worked as a journalist and teacher in São Paulo, until he was granted a scholarship to study in Madrid and Barcelona in 1980. He went to France after Spain, to study comparative literature at the Université de la Sorbonne. He taught French literature at the Federal University of Amazonas from 1984 to 1999. In 1996, Hatoum was a visiting professor of Brazilian literature and writer-in-residence at the University of California, Berkeley. He was writer-in-residence at Yale and Stanford Universities, and has received fellowships from the Fundação VITAE (Brazil), the Maison des Ecrivains Etrangers (France), and the prestigious International Writing Program from the University of Iowa. Not surprisingly, his writings are also informed by his international experience. He now lives in São Paulo and is a columnist for *O Estado de São Paulo*, one of Brazil's major newspapers.

In any case, Manaus remains a strong reference in Hatoum's short stories. Although some of his narratives are set in the Amazonas's state capital, Manaus is often either a destination or the starting point of the plot's action. In his collection, Hatoum illustrates the ways in which the local is always a segment of the global, or rather, the global is an extension of the local, as the notion of the latter cannot exist without the former. This proposition contradicts the title of his book, *A Cidade Ilhada*, which is a reference to Manaus's pseudogeographical isolation in the heart of the Amazon rainforest: "Why living in Manaus, this isolated, perhaps lost, town?"[8] asks a character in "A Natureza Ri da Cultura" (Nature Laughs at Culture, 95-102). Although at some point Manaus was called *the city of the forest*, the capital became a major port city, that is, a place of high cultural contact, particularly after it became a duty-free zone in 1967. Aware of this, Hatoum chose an ironic title as a kind of response to complaints about the city's hard-to-reach nature, because of its perceived long distance from other Brazilian major centers, such as São Paulo, Rio de Janeiro, and Brasília, the country's capital.

In *A Cidade Ilhada*, characters are often in movement. As in his other novels, they are often leaving, moving out, or returning home. There are tourists, sojourners, immigrants, and exiled as well. In "Dançarinos na Última Noite" (Dancers' Last Night, 111-19), the moneychanger who employs Porfíria and Miralvo moves from Manaus to Brasília. "Encontros na Península" (Encounters in the Peninsula, 103-10) is a love story with a sad ending told by a Brazilian living in Barcelona. It is about a Catalan woman who travels from Barcelona to Lisbon to see her Portuguese lover, where she discovers that he is married. "Bárbara no Inverno" (Bárbara in the Wintertime, 77-88) depicts a group of Brazilian exiles in Paris during the military dictatorship. From Stanford University in Palo Alto, the narrator in "Manaus, Bombaim, Palo Alto" (Manaus, Bombay, Palo Alto, 53-60) remembers a visit from a fake Indian admiral who wanted to see what the everyday life of a local writer in Manaus was like. At the University of California, Berkeley's

Bancroft Library, the protagonist of "Uma Carta de Bancroft" (A Letter from Bancroft, 23-28) finds a letter written by Brazilian author Euclides da Cunha in which he describes Manaus (25-26). The short story starts with the protagonist's visit to Chinatown in San Francisco and a conversation about Chinese immigration in the city. This is how the protagonist justifies his finding: "Mas, para onde vou, Manaus me persegue" (But, wherever I go, Manaus chases me) (26). The passage is a metafictional comment. It is evidence of Hatoum's goal of showing that everything is interconnected, and that it is literature's role to make those correlations visible.

Some short stories in *A Cidade Ilhada* take place in Manaus, such as the opening one, "Varandas da Eva" (Eva's Balcony, 7-14), which is a coming-of-age story about a group of adolescents' first visit to a brothel. Other examples are "O Adeus do Comandante" (The Commander's Goodbye, 45-52), a story of family betrayal, and "A Ninfa do Teatro Amazonas" (The Nymph of the Amazonas Theater, 89-94), a fantastical tale about the watchman of the famed Amazonas Theater. In "Dois Tempos" (Two Times, 61-67), the protagonist returns home to visit his uncle and remembers his singing teacher, who passes away during his visit. As in "Dois Tempos," most short stories that are set in Hatoum's hometown emphasize human movement and call attention to the interweaving between the local and the global. When Manaus does not "accompany" the protagonists around the world, as a character says in his autobiographical "Uma Carta de Bancroft" (26), Hatoum brings the world to Manaus. "Uma Estrangeira da Nossa Rua" (A Foreigner in Our Street, 15-22) is a childhood platonic love story in which the Amazonian narrator describes a foreign family who lived on the street in which he grew up. As the narrative explores Manaus's urban setting, it emphasizes the Doherty family's otherness, its social isolation, and cultural differences.

"A Casa Ilhada" (The Stranded House, 69-75) tells the story of a Swiss couple whose wife leaves the husband to live with a local dancer. "A Natureza Ri da Cultura" (95-102) introduces us to Armand Verne and Felix Delatour, two foreign friends of the female narrator's grandmother who live in Manaus and teach French. "Um

Oriental na Vastidão" (An Oriental in the Vastness) deals with a Japanese biologist's excursion along the Rio Negro. The retired professor seems to know a lot more about the river than the local folks: "I had the impression that he knew more than I, more than Américo."[9] At the end of the account, his ashes are deposited in the river he was so passionate about. This story suggests that one can learn about oneself upon encountering the other. As the narrator says in "A Natureza Ri da Cultura," "Travelling allows one to get along with the other . . . the emergence of a new perception."[10] Moreover, the narrative suggests that belonging is a personal choice that is not determined by one's origins or history. In "Dois Poetas da Província" (Two Poets from the Province), Hatoum contrasts Manaus with Paris, the former being portrayed as the *província*, that is, an underdeveloped place, whereas the latter is depicted as the booming metropolis. The two poets are a teacher who is so obsessed with Paris that he pretends to have visited it, and his student, who is about to start his journey to the French capital. Besides revealing Manaus's cosmopolitan nature, as international figures such as Sartre and Henri Michaux visited it, this story is, paradoxically, about the dangers of cultural colonization.

Hatoum's last book, *Um Solitário à Espreita* (A Lonely Man Lurking), named after one of the stories in the volume, was published in 2013. It is a collection of *crônicas* previously published in newspapers and magazines. *Crônicas* are short, colloquial texts, usually written in first or third person, often of ambiguous meaning, and filled with irony. They make commentaries on everyday situations, commonly focusing on social and other kinds of contrasts, which make readers identify with the kinds of situations depicted. They can be more journalistic, philosophic, humorous, or lyric. Their characters are ordinary people and they may portray either real or fictional events. Although the pieces in the volume are often read as *crônicas*, given their journalistic source and everyday nature, Hatoum warns the readers in his "Notas do Autor" (Author's Note) that they could also be read as short stories or "glimpses of memory."[11] Each of the four sections of *Um Solitário à Espreita* brings a selection of pieces covering topics as diverse as the repression and resistance during the military regime, literature, cinema, and his experiences in Brazilian and some of the world's metropolises.

The title of the collection alludes to the act of observing the everyday. It is a reference to the author's lonely task of selecting from life's moments those that merit being recorded; or rather, disclosing the hidden treasure that exists in our simplest experiences. Moreover, the title also makes a commentary on the role of the *cronista*, or rather, of the author, as a social recorder and/or commentator. Hatoum tells tales of ordinary people. Nobody escapes his pen: his family, neighbors, colleagues, friends, urban types such as street sellers and beggars, historical figures, and even his pets. He reveals how commonplace activities such as going to the dentist or seeing a doctor can be memorable. His *crônicas* explore human emotions such as fear, hope, and desire, as well as social contrasts and racial conflicts. He depicts life's vicissitudes and serendipities. Love, loneliness, aging, death, religion, and parenthood are other universal themes he explores.

The *crônicas* cover family routines and cultural traditions, such as vacations, Christmas celebrations, funerals, and carnival festivities. In a postmodern style, his narrative connects historical events to his family history, such as when he comments on the suicide of Brazilian President Getúlio Vargas (56-57). Often a personal or family story is told within the context of a global event, or the other way around. In "Sob o Céu de Brasília" (Under Brasília's Sky), for instance, the narrator writes a poem about the Vietnam War (44). In "Crônica Febril de Uma Guerra Esquecida" (Febrile Chronicle of a Forgotten War,114-15), the narrator's flu triggers a memory of his father's infection with malaria during World War II. The story of the War is told simultaneously with his family's story. By doing so, Hatoum suggests that collective historical events have repercussions on individual lives, many of which do not become "historical" per se, as they are not recorded and thus remain untold.

Throughout the *crônicas* in *Um Solitário à Espreita* we are reminded of Hatoum's Arab heritage, which has marked his literature since his first novel. As in *Relato de Um Certo Oriente*, Hatoum's ethnic background appears connected to his family stories and to the depictions of Manaus, his hometown. In his short texts, however, Manaus, rather than only a site of roots, becomes a place of connections. As in *A Cidade Ilhada*, from there, Hatoum revisits his experiences in Brazilian cities such as Salvador, Recife, Rio de Janeiro, São Paulo, Maringá, and Brasília, as well as in international locations such as Mexico City, La Paz, Lima, Buenos Aires, Paris, Madrid, Iowa City, New Orleans, New York, Boston, Toronto, and Shanghai. Sometimes he makes a point of making such correlation between the local and the global explicit. For example, in "Um Artista de Shangai" (An Artist from Shanghai, 48-50), we learn the history of a Chinese artist who lived in Manaus and died in Shanghai. At the end of the *crônica*, when the narrator visits the artist's bedroom in Shanghai, he finds a photo of the artist and his mother, who, we were told earlier, admired his work (50). Hatoum's global connections are also revealed through his intertexts. He alludes to Brazilian writers such as Machado de Assis, Carlos Drummond de Andrade, and Euclides da Cunha, as well as to international authors, including García Márquez, Stendhal, Baudelaire, Faulkner, and Flaubert. In "O Perroquet Amazone" (The Perroquet from the Amazon) (30-32), the Brazilian parrot Bonpland, whose name is perhaps a reference to the naturalist French doctor Aimé Jacques Alexandre Goujaud Bonpland, speaks French, and is said to be an "ancestral relative of Loulou, the famous *perroquet amazone*,"[12] a character in Flaubert's famous short story "Un Coeur Simple" (A Simple Heart). Hatoum calls "O Perroquet Amazone" a *conto* [short story] rather than a *crônica* per se, calling attention to its fictional nature. This short story is metafictional, as it makes a commentary on the literary influences of Flaubert's work on Hatoum's.

Hatoum is certainly one of Manaus's most distinguished writers. His work has helped to make the city, its places, history, and traditions known all over Brazil and the world. He has called attention to the region's human mobility and, thus, amalgamation of cultures, showing that notions such as *local* and *global* are interwoven, especially in Manaus and the Amazon region, where Amerindians and foreigners have always lived side by side.

Notes

1. "Fui incapaz de ordenar coisa com coisa" (165). All translations from the Portuguese into English are mine.
2. "Como um pássaro gigantesco e frágil sobre as outras vozes" (166).
3. "Um certo oriente."
4. "A cidade irá contigo. Andarás sem rumo pelas mesmas ruas" (7).
5. "Chegava gente de muitos países e de todos os cantos do mundo" (21).
6. "Jovens que iam estudar no Recife, em Salvador e no Rio de Janeiro" (21).
7. "O problema eram os pobres, o governo não sabia o que fazer com eles" (21); "As praças amanheciam com famílias que dormiam sobre jornais velhos" (21-22).
8. "Por que morar em Manaus, esta cidade ilhada, talvez perdida?" (98).
9. "Tive a impressão de que ele sabia mais coisas do que eu, mais do que Américo" (32).
10. "A viagem permite a convivência com o outro . . . surgimento de outro olhar" (101).
11. "Breves recortes da memória" (9).
12. "Parente ancestral de Loulou, o Famoso *perroquet Amazone*" (30).

Works Cited

Auden, W. H. "To Ask the Hard Question Is Simple." *W. H. Auden: Selected Poems*. Ed. Edward Mendelson. 2nd Edition. New York: Vintage Books, 2007. 18-19.

Burton, Richard, translator. *The Arabian Nights: Tales from a Thousand and One Nights*. Modern Library, 2004.

Camargo, Maria, screenplay. *Dois Irmãos*. Based on the novel by Milton Hatoum. Directed by Luiz Fernando Carvalho. Rede Globo, 2017.

Coelho, Guilherme Cezar, screenplay. *Órfãos do Eldorado*. Based on the novel by Milton Hatoum. Directed by Guilherme Cezar Coelho. Canal Brasil, 2015.

Daniels, Greg, and Michael Schur, creators. *Parks and Recreation*. Deedle-Dee Productions and Universal Media Studios, 2015.

Dois Irmãos. By Milton Hatoum. Adapted and directed by Roberto Lage. Centro Cultural Banco do Brasil, Aug. 14, 2008.

Flaubert, Gustave. "Un Coeur Simple." 1877. Portaparole, 2008.

Hatoum, Milton. *Ashes of the Amazon*. Translated by John Gledson. Bloomsbury, 2009.

_____. *The Brothers*. Translated by John Gledson. Farrar, 2002.

_____. *A Cidade Ilhada*. Companhia das Letras, 2009.

_____. *Cinzas do Norte*. Companhia das Letras, 2005.

_____. *Dois Irmãos*. Companhia das Letras, 2000.

_____. *Órfãos do Eldorado*. Companhia das Letras, 2008.

_____. *Orphans of the Eldorado*. Translated by John Gledson. Canongate Books, 2010.

_____. *Relato de Um Certo Oriente*. Companhia das Letras, 1989.

_____. *Um Solitário à Espreita: Crônicas*. Companhia das Letras, 2013.

_____. *The Tree of the Seventh Heaven*. Translated by Ellen Watson. Atheneum, 1994.

The Holy Bible, New International Version. Zondervan House, 1984.

Kaváfis, Konstantinos. "A Cidade." *Poemas*. Trans. José Paulo Paes. Rio de Janeiro: José Olympio, 2006. 139.

Machado de Assis, Joaquim Maria. *Esaú e Jacó*.1904. Autêntica, 2012.

Bernardo Carvalho or the Truth That You Can Only Know through Fiction_____

Sandra Sousa

As Brazil has become more industrialized and globalized in the last decades, these changes have been reflected in its literature. Even though the prevalent themes in the works of a new generation of Brazilian writers are as diverse as Brazil itself, it is possible to point out some general tendencies in their writing. Whereas in the past a rural or tropical environment was the usual background to writers' stories, nowadays the scenes are typically focused on an urban Brazil or even on the Brazilian experience abroad. National identity, long ago defined as a return to the countryside, that is, the "authentic" Brazil, is no longer one of the main concerns for younger Brazilian writers. Since the 1970s, Brazilian literature has become more diverse in its practices and themes: writers generally reject the theme of the nation and resist the tendency to represent the experience of the urban middle class individual wrapped in personal and subjective questions, that is, the fictionalization of the writer's life (autofiction). This younger generation of writers is also less interested in explicitly political issues such as social inequality and ideology. Nonetheless, the political impetus of a literary text does not necessarily depend on its plot or on speaking about daily life issues; the representation of violence, for example, is also a form of writing about politics, even if a specific type of political ideology is not explicit. In fact, Brazilian literature today is more in tune with the rest of world literatures, addressing universal problems common to the rest of the globe.

One Brazilian writer who does not completely fit this description and who sets himself apart from the general tendencies of contemporary Brazilian literature is Bernardo Carvalho (1960-). He is fairly critical of his contemporaries, who, in his view, center their plots too often on the theme of violence in Brazilian daily life:

The problem is that violence is so overwhelming in Brazilian reality, in daily life, that little by little art and literature end up losing their reason for being if they don't directly mention this reality. Or to put it another way, everything that doesn't directly refer to a reality that everyone recognizes, that isn't a common view of reality, ends up not being interesting. Literature takes on the function of sociology. And literature itself becomes corrupted. . . . In Brazil, the old hegemonic cliché of the tropical country, of the beaches, soccer, samba, and mulattas is being substituted by a new hegemonic cliché: that of the drug trade and police corruption. The *malandro*, who until recent decades was considered a mythical hero according to the Brazilian self-image, has been substituted by the drug dealer and the cop. All of these things exist, they are at the center of Brazilian society, but literature should not be reduced to a univocal representation. (Brizuela 18)

As Carvalho succinctly puts it in one of his chronicles, what counts for "not very original writers from peripheral countries such as Brazil is the celebration of the popular consumer product to the detriment of original creativity"[1] (*Mundo* 27; my translation).

Born in 1960 in Rio de Janeiro, Carvalho has established himself as one of its most prestigious authors in the Brazilian contemporary literary scene. He has received several prizes: the 2003 prize of the Associação Paulista dos Críticos de Arte; the Telecom Prize for Literature for his novel *Nove Noites*; and the 2008, 2010, and 2014 São Paulo Prize for Literature for his novels *O Sol se Põe em São Paulo*, *O Filho da Mãe* and *Reprodução*, respectively. He started out as a journalist for the journal *Folha de S. Paulo* during president Collor de Mello's government (1990-1992), but as he states in an interview, his decision to work in journalism was only based on financial reasons (Welle n.p.). Carvalho's first experience in the art world was with film, but he ended up abandoning this art form because of his difficulties working in a team. He also realized that what he found most interesting in cinema was the narrative. While working for *Folha de S. Paulo*, he would write the first paragraphs of novels. With this process of experimenting with first paragraphs, the solitude, the obsession with creation, everything was in place for

Carvalho to become what he was always supposed to be: a fiction writer.

His first book was a short story collection titled *Aberração* (1993). To date, he has published eleven novels,[2] the most recent one being *Simpatia pelo Demônio* (Sympathy for the Devil, 2016). Already in *Aberração* one can observe some of the traits that have come to define Carvalho as a writer committed to literature in a global world where that word has been either losing its meaning or undergoing redefinition. In that novel, we find eleven characters in search of a meaning to and an explanation of events, who end up trapped in a plot of obsessive coincidences. All the solutions they find have a double meaning that remains unresolved. These characters feel exiled in their own country, trying to find their identities in a place that is itself obliterated. All that is left for them is a hallucination of their own past.

The two novels that have received more critical attention are *Nove Noites* (*Nine Nights* 2002) and *O Sol se Põe em São Paulo* (*The Sun Sets in São Paulo*, 2007). In a recent review of *The Sun Sets in São Paulo*, the critic Rex P. Nielson states that "apparently [the novel] has little to do with a contemporary São Paulo and its urban challenges" (210-11; my translation). According to Nielson,

> The story begins and ends in the city, but the majority of the novel is focused on Japanese people and events that took place in Japan sixty years earlier. The story follows the trials and tribulations of an unnamed narrator, the grandson of Japanese immigrants, who is hired by an old woman named Setsuko to write her own story, a love story without a happy ending that begins in Japan and ends in Brazil. With a narration inside a narration, the novel is full of labyrinthine episodes, narrations with flashbacks, swapped and hidden identities, and unexpected revelations that take the reader from Brazil to Japan, from the present to the past, and vice-versa. (211; my translation)[3]

As Adenize Aparecida Franco affirms, "the topics of outcasts, aberrations and changing identities are an obsession for Bernardo Carvalho"[4] (199). In an interview granted to Natalia Brizuela and translated by Clélia Donovan, Carvalho states that one of the main ideas in *The Sun Sets in São Paulo* "is that things can only *be* as long as they are *not*; they can exist only before they are named. It's a paradox" (14). In reality, he thinks that his writing can be summed up as an attempt to put paradoxes into practice. A reader who is familiar with his novels can certainly confirm this. Carvalho's literary project, if one can affirm that he has one, has been based on the idea of traveling to write, which is more complex than simply taking a trip to other regions in Brazil or to other countries in order to find inspiration for writing. For him, it is like a leap into the unknown, a physical journey that is also a personal one, consisting of stepping outside of himself before beginning to write. In the same interview, Carvalho explains this interest in traveling:

> What interests me about traveling is the possibility of writing the novel before even starting to write it. The experience ceases to be something that you passively undergo and becomes part of the creation. The trips that I took prior to my most recent books were provocations of the experience. I deliberately put myself in a place vulnerable to experience. This position provokes what happens, as if the experience were already the novel in process. It's clear that, from that moment on, I have no control over anything; I don't control what's going to happen to me; I don't have control over the real. But what's incredible is that things happen and, surprisingly, everything converges toward the novel, as if the real were conspiring with me. (Brizuela 15)

If we now turn our attention to his novel *Nine Nights*, one of his most compelling works and the one with which the experiment with traveling began, it is interesting to expand Carvalho's account of his traveling with one of his critics' comments. Eric Moberg, in analyzing *Nine Nights*, argues that

> We follow Carvalho's intertwined narratives as they contemplate identity, but we end in each with fewer answers than questions, perhaps further from where we were at the beginning of the novel to understanding who was the privileged Ivy League graduate student Buell Quain and why he committed suicide in the Amazon while on an ethnographic expedition in 1939. (73)

Moberg argues that Carvalho's fiction poses fundamental questions about humanity in ways that interrogate our identities but which also delve into the epistemology of knowing ourselves and the reality in which we are immersed. As readers of Carvalho's novels have become accustomed, nothing is ever definitive or even knowable in his fictional world; paradoxical as it may seem, this is, for him, the only way to find truth. I agree with Moberg that Carvalho's narrative practice inventively situates the author as an unnamed narrator who mimics ethnographic style and, hence, Quain's own work decades later. Yet these accounts provide little of depth and insight concerning the details, desires, and psychology of Quain's life. Moberg ends by asserting that, "By demonstrating our inability to answer essential questions as to the nature of identity, Carvalho shows us that identity is a set of constructs from biased perspectives. Identity exists not in a stable, definitive, or coherent world of order but, rather, in a universe of chaos" (75).

Nine Nights has as its basis the mysterious story of Buell Quain, a twenty-seven-year-old American anthropologist who committed suicide in Brazil in 1939 while working among the Krahô Indians. One day, Carvalho stumbled upon a review that talked about the correspondence of a German anthropologist who was murdered by Indians in Brazil in the middle of the twentieth century. The review also talked about Quain. Carvalho became obsessed with Quain's suicide and began to carry out research about it. He found a few facts by reading Quain's own account of his work in the Amazon region:

> I was struck by the fear this man had experienced among the Indians. Quain was a young, brilliant and ambitious anthropologist from Columbia University. He came from the Midwest, from Bismarck, North Dakota. When he was offered a research post in Brazil, he knew he would have to go after the most inaccessible subject, which would put him among the legends of the ethnographic work of his time. (Carvalho, "Fiction" 3)

Quain chose the Trumai, an ethnic group that was by then almost extinct, as the subject of his research, but was denied permission by the Brazilian dictatorship. He then decided to ignore the Brazilian's government decision and went by himself to the Indian village. Before reaching it, Quain fell ill and during his stay, he suffered a fever that made him weaker. The Trumai, who had been a group of brave warriors, were now "reduced to a fretful population, victim of its own fears and demons" (Carvalho, "Fiction" 3).

By reading Quain's log, Carvalho became aware of how deeply this collective fear had affected Quain. Quain was later forced by the Brazilian government to move out of the Trumai's village. He was placed among the Krahô, whom he despised, "and he ended up killing himself a few months later, while trying to flee their village" (Carvalho, "Fiction" 3). Nothing else is known about Quain's story and that is what attracted Carvalho. According to the author,

> You are never going to find out what makes a suicidal person kill himself. That's the principle of suicide. What interested me in the story is that it is irresolvable. It was a type of detective research for which I already knew that there was no answer. It came to a point where I got stuck, there was nowhere else to go, and the fiction surfaced. I seek with my books to celebrate subjectivity and imagination, rather than being confined to the functionalism of reality. In the book, reality is, for the reader, a trap or a game. A sort of simulacrum of reality.[5] (Welle n.p.; my translation)

Carvalho adds that *Nine Nights* "was written at a moment when I was very irritated with the idea that fiction is worth less than books based on real stories, which is a very strong tendency throughout the entire world. Literature was becoming restrictive and elitist" (Welle n.p.; my translation). In this novel, there are three photographs that, at the time Carvalho was conducting his research, had a novelistic effect on him (Brizuela 18). The writer explains that he wanted to extract from these pictures a truth that he could discover only through fiction (Brizuela 18). For Carvalho, the "impossibility of knowing is, at the same time, the reason and condition of possibility for imagination, fiction, and literature" (Brizuela 18). Art is a way to bring truth to the world and some truths are only accessible through the world of imagination.

Carvalho is also a unique writer in the sense that he does not exactly fit within the postmodern notion of literature and literary writers. Carvalho's own words describe his uneasiness with postmodernity:

> The postmodern, characteristic of late capitalism, is the expression of a disenchanted, cynical and pragmatic world, after the failure of all of the projects, idealisms and utopias of modernity. To receive this disillusioned world with open arms, embrace it as an opportunistic possibility for the creation of a new corresponding style, is to settle for what was left over, and it seems to me to be not only a thoughtless attitude, but also a profoundly foolish and suicidal one. . . . In this sense, when you make art abide by the general agreement of what art should be, it isn't art anymore . . . That resistance is typical of a Western modernity that I identify with. (Brizuela 18-19)

Carvalho thus identifies himself as an anachronistic writer. He belongs to the postmodern world but feels unsettled in it; his books express that distraught existence. Referring to his own oeuvre, Carvalho declares that his project recalls an allegedly "out-of-date" modernity which is incompatible with postmodernity. Carvalho remains adamant in his view of postmodernity:

> I don't believe in the precepts of postmodernity. To accept that there is no difference between the original and the copy, that the real is reduced to its representation, that individual authorship is a farce, is to subject oneself to a perverse reasoning that can only serve to ruin the manifestation of strong and destabilizing art and literature. . . . I feel that only the consciousness of modernity's tragic condition allows me to write and that my books wouldn't make sense without this consciousness. (Brizuela 19)

In a compelling article published in the *Luso-Brazilian Review*, and previously presented as a lecture while the author held the position of writer-in-residence at the University of Wisconsin-Madison, Carvalho expounds on what he means by "Fiction as Exception." He begins by explaining that he has always mistrusted writers who talk about their own works. And since in this lecture he was going to be talking about his own work, he asks his audience not to trust him. Nonetheless, his lecture uses his books only as a point of departure for the subjects that concern him as a writer. In his view, no serious reader or literary critic would be naïve enough to follow the writer's perspectives on his own novels.

This article does permit us, however, to form a better understanding of Carvalho's thinking in a world where readers are seldom attracted to literary fiction, that is, "serious fiction," as he defines it. He positions himself as a "reactive writer," as "someone that would write like a child in tantrums, in reaction to a reality in which he does not fit" ("Fiction" 3). Carvalho's books are thus a kind of provocation where what interests him, "in a world that [is] progressively reducing literature to the direct expression of the author's experience and background" (3), is to make up his own experience as fiction. This is the main reason Carvalho travels to the places about which he writes: "It made me realize that once I put myself artificially into a reality which does not necessarily have much to do with my own, that reality begins to conspire with me in favor of the novel that I am working on" ("Fiction" 4). His main objective is to make the reader "understand that literature is creation, invention, and that to reduce it to the direct expression of the author's experience is not only misleading, but also impoverishing, since experience is something that you can create as well as suffer" (4). Nevertheless, this recreation of experience as fiction in the places where he traveled did not produce the intended reaction among his readers; instead, his works were read as autobiographies or travel logs. The writer's "struggle" against reality had backfired.

Carvalho also argues against today's world system where individualism, singularity, and rupture are not seen in a positive light, that is, where such values are challenged in the name of a "blurred idea of democracy" ("Fiction" 6). According to the author, "It is an individualism addicted to its own consumption, self-absorbed, seduced by narcissism and celebrity against any kind of individual rupture or dysfunction, seen as elitism" ("Fiction" 6). This is made possible by twenty-fist-century technological tools that encourage self-publicity and allow the fast dissemination of literary works. The downside is that everyone is judged by the same level. As Carvalho puts it, "The idea of not having a singular, dysfunctional, destabilizing author or work of art serves the presumption of a functioning system in which everyone can be a self-promoted artist or writer, equal and the same. The system has become more important and more original than any individual creation. The net is itself the new work of art" ("Fiction" 6).

This is, in Carvalho's opinion, the corporate ideology that has now impregnated the arts. One might say that it is much easier to become visible in today's world, but that such visibility is nevertheless precarious. This mass art is deprived of originality and contains only a "self-sense of originality," As a result, genius is set to the side as some kind of disease. It is obvious that Carvalho does not position himself against democracy or the benefits of the Internet, but he is still worried about the place of the writer, books, and art in today's society. He is aware of the power of a great book and of how it can communicate an understanding of the world and of human condition. Contrary trends dominate today's cultural world and that is a scary realization for someone like Carvalho who is committed to a more Romantic and modernist view of art. As he states,

> From what I have seen, heard and read in recent years, I realized that a new kind of sophistic struggle, opposing democracy to the subjective individual and, consequently, function to rupture, has taken hold of the arts. It began with post-modern relativism, was reinforced by multiculturalism and developed till subjective criteria had been disavowed as antidemocratic and elitist. ("Fiction" 7)

The truth for Carvalho, we may say, is simple: "literature is the result of a subjective, singular and individual act" ("Fiction" 8). Expecting something else is to betray oneself as a writer. Literature is then "created out of conventions and, in the case of the modern western tradition, conventions that were often conceived against conventions" ("Fiction" 8). The problem, for Carvalho, is that "a new generation is coming of age under the spell of a general corporate ideology in which you do not want to use art and literature as a means against conventions anymore, but rather against your own capacity to break with the conventions" ("Fiction" 8). Rupture, breaking with conventions, is not what is happening in our day and time; instead, becoming socially recognized as a writer now takes precedence over writing unexpected works. Instead, Carvalho, as one can attest by the type of books that he writes, creates rupture. And that is one of the reasons he is not read by more people; yet he still writes books that he himself would like to read. Perhaps the condition of great writers in their own time is to remain almost invisible until the next generation discovers them.

Carvalho's latest novel *Simpatia pelo Demônio* (Sympathy for the Devil, 2016), is certainly one that would be hard to "digest" by the masses. It is a reflection on world violence, terrorism, and war. It is also a book about the relationship between love and violence in both personal and political dimensions, as well as an exploration of the ambiguity of human feelings. One of the most impactful scenes in the book includes words expressed by a jihadist to the main character, Rato: "You, in the West, become scandalized when we destroy a statue or a pagan temple, but you don't say anything when you bury thousands of civilians, women and children, under debris and the fire of your bombs. We think that a life is worth more than a handful of statues."[6] And the jihadist continues:

> You wonder: what do these barbarians want when they knock down all these treasures of humanity? What do they gain by destroying a patrimony of humanity? I am surprised when intelligent people ask that type of question. Is that so hard to understand? Or is it that racism does not allow you to see that a life is worth more than a statue? Even if it is a dark, black life. I bet that you would not think twice before knocking down as many statues as necessary to save the life of your son. Would you? (57)[7]

As in his other novels, Carvalho is interested in the truth that can only be known through fiction, that is, "the result of a search for truth, for a truth that is not in the world we see" ("Fiction" 9). This is a truth, one might add, that destabilizes our preconceptions of the world, ourselves, and others. In this way, the literature that is "real" for Carvalho is, in his words, "more interested in the invention of what has yet to be created than with representation of what we already recognize around us" ("Fiction" 9). Carvalho continues by relating this general affirmation to his own artistic practice:

It is a tentative act that strives to say things that cannot be said, a literature . . . that uses the conventions of realism to show the frailty of the same conventions. It is a literature that rejects the already established poetic and metaphoric standards, sometimes through apparently banal, neutral and non-literary language, as it tries to show literature where is least expected. It is a literature . . . fascinated by paradoxes. It is a working-process literature, as if truth could only happen in movement, before being said and understood, and could only make sense before making sense, before being unanimously accepted as truth. ("Fiction" 9)

As a writer who does not conform to any religion or church, Carvalho has a special faith "in literature as a way of transcendence, of widening and understanding the world in which we live—not necessarily with good will and good universal feelings that become commonplace and therefore can be easily marketed, but by tackling our most contradictory, paradoxical and obscure spots" ("Fiction" 9). Literary truth is precisely "the product of authorship, of an individual subjectivity that cannot be unanimously or consensually taken, nor can it be conceived before its own creation" ("Fiction" 9). For Carvalho, the unknown is always useless, and uselessness is the great liberating factor of art, that which makes it impossible "to reduce human societies to functional copies, to formicaries"[8] (*O Mundo* 23; my translation).

Bernardo Carvalho is thus creating an innovative and ambitious literary project that sets him apart from his contemporaries in Brazil. Much like the early modernists, he harbors a certain pessimism toward the world and, more specifically, toward the world of literature and all that it encompasses. Nonetheless, his modernism goes beyond that first generation of modernists and poses important questions for the future of books, readers and literature in general. As literary critics and lovers of literature we can hope that Carvalho's project survives the corrosion of time. The question that we can raise is a simple one: in an age of speed technology, of fast-paced lives and reading habits, can Carvalho's conception of a good novel[9] prove capable of sustaining itself?

Notes

1. "[Para] escritores pouco originais de países periféricos como o Brasil, é a celebração do produto em detrimento da criação."

2. These include *Onze* (1995), *Os Bêbados e os Sonâmbulos* (1996), *Teatro* (1998), *As Iniciais* (1999), *Medo de Sade* (2000), *Mongólia* (2003), *O Filho da Mãe* (2009), *Reprodução* (2013).

3. "A história começa e termina na cidade, mas a maior parte do romance centra-se em pessoas e eventos no Japão sessenta anos antes. A história segue as complicações de um narrador sem nome, neto de imigrantes japoneses, que é contratado por uma mulher idosa japonesa chamada Setsuko para escrever a sua história, uma história de amor sem final feliz que começa no Japão e termina no Brasil. Com uma narrativa dentro de uma narrativa, o romance está repleto de episódios labirínticos, narrativas com *flash-backs*, identidades trocadas e escondidas, e revelações inesperadas que levam o leitor do Brasil ao Japão, do presente ao passado e vice-versa."

4. "A questão dos párias, das aberrações e das identidades cambiantes é uma obsessão para Bernardo Carvalho."

5. "Você nunca vai descobrir o que leva um suicida a se matar. Esse é o princípio do suicídio. O que me interessou na história é que ela é insolúvel. Era uma pesquisa detetivesca para a qual eu já sabia que não haveria resposta. Chegou um ponto em que eu empaquei e não tinha mais para onde ir e a ficção aflorou. Procuro com os meus livros celebrar a subjetividade, a imaginação e não estar confinado ao funcionalismo da realidade. No livro, a realidade é para o leitor como uma armadilha ou um jogo. Uma espécie de simulacro da realidade."

6. "Vocês, no Ocidente, se escandalizam quando destruímos uma estátua ou um templo pagão, mas não dizem nada quando soterram milhares de civis, mulheres e crianças, sob os escombros e o fogo de suas bombas. Nós achamos que a vida vale mais do que um punhado de estátuas pagãs."

7. "Vocês se perguntam: que é que esses bárbaros querem quando derrubam todos esses tesouros da humanidade? Que é que eles ganham destruindo um patrimônio da humanidade? Me admira que

pessoas inteligentes façam esse tipo de pergunta. É mesmo tão difícil compreender? Ou será que o racismo não permite ver que uma vida vale mais que uma estátua? Ainda que seja uma vida escura, negra. Aposto que você não pensaria duas vezes antes de derrubar quantas estátuas fosse necessário para salvar a vida do seu filho. Pensaria?"

8. "As sociedades humanas não se reduzam a cópias funcionais de formigueiros."

9. Bernardo Carvalho believes that a good novel should also be a book without a story in which the characters are a pretense for the drawing of a world-view.

Works Cited

Brizuela, Natalia. "Bernardo Carvalho." Translated by Clélia Donovan. *BOMB* 102, Winter 2008, pp. 14-22.

Carvalho, Bernardo. *Aberração*. Companhia das Letras, 1993.

_____. "Fiction as Exception." *Luso-Brazilian Review* 47.1, 2010, pp. 1-10.

_____. *O Mundo Fora dos Eixos. Crónicas, Resenhas e Ficções.* Publifolha, 2005.

_____. *Nove Noites.* Companhia das Letras, 2002.

_____. *Simpatia pelo Demônio.* Companhia das Letras, 2016.

_____. *O Sol Se Põe em São Paulo.* Companhia das Letras, 2007.

Deutsche Welle. Interview. "Bernardo Carvalho e a literatura como antídoto da banalidade." www.dw.com/pt-br/bernardo-carvalho-e-a-literatura-como-ant%C3%ADdoto-da-banalidade/a-15352025. Accessed 12 Dec. 2016.

Franco, Adenize Aparecida. "De metrópoles e de necrópoles: Espaços perdidos em O sol de põe em São Paulo, de Bernardo Carvalho." *Brasiliana-Journal for Brazilian Studies* 4.1, 2015, pp. 187-207.

Moberg, Eric. "Chaotic Identities in Bernardo Carvalho's *Nine Nights*." *The Explicator.* 73. 1, 2015, pp. 73-75.

Nielson, Rex P. "Reorientando a identidade nacional em *Native Speaker,* de Chang-era Lee, e *O sol se põe em São Paulo*, de Bernardo Carvalho." *Estudos de Literatura Brasileira Contemporânea* 44, 2014, pp. 193-222.

Cybertheology: The Problem of Evil in the Metanarratives of Camila Gutiérrez

Moisés Park

The focus of this chapter is to introduce the works of Chilean writer Camila Gutiérrez Berner (1985-). The blogs she wrote as a teenager were turned into a well-received feature film, Marialy Rivas's *Joven y alocada* (*Young and Wild*, 2012), which she cowrote, and later adapted into an autobiographical novel titled *Joven y alocada: La hermosa y desconocida historia de una evangeláis* (*The Beautiful and Unknown Story of an Evangelais*, 2013). The chapter will conclude by mentioning her second semiautobiographical novel, *No te ama* (*Doesn't Love You*, 2015).

Born in Chile in 1985, Gutiérrez graduated from Universidad de Chile with a degree in literature and a master's degree in journalism. She then received a master's degree in fine arts in creative writing from New York University. Gutiérrez is one of many Latin American authors (e.g., Mario Bellatin, Cristina Rivera Garza) who use social media and new media platforms as ways to draft, publish, and/or distribute the content of their metanarrative works (Paz Soldán 38). Whether the platforms of media are online, printed, nonfiction, fictional, or journalistic, Gutiérrez fearlessly incorporates intimate and personal aspects of her life (such as sexuality and religion).

Gutiérrez already had a sizable following on social media when she became a highly recognized writer, after the film based on her life became a hit on the big screen and won the Best Screenwriting Award at the Sundance Film Festival. Her writings on social media and the movie are crucial in understanding the metanarrative in her first book, *Joven y alocada*. The references, allusions, and content in the book are not only supplemented by the online posts, but also by the other two media platforms: social media and feature film. Although *No te ama* presents some narrative continuity with her previous book, *Joven y alocada*, it stands as less of a sequel and more of an in-depth spin-off of the writer's life. In particular, it concentrates on her fictionalized romantic bisexual love interests, rather than on her religiosity and the aftermath of her apostasy.

The book *Joven y alocada,* dedicated to "to apostates, with love," is a reverse conversion narrative dealing with theodical issues. Perhaps modeled after Jeanette Winterson's *Oranges Are Not the Only Fruit* (1985), Gutiérrez traces her own journey of leaving evangelicalism. The complete title of the novel echoes those of Gabriel García Márquez's novel *La increíble y triste historia de la candida Eréndida y su abuela desalmada* (*The Incredible and Sad Tale of Innocent Eréndida and Her Heartless Grandmother*) (1972) or Junot Díaz's *The Brief and Wondrous Life of Oscar Wao* (2007), but Gutiérrez's title speaks to an audience that is aware of Chile's contemporary colloquialisms. The untranslatable neologism *evangeláis* is a combination of the word *evangélico* with *peloláis*, a term referring to straight-haired rich schoolgirls that became popular amongst Chilean youth's social media.

The book follows a scriptural structure divided into three parts: 1. "The Weeping and the Gnashing of Teeth," citing Luke 13:28, which explains the genesis of the family's conversion into evangelicalism; 2. "The Apostasy," which focuses on the exodus from ecclesiastic oppression; and 3. An eschatological conclusion, "The End of Times," which is a further revelation of the aftermath of her apostasy, after her blog's content was adapted into the movie.

The film's structure reformulates Gutiérrez's sardonic online posts on evangelicalism into a narrative that follows the fictionalized Daniela in a coming-of-age discourse, more apt to the feature film form. Having said this, the book also evokes the coming-of-age form, where the main character becomes an adult. The book concludes with an open ending as the author seemingly indicates that her younger brother has also left the church, solidifying the break in an intergenerational cycle of religiosity.

While the film *Joven y alocada* emphasizes an out-of-religion coming-of-age narrative, Gutiérrez unintentionally addresses profound theological questions in her blogs and film, namely theodicy. In philosophy and religious studies, "the problem of evil" or theodicy can be summarized by variants of the following question: Why would a good God permit the manifestation of evil? The etymology of the word, "to justify God," reveals the pivotal telos that most faith-based communities must explain. One can extrapolate a myriad of theodical explanations intending to rationalize the existence of the divine, with the presupposition that the divine is indeed benevolent and evil is still present in life. Gutiérrez is skilled in challenging the assumptions some religious individuals have in regard to what is considered good and bad.

Evangelical Presence in Chile and Theodicy in *Joven y alocada*

Gutiérrez's writings reflect precisely on this "problem of evil," but at the same time they also reveal the increasing presence and rise of the (ex-)evangelical community in Chile; evangelicalism spread to all aspects of Chilean society, most notably in the 90s. The book portrays an upper middle class family navigating through a major change in their lives through the eyes and the keyboard-typing fingers of a middle child. For instance, according to her parents and extended family members who are actively involved in the evangelical church, Catholicism is evil in her former theodicy. Although Catholicism is the religious majority in Chile (up to 65 percent in some surveys), there is also a considerable number of Protestants, who, according to several studies, consider their faith an important aspect of their identity, unlike the population that identifies as Catholic. The increasing presence of Protestants in Chile has reached up to 15 percent of the population, the highest in the country's history.

Both the book *Joven y alocada* and the eponymous film identify the ideological chasm between Catholicism and Protestantism within the family and among the devotees, realistically reflecting the divide between both communities of the Christian faith. The book represents a less known aspect of Chilean society, as many assume that Chile is a *de facto* Catholic country, when in fact, the Church and state separated in 1925 and the estimated population that strongly identifies as Catholic is closer to 50 percent of the total population, although some surveys suggest up to 65 percent. The demolition of the statue of the Virgin Mary in the main character's backyard is highlighted in all three platforms (book, film, and social media), emphasizing the fact that this family is not just religious, but specifically *canuta*, a pejorative colloquial expression used to refer to Protestants in Chile. The word comes from Juan Canut de Bon Gil (1846-1896), a Spanish preacher who deserted Catholicism and became the first Spanish-speaking Protestant preacher in Chile.

Particularly in the nineteenth century, some renowned Latin American writers were known for their *costumbrismo*, an artistic and literary method or movement that focused on daily life, mundane activities, customs, and speech of particular parts of society. Often, painters and writers would represent less known members of society, doing activities that were seldom featured in previous canonical works. Gutiérrez's writing may be described as contemporary *costumbrismo*, as it innovatively mixes the rhetoric of evangelicalism, Chilean youth jargon, and upper middle class dialect. The caricature that is often represented in other Chilean cultural productions, such as Orlando Lübbert's film *Taxi para tres* (*A Cab for Three*, 2001), is not replicated by Gutiérrez. Instead, her writings are self-deprecating, yet realistic, as she initially belongs to the evangelical community, only to then criticize it and eventually depart from it. Moreover, the cybernetic rhetoric in her literary project and film successfully represent social media language by using alternate spellings and playful suffixes (replacing *-ción* for *-sound*) or the frequently used diminutives in Chilean oral colloquialism (*cosita*, *tecito*, *hermanito*, etc.). The film features blogging replies through the frequent close-up shots of erratic netizens from the computer monitor's point of view, responding to the online posts and making use of Chileanisms (*hueón*, *pololo*, *orto*, etc.).

In an interview, Gutiérrez confirmed that although her writings do not explicitly or intentionally focus on theodicy, she was aware of the topic itself from one of the innumerable sermons or workshops that she attended. Theodical modes can be traced as the narrator describes the transition into her new life as a *canuta*. She recalls the gatherings at houses where people frequently used the words *Hallelujah*, *Amen*, *Lord*, and *the enemy*. The author also noticed that they substitute the word *canción* (song) for *alabanzas* (worship songs) and that at church, they sing romantic ballads for Jesus (12). Additionally, she notices the distinct semantics and syntax used by Chilean *canutos*, such as putting the adjective before the noun, likely imitating the poetic language in earlier translations of the Bible and sermons (13). In fact, the last part of the book is a "Diccionario canuto," where the author provides succinct and comical definitions for terms such as *liberación* (exorcism), *la carne* (the sinful nature of humans) and *incircunciso de corazón* (superficially Christian, but evil at heart).

At a very young age, her speech goes through "religious correctness": some words are "good" and should be uttered frequently, while others are not *canuto*-specific, or are "evil" and should be avoided. Hamartiology, the study of sin or "good" versus "evil," is at the core of the theodical discourse, as the protagonist's speech and lifestyle are in direct opposition to sanctification, the process of becoming holy. Determining what is holy ("santo") or good and fighting ("lidiar") to become holy is seminal in understanding theodical issues. For instance, Tía Paulina compels the family to reconsider what they listen to (e.g., music by Marilyn Manson, Hanson, Fito Páez, Charly García) in hopes that they can devotedly sanctify their lives ("estar en santidad") by studying Scripture and listening to music that is appropriate, holy, and good, such as Marcos Witt's. Therefore, the hamartiological aspect of theodicy is reflected in the many punishments that the author endures, since goodness through discipline abolishes the manifestation of evil.

Gutiérrez is versed in renowned and influential evangelical leaders in the Spanish-speaking community and in globalizing American evangelicalism. She mentions Kathryn Kuhlman (15), a spiritual healer, Marcos Witt (170), the most famous Spanish-speaking Christian worship band leader, as well as conservative psychologist and founder of Focus on the Family, James Dobson. She also addresses the use of the "Reina Valera" Bible translation (171), the only one permitted in her Evangelical circle. In this way, the book gives evidence of how American Evangelicalism has reached additional aspects of life globally.

Indicating how some texts impacted her, the narrator dedicates entire pages to cite Hayley DiMarco's *Technical Virgin: How Far is Too Far* (2006, a best-seller about sexual purity and celibacy), including a passage that suggests that sexual intercourse accelerates aging (53). The narrator also mentions the belief that intercourse may have pneumatological consequences, as her friend Pía tells her how sex leads to demonic possession, according to a book she read (78). Therefore, according to this set of beliefs, promiscuous life leads to demonic possession, since the body needs to be holy, as it is the temple of the Holy Spirit (88). All of these values point to a theodical scheme that considers the church as the original source able to determine good and evil.

The first lines of the book contain daring theodical content that arguably links beauty to goodness and to political inclinations: "When I was young and a Nazi, at around four or five, I thought that Büchi—presidential candidate and lover of yoghurt—was a beauty, that blondness was a moral virtue, that families with five kids was perfection and that I, blue-eyed and blondness, was the beauty of this world"[1] (11). The book links the *canutos* with aspects of Chile's neoliberalism (e.g., Dunkin' Donuts as the Promised Land). Gutiérrez initiates a theodical mode by identifying the Eurocentric and patriarchal stance of right-wing Chilean politics as something she considers initially as "beautiful" or "good." This is noteworthy, since the narrator does not exclusively consider God as a benevolent being; rather, she connects the Christian deity to her parents, the global Evangelical church, the Republican Party in the United States, conservative Christian Life literature, and her immediate social circles linked to the church. Hence, goodness does not only pertain to an ambiguous deity, but also to a personal being that belongs to a political party and has a determined ideological agenda in all aspects of life, from its conception all the way to the afterlife.

At some point, Camila indicates that her mother had become the personification of a disciplining God (62); however, she realizes that her whole family structure is rigidly oppressed by a superego that is commanded by the church: "The worst thing about punishment is that Mother became omnipresent . . . every morning, every afternoon, every night, every morning" (68). This hyperbole describes much of the Christian theodical form that evolves into the agnostic mode. There is no certainty that God is good because her mother, who represents God, is not pleasant and seems to be a repressive force. Thus, one can infer a theodical challenge: if God is omnipresent and omniscient, how can evil be manifested? On the contrary, if God is *not* good, is God evil? Is God not God at all? Is Mother evil?

The narrator genuinely struggles with her double life and understands the relational implications of "coming into light." For example, she confesses: "I try: the problem is my parents discovering who I really am. The problem is that they discover that I always fall short because if I lie and I do things that Jesus doesn't approve, it is not because sometimes I lie. It is because I am always in sin. So if I am always in sin, I don't really believe in the Lord *like others believe.* And if things are like that, my greatest fear is coming into light fully as myself"[2] (33). Her hamartiology is initially connected to the "fear of God," evoking the well-known existential biblical literature in the Book of Ecclesiastes, often cited by preachers to draw congregants to awe and obedience. Gutiérrez understands her developing values are in direct contradiction to her family's values. Furthermore, the narrator suggests that her aunt has the virtue to turn the fear of God into the *terror* of God (34). She contests the aunt's terrifying hamartiology by insisting that her pastor-uncle and aunt's theodicy relies on an oppressive deity, rather than a loving and liberating God, defiling the theodical presupposition that "God is good" or "God is love." Instead, the protagonist challenges traditional norms by consuming and recommending "liberal Christian" resources, such as the pro-same-sex marriage documentary *For the Bible Tells Me So* (2007) or ex-Christian literature, such as Winterson's books.

The most theodically explicit statement in the book can be found at the end of chapter 22, in a description of the full immersion of the narrator-protagonist in the fundamentalist world: "Pain is one's own fault. It is never God's" (60). This echoes what other religious conservatives have stated: tragedies appropriately happen to punish transgressive societies or individuals. For example, on one occasion, the protagonist reiterates what she is told at her Christian private school or church: the 9/11 attack in the United States or the 8.8 earthquake in Chile in 2010 are God's punishments for becoming "fornicating countries" (60). The narrator finds no comfort in justifying massive human tragedy as punishments from a God who is supposedly good and loving.

Eschatological theodicy is mentioned as the narrator shares how she spent days reading Tim LaHaye's classic Christian horror works, the *Left Behind* series, while recovering from appendicitis. She imagines the rapture, the evangelical doctrine of the return of Christ who will save a select number of believers leaving large numbers of people behind. Yet again, she wrestles with seminal aspects of theodicy, sometimes with utmost fear but other times with humor (111). Her developing theodicy can be inferred: If God is so good, why will he only take evangelicals to eternal life? Or, is she good enough to be saved at the rapture? Fear is trivialized when the author recounts an anecdote where her sister mistakenly assumes the rapture occurred (75), or imagines if those who are taken will still be wearing their clothes as the ones left behind see them levitate toward a light in heaven (73-74).

In Chapter 15, we find "goodness" in the narrator's upbringing in the fundamentalist church (42-43). She calls these "momentos de felicidad" (happy moments): making fun of the gospel; playing soccer; having a "communion" of donuts and fries with her dad, who also quizzes her on country capitals; spending time with her friend, Pía; cheering for her favorite soccer team, "la U;" talking about the British girl band, Spice Girls; anime, Sailor Moon, etc. Her "momentos de felicidad" are usually unrelated to her faith, and the nostalgia of the waning happiness inevitably reformulates what she considers "good" in her own theodicy. The novel swings between declaration and confession, rebellion and remorse, while she realizes the church is increasingly taking over her entire life. In other words, these "momentos de felicidad" are diminishing because of the increasing role of the church in her life. Nevertheless, she finds happiness in her clandestine adventurous life, made public through her blog: "I was an Evangelical, I no longer am, I vent my transgressions through the cyberworld"[3] (111).

The novel explicitly refers to her clashes with conservative Christian principles and how she vented about a clandestine life that is increasingly becoming public, first through social media and eventually through the public release of the feature film. As such, social media becomes the confessional: a space that is supposedly private and intimate, the confessional, is transformed into an overtly public sphere, in anonymity under the username *joven y alocada*. In this context, feedback from social media users ironically becomes the priestly entity that "hears" the confessions of the blogging sinner. The users subvert the role of the priest or the atoning savior, and become the recipients of transgressive narratives that challenge her family's heteronormative, patriarchal, Eurocentric, politically conservative, and upper middle class Christian values. The theodical scheme is shifted, as the priest is replaced by the juvenile netizen mass that receives the confession, and instead of recommending discipline or atonement, they carefully follow her posts as cybercongregants of Gutiérrez's unique gospel.

The narrator acknowledges that her promiscuous life defies her family values. But she also confesses that although she was brought up with a deep sense of guilt, she ultimately finds "alegría" (joy) apart from churched values, choosing to meet and be intimate with loved ones as she pleases (18). In other words, the protagonist is able to break the intergenerational bond, rejecting the inherited code of ethics. She develops her own solution to the hamartiological dilemma that clashes with adolescent sexuality: "God covers me with a blanket of protection. Ignorance is the protection. Ignorance will protect me from the guilt of fornication. Not having that guilt will protect me from trauma"[4] (49).

When discussing *Oranges Are Not the Only Fruit*, the narrator explains that its author, Jeanette Winterson, "invents a character of a friend that never existed in real life. She invents her because she would have liked to have somebody good in her damn life. A tolerable fiction about an intolerable life" (72). That is, fiction becomes the only hope that allows repressed characters to tolerate life, perhaps a reason why the film included characters such as Antonia and Tomás, who allowed the protagonist, Daniela, to endure life. Among her family members, the secondary film characters, Aunt Isabel (who is absent in the book) and her older sister (Julia in the film, Virginia in the book and in real life) become a source of solidarity and hope. In fact, toward the end of the autobiography, the sister authors a cosigned letter posted on Facebook explaining their apostasy as sisters, in their own exodus out of the church. The sisters affirm that they live ethically in spite of the church's assumption that only the Evangelical church they belong to upholds the code of ethics perfectly (138), thus challenging the church's assumption that they have "resolved" theodical paradox. The fictional character that Winterson did not have in her own life is her older sister, who challenges the church's ethical superiority by condemning corporal punishment of infants (138), the unjust American war in Iraq (139), and the justification of torture (139), among many other divisive contemporary issues, positing a reformulated theodicy: If God is love/good, why would God's church not manifest love/good? If God is love, why do the followers seldom manifest it? If her older sister and she are "not good" according to the church, why do their ethical postures seem obviously more ethical than the church's?

Virginia becomes a Moses leading the Exodus out of a life of pharaonic and pharisaic oppression and into a sisterly apostasy toward the Promised Land where nihilism and hedonism flow, leading them to freedom. The freedom achieved after her independence from her parent's generation (uncle-pastor, aunt-principal, father and mother) allows the narrator's theodicy to evolve into a hamartiology that is devoid of parental influence and has matured into a fresh world-view, where she can narrate freely and find goodness, love, and hope outside the evangelical world. In the film, the intergenerational break is even more evident when the only "good" Christian, Aunt Isabel, dies of cancer at the end of the film, strengthening a generational hamartiology: nobody in her parents' generation who is involved with the church is "good."

Critical Insights

Anthropodicy in *No te ama*

Linking it to the sororal apostasy at the end of *Joven y alocada*, Gutiérrez's second novel, *No te ama* is dedicated to her sister, Virginia. However, in this work, Gutiérrez barely returns to theological questions, which are now eclipsed by issues related to identity and romantic love. If theodicy attempts to justify God as a benevolent being, anthropodicy, faithful to its etymology, justifies humankind as inherently good. This shift from the omnibenevolence of God to the goodness in human beings is not apart from theodicy. The doctrinal premises claiming that God is good and that Man is good are not mutually exclusive. However, in the reformed and evangelical traditions, there is a tendency to highlight the broken nature of humans (doctrine of total depravity in some Protestant circles), rather than the Imago Dei, that is, that since all humans are created in the image of God, humans also possess divine goodness. We find a generational communion reflecting the anthropodical fraternal affection between siblings. In Cartesian modes, "I love, therefore I exist" or "I want to be loved, therefore I exist."

Reverting the notion that a good God permits the existence of evil, one may ask: how can the nonexistence of God allow the seemingly "divine" experience of sexual attraction? Or how can the rejection of a good God permit the apparently supernatural solidarity between sisters and siblings? Addressing these questions subtextually, the search for love (Eros) in *No te ama* is at the crux of the entire narrative, as the protagonist seeks to find love from Vietnam (a young woman) or Bolivia (a young man). The second book distances itself from its nonfiction content and delves into a more fictionalized look at the past. Hence, in *No te ama*, the reciprocated love from both Bolivia and Vietnam becomes goodness and hope. In other words, the theodical scheme replaces the goodness from the religious institution with the goodness of romantic company. Both books have an evolving theodicy, where the personable, good Christian deity is replaced by the good *unknown* God(dess) and the good life with loved ones.

In that sense, *No te ama* has far more inclination toward a classical theodical mode than the first one. That is, there is no presupposition that God (and God's followers) is at all good in the *Joven y alocada* metanarratives; *No te ama* deals with a more pantheistic worldview. Superficially, destiny or karma have agency that favors the narrator. There is an inherent attribute of benevolence that sympathizes with the protagonist. This source of goodness is certainly not limited to the Christian God. On the contrary, it is extended to a humanity that mutually bond in (erotic) love, unconditional fraternal love with family members, under a "god" that is ambiguous and more universal.

The novel mildly resembles a Greek tragedy, given that the title foreshadows an unrequited love. The protagonist is *not* loved by her love interest(s) in the present indicative tense: "No te ama." The unreciprocated love, however, is not gender-specific in the Spanish-language original version, as it lacks the explicit syntactic subject that could contain gender (he or she). The romantic tension remains, given that the love triangle is not "resolved" until the end. Either Vietnam or Bolivia does not love the protagonist. This syntactic ambiguity cannot be translated into English language, as it would require the gender-specific "he" or "she" pronouns to describe "No te ama." It is either "he doesn't love you" or "she doesn't love you." We could, however, further theorize whether the subject of the sentence "No te ama" refers to the well-known evangelistic mantra: "Dios te ama" ("God loves you"). Yet, the content of the novel departs from Christian theodicy. Whichever was the author's intent, one thing is clear: while the apostate leaves the church, satisfaction from love and goodness is not easy to find. The love of the self-evident omnibenevolent God in evangelical faith is not so common in humans.

Chapter 11 cites Jaime Moreno Garrido, professor of ancient history at the Universidad de Chile, in the context of a Sumerian or Babylonian prayer. The "Penitential Prayer to Every God" mentioned by the protagonist is, in fact, a Sumerian prayer, and Gutiérrez shares the concluding lines of the prayer in two moments: "god who I know and don't know, I implore you / goddess who I know and don't know, I implore you"[5] (Francis 37-8, Weber 123). She later adds to the prayer, asking for serendipity: "may the god I know and don't know; may the goddess I know and don't know / grant us a life that we are not currently living. / grant her to be here, sitting at this table, making herself some tea"[6] (40-41). Gutiérrez reformulates the prayer into a passionate plea: that Vietnam will come back to her. With her Marian turn, achieved by imploring a goddess whom she "definitely doesn't know" she hopes for a more merciful female god who might grant that which was previously unanswered or forbidden. There is a sentimental spiritual matter in desiring divine or supernatural intervention, whoever the granting and gracious deity may be, whether anthropomorphic or celestial, known Judeo-Christian gods or unknown deity. Coincidentally, the etymology of the verb *to desire* refers to demanding or expecting from the stars (*sidere* in Latin), and *imploring* means *invoking with tears*. Thus, the dramatic invocation of deity is still sincere, in spite of the absence of a Judeo-Christian God.

The tearful supplication projects humility. The premise of the supplication is the helplessness in addressing God, whether known, unknown, male, female, omnipotent, impotent, omnipresent, present, omniscient, oblivious, omnibenevolent, obnoxious, or otherwise. The protagonist no longer has assurance in the immediacy of the answer, or in the intimacy that oftentimes evangelicalism upholds in regard to the relationship between god and man. *No te ama,* in that sense, highlights an esoteric and mystic deity, an ambiguous relationship with the unknown divinity rather than the theodically resolute attitude of the institutionalized God. To sum up, the second novel replaces the traditional theodical mode related to an ominous God with an anthropodical mode and the hope of finding love in human relationships rather than inhumane religion.

Notes

1. "Cuando era joven y nazi, como a los cuatro o cinco años, pensaba que Büchi –candidato a presidente y amante del yogur– era una hermosura, que la rubiedad era una virtud moral, que las familias de cinco hijos eran la perfección y que yo, pelo claro, ojos azules, era la belleza de este mundo."

2. "Trato: el problema es que descubran cómo soy realmente. El problema es que se enteren de que siempre estoy en falta porque si miento y si hago cosas que a Jesú no le parecen, no es porque a veces peque. Es porque siempre estoy en pecado. Si siempre estoy en pecado, realmente no creo en el Señor *como creen los demás*. Y si las cosas son así, mi temor más temor es salir toda yo a la luz."

3. "Fui evangelion, dejo de serlo, vocifero mi maldad a través del cibermundo."

4. "Dios pone un manto de protección sobre mí. La protección es la ignorancia. La ignorancia me protegerá de la culpa fornicaria. No tener culpa fornicaria me protegerá del trauma."

5. "Al dios que conozco o no conozco, yo te imploro / a la diosa que conozco o no conozco, yo te imploro."

6. "Al dios que conozco o no conozco; a la diosa que definitivamente no conozco / Que tengamos la vida que no estamos teniendo. / Que esté acá, sentada a esta mesa, haciéndose un té."

Works Cited

For the Bible Tells Me So. Directed by Daniel G. Karslake. First Run Features, 2007.

Francis, Robert Harper. "Prayers and Hymns." *The World's Great Books: Assyrian and Babylonian Literature.* Edited by Rossiter Johnson. Appleton, 1901.

Gutiérrez, Camila. *Joven y alocada: La hermosa y desconocida historia de una evangeláis.* Penguin Random House, Grupo Editorial Chile, 2013.

_____. *No te ama.* Penguin Random House, Grupo Editorial Chile, 2015.

_____. Personal interview. June 27, 2017.

Joven y alocada. Directed by Marialy Rivas, performances by Alicia Rodríguez, Aline Kuppenheim, and María Gracia Omegna. IFC Films, 2012.

Paz Soldán, Edmundo. "Cristina Rivera Garza's Tweets." *Hybrid Storyspaces: Redefining the Critical Enterprise in Twenty-First Century Hispanic Literature.* Edited by Christine Hensler and Deborah A. Castillo. *Hispanic Issues On Line* 9, Spring 2012, pp. 38-39. Accessed July 30, 2017.

Weber, Eugen, editor. *The Western Tradition, Vol I: From the Ancient World to Louis XIV.* 5th ed. Heath, 1995.

Winterson, Jeanette. *Oranges Are Not the Only Fruit.* Grove, 1997.

Labyrinths of the Literary World: The Writings of Bárbara Jacobs

Traci Roberts-Camps

The world of Bárbara Jacobs (1947-) is one of words, language, and writing in which books refer to other books, stories hide within stories, and literary theory is a central theme.[1] While Jacobs plays with the concepts of literary theory in her texts, she nevertheless gives them earnest consideration. In other words, Jacobs focuses on the way in which she writes and makes this process transparent to the reader. In this way, Jacobs's texts are simultaneously questioning the writing process and probing the meaning of this very process. When one of her characters ironically follows the precepts of some theory on creative writing, Jacobs is also analyzing her own writing. When she openly discusses literature, literary theory, and language itself, she reveals how important these are to her own view of writing. With this in mind, this chapter will examine *Florencia y Ruiseñor* (Florencia and Ruiseñor, 2006), *La dueña del Hotel Poe* (The Owner of Hotel Poe, 2014), and *Hacia el valle del sueño* (Toward the Valley of Sleep, 2014) from the following perspectives: multiple languages, linguistic analysis and word play, literary theory, the world of publishing, self-awareness, and self-analysis. Gérard Genette's theories on narrative discourse will prove helpful in discussing Jacobs's singular focus on language, literature, and the writing process.

Certain terms that Genette uses in *Narrative Discourse: An Essay in Method* (1980) are helpful in understanding Jacobs's focus on language and the formal aspects of the writing process. Genette proposes "to use the word *story* for the signified or narrative content ... to use the word *narrative* for the signifier, statement, discourse or narrative text itself, and to use the word *narrating* for the producing narrative action and, by extension, the whole of the real or fictional situation" (27). He further categorizes his study to three basic classes of determinations: those dealing with temporal relations between narrative and story, which I will arrange under the heading of *tense*; those dealing with modalities (forms and degrees) of narrative "representation," and thus with the *mood* of the narrative; and finally, those dealing with the way in which the narrating itself is implicated in the narrative . . . , this term is *voice* [which] will refer to a relation with the subject (and more generally with the instance) of the enunciating. (31-32)

While these terms and concepts have been nuanced since Genette, they are appropriate to a study of Jacobs's work. Jacobs herself refers to some of these terms when she discusses the literary process. Furthermore, her work manifestly reveals her preoccupation with the formal aspects of writing and openly discusses such concepts as tense and mood. In novels such as *Florencia y Ruiseñor* and *La dueña del Hotel Poe* (as well as most of her other texts), Jacobs makes it clear to the reader that one of her primary intents is to examine the formal aspects of writing.[2]

Other Languages

In her novels, Jacobs includes several languages in short phrases. Part of this fascination with languages stems from her personal background: both sets of Jacobs's grandparents were Lebanese immigrants; those on her father's side went to New York City and the ones on her mother's side to Mexico City. As Jacobs says in an interview with Roberto García Bonilla, "I grew up listening to several languages around me: Spanish, English, French, Arabic, and the indigenous language of my nanny."[3] Lady Rojas-Trempe recognizes Jacobs's fascination with multiple languages as early as in her short story collection *Doce cuentos en contra* (Twelve Short Stories Against, 1982), in which she includes passages in Spanish as well as English and French, the two languages of Canada where she attended high school ("La educación privada" 26-27). In another article, Rojas-Trempe analyzes a passage from the short story "Carol dice" (Carol Says) and the significance of language: "nationality, native tongue, accent and pronunciation leave a mark on the act of saying and expressing" ("La iniciación"). [4] In the same article,

Rojas-Trempe discusses the protagonist's relationship to language and her exposure to English and French in this short story "as a way of enriching her Spanish, as well as of developing her intellectual comprehension" (125). In *Florencia y Ruiseñor*, a novel in which two characters encounter each other in a mental asylum and explore theories of writing a novel, we can see that Jacobs peppers the novel with phrases in other languages, such as "justement comme un petit-maître, n'est-ce pas?" (Just like a little master, right?) (15). In *La dueña del Hotel Poe*, a novel in which the author explores various genres and the idea of a novel-within-a-novel , Jacobs uses the words "barbecue," "Coca Cola," and "teenager" (40-41) when referring to the character Galleta Cookie's stay in San Antonio, Texas. Also, when referring to Galleta Cookie (the name itself a play on languages), the narrator of *Objeto de segunda mano* (Second-hand Object)—the novel within the novel—calls her "Galleta, *my cherry* Cookie, *ma chéri*" (44). Moreover, Chapter 8 of the book within a book is titled "*Shtó eta takoe*, o ¿Qué es eso?" (What is this? What are you doing?), the first part in Russian also having an occasional negative connotation (69). This linguistic diversity is a first indication of Jacobs's attentiveness to language and how it works in narrative form.

Linguistic Analysis/Word Play

Along with other languages, Jacobs's texts reveal the author's emphasis on linguistic analysis and word play. In an interview in 2007, Jacobs discusses the relationship between literature and language and whether they are separate; she refers to literature that seeks to highlight linguistic differences and asserts: "The interest aroused by this type of literature is particularly challenging because it multiplies the problems involved not only in understanding but also in translation. I think of *Finnegan's Wake*, the quintessential conceptual and language game that James Joyce proposes to the reader as entertainment and fun."[5] In her writing, Jacobs practices this style of writing in which she plays with language as a form of linguistic analysis but also as a way of amusing the reader. In *Florencia y Ruiseñor*, Jacobs also uses linguistic analysis to advance the narrative; for example, when the narrator discusses the events leading up to Nadia's arrival, he states

> According to this, for my timid pupil, what caused the collapse that finally brought her here was the adverb in the phrase "(the skirt) no longer fits you." "Why?" Nadia was incapable of asking her mother a question as harmless as this, "Why, Mom, does it not fit me anymore?" What do you mean? Clarify yourself spatiotemporally.[6]

In this passage, Jacobs's narrator analyzes the use of the term *ya* (anymore) as it pertains to Nadia's relationship with her mother. In other words, according to the narrator, the use of this word and Nadia's inability to ask her mother for an explanation about its use are indicative of Nadia's relationship with her mother. Likewise, the narrator's use of the word *espaciotemporalmente* (spatiotemporally) parallels the language of linguistic analysis, specifically Genette's term *voice*. For the theorist, voice reflects the "way in which the narrating itself is implicated in the narrative" (31). This being said, he further develops the idea by substituting the word *voice* for *person* and then referring to the "temporal determination of the narrating instance" (216). Although Genette's use of the term is much more concerned with the technical issue of the time between the narrating instance and the narrative, Jacobs's linguistic examination of the adverb *ya* (anymore) in the passage above similarly focuses on this grammatical question of temporality.

Jacobs's interest in linguistic analysis is also evident in *La dueña del Hotel Poe*, when the narrator discusses the press she will create with her niece for their best sellers: "We named ours If Press, *if* not so much for its conditional sense in English, equivalent to *si* in Spanish, or given that, assumed that, provided that, although and even when, as for being the initials of the Latin expression *ipso facto*, which in Spanish translates to immediately."[7] Here we see Jacobs analyzing a specific word and giving synonyms. This tendency in her style is both earnest and playful, as seen also in the example above from *Florencia y Ruiseñor* and the adverb *ya* (anymore). In *La dueña del Hotel Poe*, Jacob scrutinizes the word *if* and its different meanings. In so doing, she also employs a previously mentioned technique of including various languages. In this instance, Jacobs outlines the definitions of the word in order to clarify the meaning she wishes it to have. There is the additional element of humor in the passage, as well, as the immediate impression is the first one offered—If Press is based on the conditional. This could be the conditional publication of books and the conditional existence of the press itself. Thus, while Jacobs earnestly includes an analysis of the term *if* in the above passage, she also infers the humorous or playful use of the term as a conditional state.

Another characteristic of Jacob's writing is her use of various words to describe one thing; this comes more from an analysis of language than from a desire to include flowery adjectives. For example, in *Florencia y Ruiseñor*, the narrator states: "The thing was taking a course, apart from improvisational, inevitable, interesting, intense, half-intuitive, unusual."[8] While one adjective would suffice, the narrator's (and the author's) tendency is to explore all of the linguistic possibilities. This is evident in the example of the word *if* and its definition in Spanish. A similar example is the wordplay evident in the novel within the novel in *La dueña del Hotel Poe, Objeto de segunda mano* (nouvelle *en nueve entregas*) por Ada Donada (nouvelle in nine parts by Ada Donada). When describing the protagonist's parents' home, the narrator declares: "The property of the parents of Galleta Cookie, fiefdom that quite understandably contained a greenhouse, hills, orchards, forests, meadows, farms, lakes, valleys, caves, rivers, ponds, lagoons, fountains, a pergola and, of course, a large outdoor swiming pool."[9] The words *sobreentendidamente* (quite understandably) and *por supuesto* (of course) make clear the grandiosity of the property and the parents' desire to display it. Furthermore, the long list of attributes is a playful attack on Galleta Cookie's parents' snobbery. Analogous to the inclusion of assorted adjectives, this long list of elements is at once sincere in its linguistic analysis, as well as playful and exaggerated so as to mirror the family's inflated sense of self-worth.

Literary Theory

Literary and creative writing theories play a significant role in Jacobs's texts, as well. In some texts, the author outlines theories on writing a novel; in others, she includes considerations on literary theory similar to those proposed by Genette. In *Florencia y Ruiseñor*, Jacobs plays with the theory of writing a novel through the voice of her narrator:

> It will have to have a particularity and, on the other hand, it should not deal, in any sense, with the old question of the skirt. That matter was left behind; agreed? As for the particularity, your novel, as we agreed (not to say I agreed) should not tend to, or start from, the possibility of being made into a movie. Agreed? I want the words, the language, the use, the handling that you give them, to be what awakens the reader's imagination as the best of images. Agreed?[10]

The narrator has taken Nadia under his wing, so to speak, and is giving her lessons on writing a novel. There is a definite tone of playfulness in this passage, starting with the mention of the skirt, which is the incident that eventually sent Nadia to the asylum. Second, the narrator alludes to the notion that good literature is not written with the intent of making it into a film. Later in the same novel, the narrator moves through a list of questions for Nadia, similar to those covered in a writing workshop:

> Do you catch the reader from the first line? . . . Which reader are you addressing? What are your intentions with your "novel," becoming a star, or making your character memorable? Where did you put your best effort, in the story or in the form? In what age do you live and in what age did you situate your novel? How many conceptual and formal planes do you have? What quality? What is your tone? To what novel genre does it belong?[11]

Like the suggestions in the previous passage, these questions approximate a list one would receive in a writers' workshop. They also allude to Jacobs's own exploration of writing, as her works tend to test these ideas. For example, the author seems to have several readers in mind in her novels. Furthermore, Jacobs plays directly with the idea of the bestseller and becoming a well-known writer in *La dueña del Hotel Poe*. She consistently explores the line between content/form, which is the focal point of her texts. Finally, *La dueña del Hotel Poe* is a prime example of the author's explorations on genre, as she offers an entire section dedicated to different genres, discussed below.

There is a similar play on the theory of writing a novel in the beginning of *La dueña del Hotel Poe,* in the passage where the narrator/writer concocts a plan with her niece to write novels in order to help the niece with her fear of publishing. The beginning of the novel sets up a novel-within-a-novel . As in *Florencia y Ruiseñor*, the narrator summarizes a theory for writing a novel, this time a bestseller, so that the niece can avoid worrying about her perfectionism, reception among critics, or the intellectual sophistication of the book:

> We both encouraged each other to organize ourselves and sit down to write in nine days each their best seller. As in a laboratory, we first reviewed what we had, elements such as the time my niece had left for the visit, which in the end determined the extension of our novels, which perforce would have to be brief, more like a long story or short novel than a proper novel, pointing to that intermediate genre that in French is called *nouvelle*, word that you have seen and that is sufficiently established, so much so that even English has incorporated it into its vocabulary, or *noveleta* in Spanish, a term however that I rather dislike.[12]

In this passage, we have a discussion of the theory of writing a novel, as well as a brief examination of genre and literary terms. Moreover, the playful and slightly ironic tone coincides with the narrator's tone in *Florencia y Ruiseñor*. Here we have a discussion of a bestseller, which parallels the narrator's questions in *Florencia y Ruiseñor* concerning Nadia's desire to become a well-known author or write for film, versus an author dedicated to the craft of creating literature. Moreover, there is a discussion of the genre, *nouvelle,*and its English and Spanish equivalents. Here again, we see Jacobs exploring other languages and the nuances between them.

The narrator in *La dueña del Hotel Poe* continues to lay out the theory for the bestsellers, including theme, style, counterpoint, and tone: "The physical and emotional maturity of women . . . to disturb the reader, or to upset or confuse the reader" . . . "the natural envy that women feel of men" . . . "it would have to be of ridicule."[13] This list of theme, style, counterpoint, and tone mirrors the "writers' workshop" discourse given by the narrator in *Florencia y Ruiseñor*, analyzed above. Both theories include specific questions the writer must ask before writing the novel. As with the rules set out by the narrator and her niece in *La dueña del Hotel Poe*, we see a desire to know the rules and regulations of writing. The discussions in these passages are both in earnest—as they correspond to Jacobs's own desire to probe the process of writing a novel—and in play—as both narrators play with the idea of writing a novel and whether one must follow the rules and regulations. Furthermore, these postulations highlight Jacobs's interest in the theory and formal aspects of narrative. To return to Genette's terms *mood* and *enunciation*, for example, we see that Jacobs is interested in exploring the ways in which a narrative can be enunciated or communicated and how the narratee (the person receiving the narration within the narrative) and the reader perceive the enunciation. In this instance above, Jacobs relies heavily on satire and humor in her novel-within-a-novel to convey a certain mood.

In an interview with Kristine Ibsen, Jacobs shares: "I am very interested in experimenting precisely with genre, voice. I like to surprise, even confuse."[14] *La dueña del Hotel Poe* includes a section that explores different genres, a clear reference to the novel's self-awareness. In "Muestrario," Jacobs includes an interview, a chronicle, a day-in-the-life, a clinical history, dreams, an article, a riddle. This section begins:

> The sample of genres follows in which the author begins to create the character of the owner of Hotel Poe, who is the one who writes them. As will be seen, the collection delineates a very literary writer, but with an identity in conflict, as if looking for herself in a character and at the same time wanting to escape the confrontation.[15]

Returning again to Genette and his term *mood*, the theorist explains narrative mood: "Narrative 'representation,' or more exactly, narrative information, has its degrees: the narrative can furnish the reader with more or fewer details, and in a more or less direct way, and can thus seem . . . to keep at a greater or lesser *distance* from what it tells" (162). As seen in the statements above by Jacobs, the author seeks to surprise and confuse, at times by withholding information or not offering all of the details. Similarly, as in the quote from "Muestrario" in *La dueña del Hotel Poe*, Jacobs delineates the main character in the larger narrative of the novel (as opposed to the one in the novel within the novel); however, this delineation is never completely clear. In fact, Jacobs chooses to withhold some facts while revealing others. In this sense, Jacobs experiments with Genette's concept of *mood*.

World of Publishing

Part of Jacobs's analysis of literature is her consideration of the publishing world, including editors and literary presses. In *La dueña del Hotel Poe*, the author examines this world in a segment where the main narrator reports:

> No one laughs at the justification of powerful editors who reject a project by referring to their lack of budget, or to excessive offers, or to the strictness of schedules, or to the need to stick to a policy of themes or genres or who knows what, or this or any other principle or occurrence; nobody laughs at the idea of being considered a nobody.[16]

Later in the same segment, the narrator proclaims of the "juego editorial" (editorial game):

> On this occasion and circumstance, the two of us were continually pushed aside by diligent employees who, by their demeanor and presence, implied that they, not we, were the owners and masters of all the space around us; or by authors, who were most of them, who entered the various offices, disheartened and crestfallen, with manuscripts they seemed to want to hide; or by authors, who were the least, who emerged from the various offices emboldened and with

their heads held high, with a shining copy of some title that they waved and flailed with ostentatious pride.[17]

Both passages reflect the difficulties of publishing and authors' feeling of powerlessness when confronted with the money and power of the publisher. Likewise, Jacobs presents the hierarchy among the employees of the presses as well as the authors themselves who are continually jockeying for the position of published author. These examples are Jacobs's reflections on the external and more practical aspects of literature and complement her deliberations on the internal structure of literature and writing. In an interview with Kristine Ibsen, Jacobs discusses this world of publishing, recognizing that during her writing process, gender plays no role in the quality of her writing. However, she affirms that gender does influence decisions about what is published: "Before the blank sheet of paper, I only face an artistic problem; but, to the outside, composed of editors, teachers, booksellers, critics, translators, readers and colleagues, I am effectively facing a battle."[18] Again, this is a reflection of the external and practical aspect of literature, which is the world of publishing. Jacobs recognizes all of the people involved in this external world.

Self-Awareness/Self-Analysis

Many of the examples above represent Jacobs's style but also a play on her style, as if she were laughing at herself or treating her own writing with a hint of satire and irony. She does this by analyzing her own tendencies through fictional writers in her novels, specifically the narrators of *Florencia y Ruiseñor* and *La dueña del Hotel Poe*. Possibly, the latter is the author's most self-exposing, as it includes such a variety of styles—not all of which are part of Jacobs's typical repertoire. In *La dueña del Hotel Poe*, when the narrator/writer meets with an employee of a publishing house to discuss *Objeto de segunda mano*, the employee asks: "But, tell me, do you think it is appropriate to introduce phrases in other languages in a text basically in Spanish? What a useless occurrence, and not very original, on the other hand!"[19] As we know, this is precisely what Jacobs does in this novel and others. The editor goes on to say: "Tone it by emphasizing the sharply dramatic slant it has. Don't imply that the author is making fun. Induce the reader to cry, seriously, but not to laugh!"[20] These commentaries relate directly to Jacobs's style of writing, in which she introduces phrases in other languages, plays with the reader, and elicits laughter. Also in *La dueña del Hotel Poe*, in a section analyzed above, the narrator refers to the writer within the novel: "It is the writer who is mature enough to sketch or adopt certain principles, but immature enough to need the approval of the teacher to put them into practice. It is the writer who wants to belong to her profession but who knows herself incapable. . . . It is the writer who fears that seeing what she sees when writing will lead her to lose her mind."[21] This passage reveals Jacobs's interest in examining the very act of writing and being a writer and it also possibly hints at her own thoughts about the writing experience. The last line also corresponds to other writings of Jacobs that deal with the idea of mental sanity, for example, *Florencia y Ruiseñor* and *Atormentados* (essays, 2002). This passage from *La dueña del Hotel Poe* reveals a rare tendency of Jacobs's toward self-analysis as an author, as well as a tendency to write what would be considered metanarrative.

Jacobs explores the idea of self-reference later in *La dueña del Hotel Poe*:

> I am the same, but I am another. (In parentheses I will tell you that I am not the only character who experiences this state of things.) In literature, as in life, the story of the double is illustrious and long. To quote the examples I know, "William Wilson," by Poe; *The Haunted Man* by Dickens; *The Strange Case of Dr. Jekyll and Mr. Hyde* by Stevenson; *The Portrait of Dorian Gray,* by Oscar Wilde; "El doble," by Borges; *The Cloven Viscount,* by Italo Calvino ...).[22]

This passage reveals Jacobs's passion for and knowledge of other literatures, as she tells Kristine Ibsen in an interview that in her youth she had almost exclusively read European and North American literature (48).[23] In her interview with Roberto García Bonilla, she calls herself one "of the writers who nourish themselves through

Critical Insights

literature."[24] Likewise, in her essay on *Atormentados*, Bados-Ciria asserts that "each one of the characters in an essay takes us to several books."[25] Elsewhere, Bados-Ciria affirms, "her work is a rereading, a rewriting, and a readjustment of what we consider her literary 'parents' and 'mothers.'"[26] The passage above also plays with the idea of self-reference within the novel. The author creates a double within the novel, a double that also might refer to Jacobs herself in some instances. She further plays with this idea and with the reader's assumptions:

> Not to be named, or not being able to name her, with anything but the epithet "the owner of the Hotel Poe," with the pseudonyms Ada Donada or Alpha Sigma, or the initials BD, which have begun to break through the mist, denotes without doubt to say the least an identity in conflict of one of the authors, the real one, that refers to me (Me? And who are you?), Or the one that represents the real one, that is her. W refers to her as "the doctor." What's her name? Who is she?[27]

Readers unremittingly look for clues about authors in the narrators and characters of their books. In this passage, Jacobs toys with the reader's desire to find her in the novel, including such tidbits as BD (Jacobs's full name is Bárbara Dian Jacobs Barquet). The self-reference game continues in sections where Jacobs includes other pieces of information that pertain to her own life, for example: "I live very well with W in Cuernavaca."[28] Bados-Ciria confirms: "Barbara Jacobs points to a process of self-integration with language that allows her to reveal certain features of her identity using self-concealment, to give the text a partial self-identification that we assume to be conscious and premeditated."[29] Bados-Ciria recognizes the intentional and partial self-identification of these passages. Furthermore, this style of writing places Jacobs within a group of writers, such as Borges, who deliberately play with the reader. Returning to Genette's comments on *mood*, Jacobs also experiments with the amount of information she reveals: "the narrative can furnish the reader with more or fewer details, and in a more or less direct way" (162).

According to Bados-Ciria, "Jacobs's work is characterized by channeling her subjectivity through different autobiographical acts that allow her to articulate different incursions in search of an identity formed by the exchange of the different traditions and cultures that converge in her individual 'I.'"[30] Bados-Ciria goes on to examine how Jacobs upends the rules of Western autobiography in her work: "She raises the conflicting relations between the 'decolonized' female subject and the Western autobiographical genre.'[31] Bados-Ciria outlines the unique elements of Jacobs's style of autobiography, including fragmentation that breaks the rule of the unified subject; intertextuality that necessarily comes from the dialogue that is so important in the author's work; and irony and parody that demystify themes and important figures (*Vida con mi amigo* 58-59). Moreover, Jacobs's originality stems from dialogue, which permits multiple points of view and allows for "rupturas creativas" (creative breaks) that further develop existing narratives (*Vida con mi amigo* 60). Jacobs's style of autobiography also includes the following: "Self-construction of herself as a writer," "constant creative reflection," and "an emotional detachment."[32]

Another element of self-awareness in Jacobs's work is her return to previous books. Jacobs tells Kristine Ibsen in an interview that her texts are "almost interdependent" (52). Bados-Ciria identifies this in *Juego limpio*: "her way of seeing literature as a rewriting and rereading of her previous works."[33] Jacobs's 2014 essay *Hacia el valle del sueño* is a nonfictional return to her early novel *Las hojas muertas* (1987). *Las hojas muertas* is a biographical novel based on the author's father and his relationship with his children, including a fictional character based on the author as one of the protagonists named *nosotros* (us). As the author describes in an interview with Kristine Ibsen, this early novel is divided into three sections: before knowing their father's story, their father's story, and their father's present (50). *Hacia el valle del sueño* returns to the author's father and relates the rest of his story, a large part of which is his participation in the Spanish Civil War as a member of the Lincoln Brigade.[34] Despite all of his effort in this regard, he and many of his fellow fighters were never officially recognized. In a documentary about the Lincoln Brigade, *Extranjeros de sí mismos* (Foreign to Themselves, Madrid, 2001), the author's father laments: "I want you to go and find someone to interview. You are not looking for me. I am a failure. I wanted to help but I had no way of doing so. I never had anything to offer."[35] According to Kristine Ibsen, "the central conflict in the novel is perhaps rooted less in separation anxiety than in the narrators' need to reconcile their admiration for the public figure shortchanged by history and their ambivalence toward the private man who denied them his affection" ("Their Heart Belongs to Daddy," 178-79). *Hacia el valle del sueño* returns to this point of the father being "shortchanged by history." In a series of letters, Jacobs chronicles her efforts to restore a vestige of her father's pride in his participation in the Lincoln Brigade by helping him claim the Spanish citizenship promised to the participants of the group in 1996. As she discovers in her correspondence with officials, the promise seems to be an honorary one and not a true offer of citizenship.[36] The inclusion of letters in this essay echoes what Bados-Ciria recognizes in *Vida con mi amigo*: "conversation as a discursive strategy."[37] Here, the conversation is through letters, although at times it seems more like a one-sided discussion as some of her letters are ignored.[38] The idea of conversation also harkens back to the notion that *Hacia el valle del sueño* is in dialogue with *Las hojas muertas*, a conversation that Jacobs initiates between her own texts. Through this conversation, the author enriches both texts and the reader's experience with each text. Again, this implies a level of self-awareness in Jacobs's work that plays out in these dialogues between texts and references to her own life.

Through her explorations of multiple languages, linguistic analysis and wordplay, literary theory, the world of publishing, self-awareness, and self-analysis, Jacobs reveals a deep awareness of the formal aspects of writing. In her texts, the author unceasingly examines how her texts interact with each other as well as with those of other writers. In so doing, she reveals a depth of knowledge about literature and an exceptional openness to self-exploration. Furthermore, her style is at once earnest and playful, delving into the formalities of writing while at the same time questioning the need to do so. In Jacobs's world of words, language, and writing, we encounter an ever-connected web of ideas spanning from her first to last publications. Her work establishes the author's true passion for the craft of writing and the creation of literature.

Notes

1. Bárbara Jacobs (1947, Mexico City), Mexican author of Lebanese descent, has published novels, short stories, essays, and translations. Since 1993, Jacobs has published semimonthly with the Mexican journal *La Jornada*. She received the prestigious Premio Xavier Villaurrutia in 1987.

2. I have explored Jacobs's interests in form previously, in "La técnica del extrañamiento en *Las hojas muertas* y *Adiós humanidad* de Bárbara Jacobs" (*Revista de Literatura Mexiana Contemoránea* 8.15, 2002, 55-61).

3. "Crecí oyendo varios idiomas a mi alrededor: español, inglés, francés, árabe y la lengua autóctona de mi nana" (159). All translations are mine.

4. "La nacionalidad, la lengua nativa, el acento y la pronunciación imprimen una huella en el acto de decir y de expresarse" ("La iniciación" 120).

5. "El interés que despierta este tipo de literatura es particularmente desafiante porque multiplica los problemas que implica no sólo de comprensión sino de traducción. Pienso en *Finnegan's Wake*, juego conceptual y de lenguaje por excelencia que James Joyce propone al lector como entretenimiento y diversión" ("Encuesta," 727).

6. "Según esto, a mi apocada alumna, lo que le ocasionó el derrumbe que finalmente la trajo aquí fue el adverbio en la frase '(la falda) *ya* no te sienta.' '¿Por qué?' Nadia fue incompetente para hacer a su mamá una pregunta tan inofensiva como ésta, '¿Por qué, mamá, *ya* no me sienta?' ¿A qué te refieres? Defínete espaciotemporalmente" (25-26).

7. "A la nuestra le pusimos de nombre If Press, *if* no tanto por su sentido condicional en inglés, equivalente al *si* en español, o *dado caso que, supuesto que, con tal que, aunque* y *aun cuando*, como por ser las iniciales de la expresión latina *ipso facto*, que en español se traduce como *inmediatamente*" (28-29).

---

8. "La cosa tomaba un rumbo, aparte de improviso, inevitable, interesante, intenso, intuido a medias, inusitado" (35).

9. "La propiedad de los padres de Galleta Cookie, feudo que sobreentendidamente contenía un invernadero, montes, huertos, bosques, prados, granjas, lagos, valles, cuevas, ríos, piletas, lagunas, fuentes, una pérgola y, por supuesto, una gran piscina descubierta" (32).

10. "Tendrá que tener una particularidad y, por otra parte, no deberá tratar, en ningún sentido, de la vieja cuestión de la falda. Ese asunto quedó atrás; ¿de acuerdo? En cuanto a la particularidad, tu novela, según acordamos (por no decir acordé) no deberá tender a, ni partir de, la posibilidad de ser llevada al cine. ¿De acuerdo? Quiero que las palabras, el lenguaje, el uso, el manejo que les des, sean lo que despierte la imaginación del lector como la mejor de las imágenes. ¿De acuerdo?" (29)

11. "¿Atrapa usted al lector desde la primera línea? . . . ¿A qué lector se dirige? ¿Cuáles son sus intenciones con su 'novela,' convertirse usted en estrella, o hacer memorable a su personaje? ¿En dónde puso su mayor empeño, en el fondo o en la forma? ¿En qué época vive usted y en cuál situó su escrito? ¿Cuántos planos conceptuales y formales tiene? ¿De qué calidad? ¿Cuál es su tono? ¿A qué género de novela pertenece?" (41).

12. "Las dos nos dimos ánimos para organizarnos y sentarnos a escribir en nueve días cada una su best seller. Como en un laboratorio, primero revisamos con qué contábamos, elementos como el tiempo que le quedaba de visita a mi sobrina, lo que de paso determinó la extensión de nuestras novelas, que por fuerza tendrían que ser breves, más parecidas a cuento largo o novela corta que a novela propiamente dicha, apuntando hacia ese género intermedio que en francés se llama *nouvelle*, palabra que viste y que está suficientemente establecida, tanto así que incluso el inglés la ha incorporado a su vocabulario, o *noveleta* en español, término que sin embargo a mí más bien me disgusta" (24).

13. "La maduración física y emocional de la mujer . . . inquietar al lector, o disgustarlo, o confundirlo" . . . "'la envidia natural que la mujer siente del hombre'" . . . "tendría que ser de burla" (26-27).

14. "Me atrae enormemente experimentar precisamente con el género, la voz. Me gusta sorprender, incluso confundir" (46-47).

15. "Sigue el muestrario de géneros a través de los cuales la autora empieza a conformar al personaje de la dueña del Hotel Poe, que es quien los practica. Como se irá viendo, el conjunto va delineando a una escritora muy literaria, pero con una identidad en conflicto, como si se buscara a sí misma en un personaje y al mismo tiempo quisiera escapar de la confrontación" (93).

16. "A nadie lo hace reír la justificación de los editores poderosos que rechazan un proyecto aludiendo a su falta de presupuesto, o al exceso de ofertas, o al rigor de las programaciones, o a la necesidad de atenerse a una política de temas o géneros o qué sé yo qué, o a este o cualquier otro principio u ocurrencia; a nadie lo hace reír ser considerado nadie" (82).

17. "En esta ocasión y circunstancia, los dos éramos continuamente hechos a un lado por empleados diligentes que, por su porte y presencia, implicaban que ellos, no nosotros, eran los dueños y señores de todo el espacio a nuestro alrededor; o por autores, que eran los más, que entraban a las diversas oficinas desalentados y cabizbajos, con manuscritos que parecían querer ocultar; o por autores, que eran los menos, que salían de las diferentes oficinas envalentonados y con la cara en alto, con un ejemplar reluciente de algún título que más bien blandían y enarbolaban con ostentoso orgullo" (83).

18. "Ante la hoja en blanco, yo sólo me enfrento a un problema artístico; pero, ante el exterior, compuesto de editores, profesores, libreros, críticos, traductores, lectores y colegas, efectivamente me enfrento a una batalla" (47).

19. "Pero, dígame, ¿le parece adecuado introducir frases en otros idiomas en un escrito básicamente en español? ¡Qué inútil ocurrencia, y poco original, por otro lado!" (84-85).

20. "Tonalícelo haciendo énfasis en el sesgo agudamente dramático que tiene. No implique que el autor se esté burlando. Induzca al lector a llorar, de plano, pero no ¡a reír!" (86).

21. "Es la escritora lo suficientemente madura para esbozar o adoptar determinados principios, pero tan inmadura que necesita el visto bueno del maestro para ponerlos en práctica. Es la escritora que quiere pertenecer a su medio pero que se sabe incapaz. . . . Es la escritora que teme que ver lo que ve al escribir la lleve a perder la razón" (93).

22. "Soy la misma, pero soy otra. (Entre paréntesis te diré que no soy el único personaje que experimenta este estado de cosas. En la literatura, como en la vida, la historia del doble es ilustre y larga. Por citarte los ejemplos que conozco, 'William Wilson', de Poe; *The Haunted Man*, de Dickens; *Strange Case of Dr. Jekyll and Mr. Hyde*, de Stevenson; *The Portrait of Dorian Gray*, de Oscar Wilde; 'El doble', de Borges; *El vizconde demediado*, de Italo Calvino...)" (99).

23. As Bados-Ciria quotes from Jacobs, the current list of authors would also include classic Greek and Latin, Spanish, classic and modern English, French, German, Italian, Russian, and Latin American (*Vida con mi amigo* 63).

24. "De los escritores que se nutren de la literatura" (162).

25. "Cada uno de los personajes de un ensayo nos lleva a varios libros" ("Atormentados," 92).

26. "Su obra es una relectura, una reescritura, y un reajuste de los que consideramos sus 'padres' y 'madres' literarios" ("*Las siete fugas de Saab*, 87). Rojas-Trempe examines the short story "Carol dice" in *Doce cuentos en contra*: "En 'Carol dice' gobierna la oralidad y la escucha propias de las adolescentes y se rinde tributo a la escritura y a la lectura como posibilidades de desarrollo individual y profesional" ("La iniciación" 127).

27. "No nombrarse, o no poder nombrarla, más que con el epíteto de "la dueña del Hotel Poe," o con los seudónimos Ada Donada o Alfa Sigma, o con las iniciales BD, que han empezado a abrirse paso entre la bruma, denota sin duda por decir lo menos una identidad con conflicto de una de las autoras, la real, que se refiere a mí (*¿A mí?* ¿Y tú quién eres?*), o la que representa a la real, que es ella. W hace referencia a ella como "la doctora." ¿Cómo se llama? ¿Quién es?" (109).

28. "Vivo muy bien con W en Cuernavaca" (112).

29. "Bárbara Jacobs apunta un proceso de autointegración con el lenguaje que le permite desvelar ciertos rasgos de su identidad haciendo uso de la auto-disimulación, para trasladar al texto una parcial autoidentificación que suponemos consciente y premeditada" ("*Las siete fugas de Saab*" 84).

30. "La obra de Jacobs se caracteriza por canalizar su subjetividad a través de diferentes actos autobiográficos que le permiten articular distintas incursiones en búsqueda de una identidad conformada por

el intercambio de las diversas tradiciones y culturas que confluyen en su 'yo' individual" (*Vida con mi amigo* 57).

31. "Plantea las relaciones conflictivas existentes entre el sujeto femenino 'descolonizado' y el género autobiográfico occidental" (*Vida con mi amigo* 57).

32. "La autoconstrucción de sí misma como escritora, la reflexión creadora constante, and un distanciamiento emocional" (*Vida con mi amigo* 65).

33. "Su modo de ver la literatura como reescritura y relectura de sus trabajos anteriores" (*Vida con mi amigo* 62).

34. The Lincoln Brigade was a group of American volunteers who went to work and fight in the Spanish Civil War with the Spanish Republicans against Francisco Franco.

35. "Quiero que se vayan y busquen a quién entrevistar. No me están buscando a mí. Yo soy un fracaso. Quería ayudar pero no tenía cómo hacerlo. Nunca tuve nada que ofrecer" (n.p.).

36. "Pero o la justicia no existe, o llega tarde o, como la Ley de la selva, es una carrera de obstáculos que sólo el más apto libra, porque lo cierto es que, en 2013, a setenta y cinco años de la promesa que Negrín hizo en la despedida de las Brigadas Internacionales en 1938, de conceder la nacionalidad española a los brigadistas internacionales, y a diecisiete de la aprobación de la ley en 1996, el Real Decreto, redactado en noviembre de 2008 por Mariano Fernández Bermejo, aún tiene que ser informado por el consejo de Estado y volver al Consejo de Ministros para que éste lo apruebe y lo mande a las Cortes y, algún día, quizá, se haga realmente efectivo" (n.p.).

37. "La conversación como estrategia discursiva" ("Atormentados" 94).

38. Jacobs also explores dialogue through letters in *Un amor de Simone* (2012), in which the author examines Simone de Beauvoir's life through her correspondence with the American Nelson Algren. As Jacobs explains, these letters reveal a different side of de Beauvoir.

Works Cited

Bados-Ciria, Concepción. "Atormentados, de Bárbara Jacobs: Ensayos de opinión y posmodernidad." *Revista de literatura mexicana contemporánea* 9.20, 2003, pp. 88-95.

_____. "*Las siete fugas de Saab, alias el Rizos*: Sugerencias autobiográficas entre prácticas de ficción." *Revista de literatura mexicana contemporánea* 1, 1995, pp. 84-89.

_____. "*Vida con mi amigo* y *Juego limpio* de Bárbara Jacobs: Alternativas de la autobiografía." *Revista de literatura mexicana contemporánea* 4.9, 1998), pp. 57-65.

"Encuesta a los escritores mexicanos presentes en *La Mar de Letras* Cartagena (Murcia)." *Insula* 727-28, 200, pp. 22-23.

García Bonilla, Roberto. "Bárbara Jacobs." *Hispamérica* 27.80/81, 1998, pp. 159-69.

Genette, Gérard. *Narrative Discourse: An Essay in Method*. Translated by Jane E. Lewin. Cornell UP, 1980.

Ibsen, Kristine. "Entrevistas: Bárbara Jacobs/Carmen Boullosa." *Chasqui* 24.2, 1995, pp. 46-63.

_____. "Their Heart Belongs to Daddy: *Las hojas muertas* and the Disintegration of Patriarchal Authority." *Cincinnati Romance Review* 15, 1996, pp. 174-83.

Jacobs, Bárbara. *Atormentados*. Alfaguara, 2002.

_____. *La dueña del Hotel Poe*. Era/Consejo Nacional para la Cultural y las Artes, 2014.

_____. *Florencia y Ruiseñor*. Alfaguara, 2006.

_____. *Hacia el valle del sueño*. Universidad Autónoma de Nuevo León, 2014.

_____. *Las hojas muertas*. Alfaguara, 1996.

_____. *Un amor de Simone*. Consejo Nacional para la Cultura y las Artes, 2012.

Jiménez de Báez, Yvette. "Marginalidad e historia o tiempo de mujer en los relatos de Bárbara Jacobs." *Mujer y literatura mexicana y chicana, cultural en contacto*. Vol. II. Edited by Aralia López González, Amelia Malagamba, and Elena Urrutia. Colegio de México, 1990, pp. 127-37.

López-Linares, José Luis and Javier Rioyo, dir. *Extranjeros de sí mismos*. Alma Films, Alta Films, 2001.

Patán, Federico. "La percepción de la otredad en cuatro narradores." *Anuario de letras modernas* 6, 1993-1994, pp. 99-114.

Rojas-Trempe, Lady. "La educación privada en Montreal en dos cuentos de Bárbara Jacobs." *Alba de América* 14, 1996, pp. 26-27.

_____. "La iniciación y el discurso de dos adolescentes en 'Carol dice' de Bárbara Jacobs." *Cuento contigo (La ficción en México)*. Universidad Autónoma de Tlaxcala, 1993, pp. 117-27.

Roberts-Camps, Traci. "La técnica del extrañamiento en *Las hojas muertas* y *Adiós humanidad* de Bárbara Jacobs." *Revista de Literatura Mexicana Contemporánea* 8.15, 2002, pp. 55-61.

Daniel Sada and the Everyday Baroque_____

Mark Anderson

> Lo demás es lo de menos. Bosquejos y replanteos. Nudos para desatar.
> (Everything else is insignificant. Drafts and reformulations. Knots to
> untie.)
>
> (Daniel Sada, *Porque parece mentira*)

Although not as well known abroad as some other writers of his
generation, Daniel Sada (1953- 2011) was considered by many of his
contemporaries to be one of Mexico's most consistently innovative
novelists of the turn of the twenty-first century. Writing at a time
when the urban internationalism and straightforward realist style
of Mexico's Generación del Crack and Chilean transplant Roberto
Bolaño dominated the literary market and critical discussion of
Mexican writing in Europe and the United States, Sada published
novel after novel in a highly unique, somewhat convoluted style
that honed in on what he called the *paisajes internos* (internal
landscapes) of arid, predominantly rural Northern Mexico. From his
earliest novel, *Lampa vida* (Bare Life, 1980), up through milestones
in his oeuvre like *Albedrío* (Free Will, 1989), *Porque parece mentira
la verdad nunca se sabe* (Because It Seems Like a Lie, the Truth Can
Never Be Known, 1999), *Casi nunca* (*Almost Never*, 2008), and his
short story collection *Registro de causantes* (Register of Causatives,
1990), to his final, posthumous novel *El lenguaje del juego* (The
Language of the Game, 2012), his narrative constructs meticulous
linguistic landscapes that converge multiple, often conflicting
points of view into a single cultural geography that is nevertheless
always open and purposefully incomplete, since no story is ever
self-sufficient.[1] In the majority of Sada's works, these linguistic
landscapes are those of Northern Mexico, although several stories
and three of his novels, *Luces artificiales* (Artificial Illumination,
2002), *Ritmo delta* (Delta Rhythm, 2005), and *La duración de los
empeños simples* (The Duration of Simple Endeavors, 2006) are set

---

in intimate spaces in Mexico City, where he resided during much of his professional life, while *Casi nunca* begins in Oaxaca and then follows its protagonist northward to Coahuila.

Sada's first novel, *Lampa vida*, recounts the tale of Hugo Retes and Lola Tuñín, a young couple who has absconded from the small town of Comoatí because Lola's father is opposed to their union. The plot centers on their escape and wanderings as they search for a place to make a life together. This somewhat traditional storyline is complicated by Retes's desire to withhold his profession from his lover: he is a clown who is unable to make his audiences laugh. After being run off the stage in the village of Maloja, Retes convinces Lola to flee on foot to Fanance, a larger town about a week's journey away. They soon become lost in the desert, where they nearly die of thirst and hunger before being found by the inhabitants of a local settlement called El Oro. Despite their misgivings, Lola and Retes end up adapting to the slow rhythm of life in the tiny hamlet; Retes gives up his dream of becoming a successful entertainer in Fanance and Lola postpones her plans to leave Retes and return to her family to see if they can make their relationship work in El Oro, a land beyond the reach of family, capitalism, government, and church. This is the *lampa vida*, that is, social life at its barest, its most ungoverned, and yet most essential.[2]

Although not as polished as some of Sada's later novels, this first effort unveils his trademark style and several of the themes that characterize his later works. The overarching theme of nomadic migration appears in nearly all of Sada's narrative, along with the motif of the fruitless search for direction and the implicit maxim that meaning must always be forged provisionally by each traveler through their experiences and relationships. Other common themes include economic and social failure, the roles of spectacle in society, the vagaries of truth and perception, and the radical otherness of even those who seem closest to us, which is underscored in this case by the fact that Retes's identity coalesces almost exclusively around being a clown, a truth that he hides from his partner, as well as by the paradox that he hides from himself: that he is not funny. Sada also developed several of his distinctive techniques in this novel, among them the use of satirical place and person names, local speech rife with archaic expressions, a mixture of circuitous sentence structures and bold understatement, a narrative chronology marked out by the spatiality of an arbitrary journey, and, perhaps most notably, that of using a seemingly omniscient and yet surprisingly intimate narrator to draw together the perspectives of a wide range of characters. This narrator soon reveals himself to be highly unconventional in flitting in and out of his focalization on particular characters' points of view, interspersing narration with commentary reminiscent of more interactive, oral storytelling, but also drawing attention to its literariness, to the way in which he is crafting the storyline, particularly with regard to his stylistic choices and manipulation of the narrative chronology. A stock voice in all of Sada's prose, this narrator often addresses his readers directly, yet he also plunges fearlessly if ambiguously into the minds of the characters, revealing to us their thought processes only to question their motives or to reveal his own narration as speculation, since we may never really understand fully what motivates even ourselves, never mind the other. In this fashion, Sada draws attention to the processes by which worlds are created as stories, from the retelling of the interplay between multiple subjectivities and the societies and environments they inhabit.

Together with migration and the ineffability of the other, violence completes the triad of recurrent themes in Sada's works. While violence appears in *Lampa vida*, particularly when Retes is stoned by disappointed audiences for failing to entertain them, it is in *Albedrío* that it comes into its own as a major theme. Stoning is again the primary form of violence, which highlights the intimacy of the violent act itself, since in stoning there is not the sense of detachment or mediation one might experience with modern technologies of violence such as firearms. Stoning draws attention to the relationships between violence and territoriality, since the land itself becomes an instrument of violence, but it also marks the ahistoricity of violence as a coercive response to difference, given the prevalence of stoning in biblical and other key narratives in the Western tradition. In this case, the targets of the violence are a band of *húngaros* (gypsies), who travel from town to town performing theater and other acts, as well as showing a film that is itself a murder mystery in which the spectators must deduce the motive behind the killing—revenge for another act of violence, which belies any causal explanation or historical origin: the cause of violence is violence.

Albedrío's plot revolves primarily around the húngaros' travels and the induction into the group of Chuyito, a small boy from the town of Castaños who runs away to join them because he has tired of school and his father's frequent punishments. The *albedrío* (free will/caprice) of the title is related primarily to this character and the repercussions of his impulsive decision to run away, but the novel foregrounds the arbitrariness of the logic that all of the characters use to make choices. The plot's erratic movement captures the impulsiveness of the characters' decision-making and the reality that the only inevitable destiny that governs their lives is that they must make choices, some of which alter their lives forever and others that are seemingly inconsequential. There is no clear chain of causality leading to an outcome; choices are crossroads whose routes lead nowhere but away. In keeping with his nomadic imagery, Sada frequently uses the word *derrotero* to describe these potential lifeways, a word that means *direction* or *course*, but that also suggests phonetically *derrota*, failure.

It is thus fitting that the logic governing violence in the novel is almost entirely arbitrary, even if it does generally follow certain rules of engagement related to defining the bounds of community. In the end, the enactment of violence in *Albedrío* depends only on the fine line between perceiving difference as entertainment and apprehending it as a threat, a line that is as diffuse for the communities that the húngaros visit as it is for the húngaros themselves. Contrary to what one might expect, the violence against the húngaros cannot be framed accurately as ethnic violence. The use of the term *húngaro*, rather than the more common *gitano* or the more politically correct *romaní*, displaces the focus from a concrete ethnic identity toward a vague nationality whose defining feature, in the novel, is that it is seemingly nationless. It is never clear that any of the "Hungarians" are actually from Hungary or have any Romany ancestry at all; rather than their birth ethnicity, it is their choice to follow a nomadic lifestyle and perform practices associated with the húngaro identity (nomadic wandering, acting, performing magic, fortunetelling, and stealing) that defines them as such. Even the leader of the group, the satirically named Manducho, is of mestizo Mexican ethnicity and nationality, although he was given as a child to a group of purported húngaros and was raised in their culture. More than an ethnic term, then, húngaro connotes a range of specific positions with respect to the local social order, those ascribed to the stranger and the outcast, but also the entertainer, whose difference lies primarily in the subversion of everyday language and behavior. The violence to which the húngaros are routinely subjected in the novel—especially stoning—is thus not portrayed as an ideological violence against their ethnicity, but rather as part of the practical negotiation of their position and relations within each community they visit. This negotiation occurs specifically within the economy of the spectacle that disrupts the everyday productive economy, that is, the daily routine of these communities.

Entertainment, theft, and sex are all forms of exchange through which the húngaros engage these communities, forms of exchange that rely more directly on relations of affectivity than productivity or reproductivity, although they still imply the twin movements of giving and taking. It is the húngaros' insistence on establishing these frequently unwanted relationships of reciprocity that obligates the community to respond, either with gifts or with violence. And, in many instances, this is quite an intimate process that threatens to reshape the community's boundaries. This is certainly the case when Concho and Filiastro break into a house in a settlement called La Polka to steal while the rest of the troop performs for the local people. It turns out that the house in question is the residence of a man who claims to be their former comrade Policarpo, a renowned húngaro actor whom they believed to have been lynched years before by a mob for seducing a local married woman. Policarpo is unrecognizable to the húngaros, however, because he has become sedentary, a ghost of his former self. In a fit of anger, confusion, and jealousy, Concho smashes photos of Policarpo performing successfully (without the group) as a film and theater actor, while Filiastro steals his trunk full of costumes and mementos. Eventually, it is revealed—in very ambiguous fashion, since all the characters' memories are unreliable and subject to fantasy—that Concho himself was originally from La Polka and that he had dated and perhaps had a child with the woman Policarpo seduced and was later forced to marry. This revelation leads one to surmise that Concho himself may have actually been the cuckolded husband, who ended up replacing Policarpo in the troop of húngaros. Concho resumes his relationship with the woman, thereby hinting at his possible reintegration into the community, but then Policarpo is killed as he migrates to the United States in search of more stable employment, and Concho comes to feel entrapped by the encroachment of an ordered life, of the pressure to replace Policarpo in the household. In the end, he ransacks the house of everything of value and flees alone on foot. Meanwhile, the townspeople realize that the house has been robbed by húngaros and begin stoning Manducho, Chuyito, and the other actors in the performance.

In this way, the boundaries between the community and the húngaros come into question, revealed as entirely contingent on the kind of identity that is being performed. As the narrator states at one point, the húngaro identity is simply "a vagabond life that requires nothing more than applying a technique."[3] Policarpo ceases to be an húngaro by living a sedentary life, while characters like Chuyito and Concho become húngaros by engaging those "techniques" and performing them before an audience. And there is always an audience: as Mora Ordóñez notes in her discussion of Maffesoli's and Deleuze and Guattari's theorizations of nomadism, unlike the sedentary tendency to delineate territories and build enclosures, the impulse to wander (the vagabond life) always implies a "march towards the other" and the desert, as an environment that is only semihabitable, makes that march an inevitability (119-20). At the same time, the stonings themselves are performative of community; they represent a violent breaking of the "fourth wall" separating the audience from the actors, another form of engagement designed to police the rules of affective engagement through entertainment as well as to restructure the broken bounds of the community.

In the 1990s, when frequently schematic representations of drug trafficking and violence along the US/Mexico border became fashionable, Sada continued to deal primarily with these interior landscapes that inevitably incorporated violence, but that confounded the reductive causal chains established in many works of what has come to be known as narcoliterature.[4] In Sada's works, violence is not some exotic manifestation engendered in the barbaric convergence of environmental and cultural otherness—the "narco culture" of arid Northern Mexico—but rather an interpersonal encounter that is always negotiated and in which everything is contingent on factors that can never be fully explained or controlled. Sada's representations break with the typified characterization of Northern Mexico as an inherently violent or barbarous region due to the "hostility" of the desert environment and/or its location as a criminal "no-man's land" bordering the United States. They portray it instead as a distinctive sociocultural landscape with a profoundly ambivalent relationship with cultural modernity, economic modernization, and the centralized modern national state, an ambivalence that is simultaneously a space of creative encounter and of desperate conflict.[5] This ambivalence is captured in the language he employs, a rambling, purposefully hesitant montage of the modern and the archaic, of avant-garde technical experimentation with syntax and wordplay and octosyllabic *corrido* verse, which despite its popularity in contemporary Mexican music, traces its roots back to medieval Spain.[6]

Much of the violence in Sada's works emerges in response to the encroachment of modern forms on traditional ways of life, both in the violent reactions of rural communities to cultural change and in the violence inherent in modern economic and political processes themselves (displacement, commodification, massification, biopolitical institutionalization, state repression, exclusion, alienation, etc.). In *Albedrío*, modernity still appears largely tangential to the daily lives of the communities that the húngaros visit, and yet the húngaros themselves, despite their professed superstitions and mysticism, are closely linked with two highly transformative modern technologies: film and the automobile. On the one hand, film is incorporated seamlessly into the spectacle that the húngaros provide, but it also displaces traditional acting—on several occasions, the townspeople prefer to see the húngaros' film with no accompanying theatrical performance. As Walter Benjamin noted famously, the mechanical reproduction of images in film disrupts both cathartic identification between audience, character, and actor (the audience identifies with an image instead of a real-life actor) and the critical estrangement effects that are so important in theater; the violence portrayed in the húngaros' film reenacts the violence that film itself as a genre does on theater and its actors (228-34). In this sense, the novel captures the earliest moments of the modern movement away from a sense of community rooted in the affective bonds of social interactions toward a mass society unified by the virtuality of shared imagery. Tellingly, the húngaros are never stoned when the film alone is displayed; stoning is thus a form of affective disengagement closely related to the shared, participatory nature of violence and theater. Encounter becomes impossible when the actors are not real, only images.

On the other hand, the húngaros' truck is not only their most important possession, which enables them to embody the nomadic identity and perform their work as entertainers, but it also manifests a powerful symbolic presence. As many theorists have noted, the automobile exemplifies modernity's freedom of movement, the ability to migrate as a form of social mobility, as well as the power of a specifically modern energy regime and its derivative patterns of production and consumption—that of petromodernity. Manducho frequently asserts his decision-making authority as owner of the truck, but his absolute dependence on modern distribution networks is exposed when the truck runs out of gas. Furthermore, the truck also draws attention to the commodification of human bodies (the actors) that are transported in all directions to be displayed for money, wherever the market will support them. The truck thus becomes a powerful motif symbolizing the surreptitious arrival of modern capitalism in the novel's traditional rural villages, while both the truck and the film's association with the húngaros captures the otherness that new technologies present to rural communities. The truck comes to symbolize metonymically the nomad/migrant, the contradictory figure who has been displaced violently by social and economic forces, yet has at the same time been freed to find meaning in the journey itself.

The truck symbol takes a darker turn in Sada's masterpiece, *Porque parece mentira la verdad nunca se sabe,* which opens with the arrival in the small Northern town of Remadrín of a truck full of cadavers that the driver and his helpers unload onto the sidewalk so that they may be identified by family members. Despite his overpowering apathy, narcoleptic kiosk-owner Trinidad is woken from his siesta and cajoled by his wife Cecilia into going to see whether their disappeared sons Papías and Salomón are among the dead. When he does not find them, Cecilia convinces him to travel to a nearby cave, in which it is rumored that the sons have taken refuge. The cave is empty of all but echoes, however, and it turns out that the rumor was a trick of a neighbor who attempts to seduce Cecilia in Trinidad's absence. In this way, the opening chapter brings to bear the motif of the fruitless search, which fugues into a massive, 600-page novel packed with meandering subplots, many of which have to do only tangentially with the central "truth" to which the title refers: the facts regarding the events leading up to the massacre and disappearance of 300 protesters who marched to the state capital to protest electoral fraud. Each of these subplots is narrated from the perspectives of a multitude of major and minor characters, but the limited knowledge, dependence on rumors and misinformation, and untruthfulness of many of the characters make it impossible to arrive at a definitive synthesis of the facts of the case. In this way, the writing of the novel itself reflects the search for a truth that becomes indistinguishable from the whole or partial fictions fabricated by the characters. Thus the novel's title: despite the existence of empirical facts, the truth can never be wholly known, because it is always subjective, partial, and calculated or inferred, never fully objective.

In fact, the very possibilities of writing as a vehicle for explaining truth or history come into question in the novel's final scene. The fallout from the theft of voting urns by masked men working for the ruling party and the subsequent massacre of protestors by governmental soldiers spreads virally, as its echoes reverberate throughout the entire region, affecting all the characters to some degree, even when causal chains cannot be distinguished clearly. As the narrator states at one point: "The causes will be left out because they involve getting into obscure minutiae. The effects are more worthwhile."[7] The primary effect is that Remadrín is eventually abandoned following months of fruitless protests. The continued political uncertainty, the threat of further violence, and the absence of mayor Romeo Pomar bring the economy to a standstill, leading to a situation in which it is impossible to find even basic goods. Reminiscent of Juan Rulfo's iconic cacique, Pedro Páramo, Pomar's voracious corruption over decades has structured the entire local economy around his personal control, leading to a gradual but inexorable collapse of the social and political order when the governor decides to sequester him and the other mayors involved in the electoral fraud on his personal ranch until the storm blows over.

Trinidad and Cecilia are among the last to leave Remadrín. Before going, they post a cardboard note with their new address in Cecilia's birth town on their door for their sons to find. The novel ends with this note being carried by the wind into the branches of a dead cactus far from their home. This apparently innocuous ending is in reality deeply symbolic. The writing on the cardboard proclaims a simple, ostensibly true fact—the whereabouts of Cecilia and Trinidad, should their sons come looking for them—but it has little meaning because it has been removed from its context, that is, the door of their house. The sign could conceivably still be found by someone, but it is unlikely that the message would have any importance for that person. Its meaning is extraneous to its new context. On the other hand, it is equally likely that its words will fade into illegibility before anyone sees them; the written word has simply become litter strewn on the desert.

Given the fact that the author wrote nearly 600 pages before this final descent into illegibility occurs, it would seem quite nihilistic if his final message were that writing has no meaning. Rather than falling into this overly simplistic conclusion, one must take into consideration the sociocultural processes that have led to this point in which both written and oral communication lose nearly all possibilities for transmitting truth. Rather than failures within the communicative media themselves, the disappearance of the protestors and the subsequent migration of the townspeople due to political repression and economic corruption mean that the communicative network has been disrupted almost entirely; there remain no readers to receive a message and validate it as truthful or not. The truth explaining the causes of the apocalypse becomes irrelevant before its overwhelming effects. When life is no longer possible, there is no point in assigning guilt or meting out justice.

Nevertheless, it is only in the world of the novel that there are no readers left, and Sada's novel resonates powerfully with contemporary readers familiar with the history of political corruption, electoral fraud, and forced disappearances in Mexico, particularly given recent events such as the 2014 massacre and disappearance of student activists from Ayotzinapa, Guerrero. *Porque parece mentira* represents a penetrating study of the way in which the manipulation of information and the apathy of the citizenry in the face of political abuses make necropolitics—that is, the state use of mass killing and other coercive tactics against its own citizens—possible. The novel's brilliance lies precisely in its refusal to provide a convincing causal explanation for the political violence; it is the system-wide culture of impunity and deception that creates these conditions. Indeed, even though Trinidad redeems himself at the end of the novel by becoming a protest leader, up until that point he had been a paragon of civilian apathy (arguing against his sons' political activism), corruption (he steals from his own father), and the manipulation of information: after an altercation that results in his sons spitting in his face and Cecilia kicking them out of their home, he tricks his sons into attending his and Cecilia's wedding anniversary party to take a family portrait that deceptively communicates family harmony.

These are Trinidad's tragic flaws, the flaws that are shared by Remadrín as a community (and which lead to its abandonment) and Mágico (Sada's satirical name for Mexico) as a whole.

In this sense, the novel provides a fascinating take on the phenomenon of migration and abandonment that affected rural Mexico throughout the twentieth century, and which has intensified in the twenty-first with the concentration of wealth in urban areas and increased violence in the countryside, largely due to the war on drugs declared by then president Felipe Calderón in 2006. Rather than the stereotypical modernist explanation of rural exile as a movement toward economic opportunities and modern comfort in urban areas, here it is the dark underbelly of modernity—political repression facilitated by the machinery of modern necropolitics and citizen disengagement arising from the manipulation of information and the formation of mass society—that leads to the collapse of rural communities. In Sada's representations, corruption and apathy are killing the political and productive economy in small towns throughout Northern Mexico.

Sada's final, posthumous novel, *El lenguaje del juego*, revisits the familiar themes of migration, otherness, violence, and rural exodus within the context of the rise of the illicit narcotics economy in rural Northern Mexico. The novel recounts the return to his hometown of San Gregorio of migrant Valente Montaño, who has decided to invest the money he has saved over years of hard work and privations in the United States in a pizza restaurant. The novel deals with the complexities arising from the implementation of two competing and yet complementary forms of transnational capitalism: on the one hand, the "remesas" (remittances) immigrants bring back to Mexico and their effects in generating cosmopolitan consumer lifestyles linked to the global economy (symbolized by the pizzeria as well as the clothing styles chosen by Valente's teenage children, Candelario and Martina), and narcotic production and distribution on the other, embodied in the mysterious dealings of Candelario's friend Mónico Zorrilla and his father. These parallel economies converge when drug traffickers start appropriating public space; first, by appearing fleetingly on the town's streets in black BMW

SUVs, then by invading the pizzeria and demanding free meals. Eventually, a rival cartel led by Flavio Benavides assassinates the mayor and drives the Zorrilla band out, taking absolute political and economic control of the town. The entire family becomes complicit in some way with the narcos: Candelario joins the Zorrilla band and then, following its collapse, another, more powerful cartel for whom he ends up heading a local office in Acapulco; Martina becomes the lover of one of the invading traffickers; and Valente is forced to accept the "friendship" of the new capo in exchange for surveilling members of the rival band. Things can't but end badly: Mónico Zorrilla and his father die of overdoses in Los Angeles after binging on drugs for months, Martina is murdered by her abusive lover when she tries to leave him, and the novel ends when Candelario, sensing that he will be killed upon returning to San Gregorio to extract his parents, decides to abandon them and San Gregorio permanently. In all cases, it is clear that there is no return.

The novel's title, *El lenguaje del juego*, alludes to the vulgarity-laced idiom that the cartel members use in their everyday speech, which shocks the conservative townspeople, as well as the violent messages they communicate using mutilated cadavers. In more general terms, however, it refers to the shift in cultural codes and practices due to the rise of the tenuous new economic regime, which depends on constant informal "jugadas" (deceptive maneuvers) rather than a long-term economic strategy and structure. Tellingly, the pizzeria becomes an unviable business when it is incorporated into the drug-trafficking economy, both because its producers abandon vegetable production to grow marijuana and because its regular customers stop coming when it becomes affiliated with the drug traffickers. As in *Porque parece mentira*, the long-term inhabitability of San Gregorio comes into question, as does that of the entire nation; rather than representing the margins, the North becomes exemplary of Mexico as a whole: "Poor Mágico, poor country sinking into an inexorable black hole."[8] In this sense, *El lenguaje del juego* represents a final, pessimistic return to Sada's preoccupation with the theme of modernity's transformations of rural areas, updated for recent events in Mexico.

As much as for his regionalist focus on Northern Mexico, Sada is known for his word craft and his attention to local speech. He experiments freely with the popular lexicon of rural Mexico and archaic linguistic forms (*arcaísmos*) that are still used in some rural areas of Latin America and the Southwestern United States, but that have largely disappeared from "standard" usage, as well as with others gleaned from Spanish literary history, turning them to his own literary uses: words like *adrede, contimás, dizque, medroso, redor, postrer*, and verb forms that are used in ways not commonly found in either contemporary speech or writing. It is the sumptuousness of the linguistic texture of his writing that has led many critics, including the frequently cited Roberto Bolaño, to describe his style as being somehow "baroque." This term fits Sada's aesthetics intuitively, but it nevertheless seems problematic given its historical and geographical removal from the cultures that gave rise to baroque aesthetics: the seventeenth century Spanish Empire of Quevedo and Góngora, the colonial New World of Sor Juana Inés de la Cruz and Carlos Sigüenza y Góngora, and the intricately racialized, postcolonial Caribbean environment from which the tropicalist neobaroque of mid-twentieth century Cuban authors Alejo Carpentier, José Lezama Lima, and Severo Sarduy emerged.[9] These historical and geographical distances logically lead one to wonder, along with Bolaño: what are baroque aesthetics doing in the Sonoran desert?

Oswaldo Zavala attributes Sada's style to his early readings of classical and early modern Spanish writers, which were the only ones to be found in the sole library to which he had access growing up in the small town of Sacramento, Coahuila: a teacher's small personal collection (73). In particular, these readings would inform the verse-like structure of his prose, the use of octosyllables in *Albedrío, Una de dos*, and the corrido of Rosita Alvírez that he rewrote in *Ese modo que colma*, but also the hendecasyllables and alexandrines that appear in several works, including *Porque parece mentira*.[10] And yet, when one reads Sada's works, his style inevitably feels much closer to the popular culture of Northern Mexico than to the formal ostentation characteristic of the Hispanic baroque, with its colonial and postcolonial preoccupation with eloquence and wit that, according to John Beverley, served to reinforce class and racial lines (5-8). Indeed, Sada turns cultural elitism on its head: his baroque is not allusive, there is little of the highbrow intertextual play that one commonly associates with the imperial and postcolonial baroque, nor does it rely on the allegorical figures or elaborate chains of extended metaphor that are usually found in baroque and neobaroque writing. As Héctor Iván González notes, Sada studiously avoided casting intellectuals or the cultural elite in his works, which leads González to a diagnosis of "anti-intellectualism" (10-11). When he did eventually write a character who claimed to be an avant-garde poet in *La duración de los empeños simples*, he was satirized mercilessly, as was the literary industry as a whole in *Ritmo delta*. In the end, Sada's narrators are closer to Sancho Panza than to Alonso Quijano, or perhaps to Sancho Panza imitating Don Quixote's speech. Orality takes precedence over literariness, but that orality is itself unquestionably, emphatically literary.

If Sada shies away from Lezama Lima's and Sarduy's neobaroque fascination with the obscure reference, he nevertheless shares with Sarduy the preference for the elliptical form that, rather than converging centripetally on a central meaning, coalesces around a destabilized, ambivalent system of partial meanings. Sada's narrators exploit the eloquence of partial meanings, provisional associations, and incomplete metaphors and syntactic structures. He makes frequent use of punctuation and other textual elements that are rarely seen in literature, such as colons, parentheses, ellipses, and etceteras. It is this dense montage of partial forms that generate the baroque texture of Sada's writing, a baroqueness that is not like the gold-filigreed, finely embossed surfaces of the Spanish colonial cathedrals but rather an intricate entanglement of half-formed thoughts and expressions, indecisive acts, inexplicable events, and unfinished stories, a baroque aesthetics that reflects without mirroring the convoluted fabric of everyday life in Northern Mexico.

Notes

1. In this brief summary, I have included only Sada's works of narrative that have attracted the greatest critical acclaim and/or won national or international prizes. In addition, Sada published *Un rato* (short stories, 1984); *Juguete de nadie y otras historias* (short stories, 1985), *Tres historias* (novellas, 1990), *Una de dos* (novel, 1994), *El límite* (poetry and stories, 1997), *Luces artificiales* (novel, 2002), *Ritmo delta* (novel, 2005), *La duración de los empeños simples* (novel, 2006), *A la vista* (novel, 2011), and *Ese modo que colma* (stories, 2010). Sada also wrote three volumes of poetry: *Los lugares* (1977), *El amor es cobrizo* (2005), and *Aquí* (2007).

2. Sada's usage of *lampa* is likely derived from the Náhuatl suffix *tlampa*, meaning *interior* or *behind* (perhaps referring to the premodern lifestyle in El Oro), although it could also come from the Greek *lampas* (lamp, but also burning desire), or, given his predilection for wordplay, both.

3. "Una vida vagabunda que no exige más que aplicar una técnica" (147). All translations are the author's own.

4. Rafael Lemus criticizes the predominant trend within narconarrative as "realismo ramplón" (tacky realism), noting that it generally relies on a formulaic mixture of costumbrismo, melodrama, and picaresque plotlines that weaken any critique that it may present of the economic, political, and social conditions that converge in the phenomena of illegal narcotic trafficking and the drug war (n.p.). Of course, there are exceptions to this rule, including Sada's own *El lenguaje del juego*.

5. For a discussion of the stereotypes and myths associated with Northern Mexico, see Viviane Mahieux and Oswaldo Zavala's "El nomos del Norte."

6. Critic Vicente Francisco Torres first drew attention to Sada's use of the octosyllable in his prose, a technique that was later confirmed by the author in an interview (see Beltrán Félix 118).

7. "Las causas quedan aparte porque significa entrar en oscuros pormenores. Los efectos valen más" (79).

8. "Pobre Mágico, pobre país sumergido en un inexorable hoyo negro" (85).

---

9. See Roberto Bolaño's interview with Daniel Swineburn in *El Mercurio*.

10. See Oswaldo Zavala, "Daniel Sada" (73) and Oswaldo Estrada, "Versos que violentan" (1133).

Works Cited

Beltrán Félix, Juan Geney. "El fabulador en octosílabos o el corridista culto. La prosa rítmica de Daniel Sada." *Revista de Literaturas Populares* 3.1, 2003, pp. 117-40. http://ru.ffyl.unam.mx/handle/10391/2616. Accessed 9/28/17.

Benjamin, Walter. "The Work of Art in the Age of Mechanical Reproduction." *Illuminations: Essays and Reflections.* Edited by Hannah Arendt. Schocken, 2007.

Beverley, John. *Essays on the Literary Baroque in Spain and Spanish America.* Tamesis, 2008.

Bolaño, Roberto. "Catorce preguntas a Bolaño." Interview with Daniel Swineburn. *El Mercurio*, March 2, 2003. n.p. http://www.bibliotecanacionaldigital.cl/bnd/628/w3-article-281762.html. Accessed 9/28/17.

Estrada, Oswaldo. "Versos que violentan historias: Daniel Sada y el corrido de Rosita Alvírez." *Bulletin of Spanish Studies* 92.7, 2015, pp. 1129-43. http://www.tandfonline.com/doi/abs/10.1080/1475382 0.2015.1041331?journalCode=cbhs20. Accessed 9/28/17.

González, Héctor Iván, editor. "El heliogábalo lingüístico." *La escritura poliédrica: Ensayos sobre Daniel Sada.* CONACULTA, 2012, pp. 9-24.

Lemus, Rafael. "Balas de salva." *Letras Libres*, Sept. 30, 2005. n.p. http://www.letraslibres.com/mexico/balas-salva. Accessed 9/28/17.

Mahieux, Viviane, and Oswaldo Zavala. "El *nomos* del Norte." *Tierras de nadie: el Norte en la narrativa mexicana contemporánea.* Ed. Viviane Mahieux and Oswaldo Zavala. CONACULTA, 2012.

Mora Ordoñez, Edith. "Tres circos, tres novelas buscando un lugar en el desierto mexicano: la territorialización de los confines." *Taller de Letras* 55, 2014, pp. 113-29. http://tallerdeletras.letras.uc.cl/images/55/d03.pdf. Accessed 9/28/17.

Sada, Daniel. *A la vista.* Anagrama, 2011.

_____. *Albedrío*. Tusquets, 1989.

_____. *El amor es cobrizo*. Ediciones sin Nombre, 2005.

_____. *Antología presentida*. CONACULTA, 1993.

_____. *Aquí*. Fondo de Cultura Económica, 2007.

_____. *Casi nunca*. Anagrama, 2008.

_____. *La duración de los empeños simples*. Joaquín Mortiz/ Planeta, 2006.

_____. *Ese modo que colma*. Anagrama, 2010.

_____. *Juguete de nadie y otras historias*. Fondo de Cultura Económica, 1985.

_____. *Lampa vida*. Mexico City: Premià, 1980.

_____. *El lenguaje del juego*. Barcelona: Anagrama, 2012.

_____. *El límite*. Vuelta, 1997.

_____. *Los lugares*. Universidad Autónoma Metropolitana, 1977.

_____. *Luces artificiales*. Joaquín Mortiz/Planeta, 2002.

_____. *Porque parece mentira la verdad nunca se sabe*. Tusquets, 1999.

_____. *Un rato*. UAM-Itzapalapa, 1984.

_____. *Registro de causantes*. Joaquín Mortíz/Planeta, 1990.

_____. *Reunión de cuentos*. Fondo de Cultura Económica, 2012.

_____. *Ritmo delta: novela*. Joaquín Mortiz/Planeta, 2005.

_____. *El temple deslumbrante: Antología de textos no narrativos de Daniel Sada*. Edited by Adriana Jiménez and Héctor Iván González. CONACULTA, 2012.

_____. *Todo y la recompensa: Cuentos completos*. Plaza y Janés, 2002.

_____. *Tres historias*. Cuadernos del Nigromante, 1990.

_____. *Una de dos*. Alfaguara, 1994.

Zavala, Oswaldo. "Daniel Sada." *The Contemporary Spanish-American Novel: Bolaño and After*. Edited by Wilfrido Corral, Nicholas Birns, and Juan E. Decastro. Bloomsbury, 2013, pp. 72-76.

The Labor of Gender: Cristina Rivera Garza, a Feminist Pedagogy_____

Laura J. Torres-Rodríguez

"I am not an advocate of ignorance, of course. But in the world of writing, which is a world marked by uncertainty and nuances, knowing often means knowing too much," says Mexican author Cristina Rivera Garza (1964-).[1] This statement captures my own experience with her writing, a relationship forged through pedagogy, through the practice of reading for and with others. Indeed, her work invites a constant interrogation of the "reading comprehension" imperative as a pedagogical objective. Rivera Garza adopts uncertainty as a writing method, opposes the formulation of certainties. This is why her teaching exhorts that we "read" our own desire for understanding, demanding that we put comprehension itself up for reading.

For the purposes of this volume dedicated to the study of contemporary literature, Rivera Garza's reflections are fundamental for questioning what *contemporary* means, beyond a positivist perspective of *contemporary* as whatever is most recent. For her, writing is a way of producing the present: "Knowing what the temporal sense of such contemporaneity consists of is . . . the duty of every writer who doesn't want to live under the shadow of the past or the imagination of the future."[2] Contemporaneity, then, is not a specific condition, but a *duty* that consists of writing in ways that show the material conditions and the kinds of relationships and sociability implicated by the historical aspect of every creative act.

This chapter traces a path through some of Rivera Garza's texts that have been central to a reconceptualization of contemporary writing in my teaching praxis. The guiding thread that I follow on this path is how the author has reformulated the operational codes for studying literature based on a theorization of the type of (re) productive relation that every creative act entails. With this I want to emphasize Rivera Garza's link to a broader feminist tradition dedicated precisely to revealing *forms of labor* not recognized as such—for instance, domestic work—that are commonly associated with the maintenance and organization upon which our daily life depends. Given this, I define reproductive labor "as the complex of activities and relations by which our life and labor are daily reconstituted" (Federici 5).[3] Hence, Rivera Garza's feminist perspective is not necessarily manifested through a specific representation of gender or of women—although the critique of her work along these lines has been extremely fruitful—but can rather be found in a positioning articulated around the question of reproductive work upon which contemporary society is built, and against which every notion of contemporary literature should be put to the test.

"Revolution at Ground Zero": The Works of History

The importance of labor as a theme in Rivera Garza's work can be observed beginning with her first well-known novel, *Nadie me verá llorar* (*No One Will See Me Cry*, 1999). This text represented an incursion into the historical novel and was written in counterpoint to her doctoral thesis. Indeed, in addition to being one of the most prolific contemporary authors in Latin America—to date she has published six novels, three collections of short stories, five books of poetry, and four nonfiction books—Rivera Garza has a doctorate in Latin American history from the University of Houston, and has had a successful university career in both Mexico and the United States as a professor of creative writing.

Thus, *No One Will See Me Cry* offers two perspectives on work that she will continue to develop in her later production. First, an explicit relationship of methodological promiscuity is established between *archival work*—the author's material contact with the traces left by other bodies—and the novel. *No one* was composed based on the medical archives of La Castañeda, the Mexican psychiatric asylum founded by the dictator Porfirio Díaz in 1910. It is a question of exploring the possibility that the novel could become a different exteriority for the medical archive that was originally used to institutionalize and discipline, "the possibility that this 'outside' [of the archive] prints a new skin" (Guerrero).[4] Indeed, as the critic

Javier Guerrero explains, the institutional archive pushes toward silencing and disciplining, but also, because of its material aspect and its exhibitionist nature, it harbors the possibility of producing new ways of being read for the future (45).

Second, the novel also points toward a (historical) rereading of an era of political transition from forms of labor not recognized as such: "In contrast to other historical novels that narrate the first two decades of the twentieth century in Mexico from the angle of the [Mexican] Revolution, this is dedicated to telling the peripheral histories that have been steamrolled by the hegemonic narration that arises in the years after the constitutionalist triumph" (Price).[5] I would also add that the novel narrates how work generated gender.[6] Rivera Garza seems to suggest that in order to understand Mexican modernity—founded in the Mexican Revolution (1910)—we must look to the struggles for control of the body and the labor of the subjects who were produced as women, that is, to the revolutionary event at one of its ground zeros.[7]

The novel begins in 1920 with the third encounter in La Castañeda between Joaquín Buitrago—a photographer hired to portray the mentally "ill" patients—and Matilda Burgos, a patient at the institution. The text opens with Matilda trying to provoke Joaquín: "How does one become a photographer of crazy people?" (1).[8] The work of the novel is to reverse the (photographic, documentary) archive, to show the body of the photographer who tries to "see without being seen" (169); it dislocates the subject/object distinction, the syntax that organizes that relationship. The portraitist becomes portrayed; he also becomes a (masculine) subject in crisis or in production: "Joaquin, unaccustomed to hearing the voices of the subjects he was photographing, thought it was the whispering of his own conscience" (3).[9] The words that supposedly name things or subjects are returned to the chaos to which they belong: *photographer*, *crazy woman*, each one slips or is derailed over the course of the novel: "Have you ever noticed that all mistakes begin with a name?" (168).[10]

Rivera Garza chooses to recount the Revolution from a bureaucratic perspective, an archive that is not normally considered central to studying the war as a political event. Critics have noted that the novel's characters dwell on the fringe of revolutionary events; however, this fringe is relative. In the medical archives, Rivera Garza finds an overlooked history of the Revolution: the movements of Mexican working women during these years of political transition. She discovers the bodily imprint of daily life that shows the instability inherent in official attempts to inscribe women's bodies on a modernizing (re)productive order.

Some of these movements are brought to life in the character of Matilda. The second chapter recounts Matilda's migration in 1900 from Papantla, Veracruz, to Mexico City. The novel points to a certain feminization of the country-to-city migration, which today is fundamental for understanding the global processes of division of labor. In Mexico City, her uncle, a doctor and public health specialist, made her the object of his civilizing experiments; he wanted to combat the "barbarism" represented by Matilda's countrified body through domestic labor. There, Matilda quickly realizes "that the attributes of femininity are in effect *functions of work*" (Federici 8). She leaves her uncle's home in 1907 after the disappearance of her friend Diamantina during the Porfirian suppression of the strike by the textile workers of Río Blanco. After this, she gets a job as a laborer in a cigarette factory. She also works as a teacher, healer and midwife in the women's community where she lives, thus earning the nickname "la doctorcita" (the little doctor). After her roommate, Esther, dies due to the extremely precarious working conditions in the cigarette factory, Matilda is fired for missing one day of work to take her friend to the hospital. From there, she goes on to swell the ranks of sex workers in order to support Esther's children.

By exploring the very unstable conditions under which migrant women were integrated into Mexico City's system of productivity, the novel offers an innovative perspective on the changes in working conditions that would contribute to the Revolution. The exorbitant number of sex workers in the city was a favorite topic of discussion among doctors and urban planners of the period, who showed an ambivalent fascination for these statistics that somehow indicated the achievement of modernity—*à la mode parisienne*—but by spurious

---

means. The bureaucratic archives on the regulation of prostitution demonstrate the anxiety over the figure of the *working woman*, since so many believed that all paid women's work *is already sex work*. The construction of the prostitute as the enemy *par excellence* of public health—with "public" being defined in masculine terms—was based on controlling and discursively mapping the ways of organizing women's work. As Rivera Garza says, "When it came to women, wage labor and vice were synonyms in Porfirian Mexico" ("The Criminalization" 154). The novel reveals the link between the lack of workforce protections for working women and prostitution at the beginning of the twentieth century:

> In Mexico City, twelve percent of the women between fifteen and thirty years of age were prostitutes, or had been at some time. Many of them were orphans and single women, although there were also widows, married women, even women with children. They had been maids, seamstresses, washerwomen, machine operators, and street vendors, and they had probably never earned more than twenty-five centavos a day. (152)[11]

The novel reads the Revolution through this massive number of women who represent a cornerstone of the modernizing order of Mexico City. It is precisely because of the undeniable visibility of working women that the bureaucratic ranks of scientists considered the regulation, medicalization, and criminalization of their bodies to be essential to controlling the reproduction of an order that was questionable from the outset. They tried to marginalize the subjects who made modernity possible: "Rivera Garza 'blast[s] out of the continuum of history,' . . . people and experiences previously construed as modernity's 'peripheral side-effects,' and instead shows them to be 'central intertwining elements' of it" (Silverstein 541). Rivera Garza thus begins from this legal and medical archive not to show how bureaucratic repression acted on the daily lives of working class subjects, but rather to read in those zones where such control was confused, disconnected from the reality of forms of social organization. Revolution as promise was also articulated from the alternative ways in which subjects organized themselves, despite the fact that the postrevolutionary government continued the Porfirian practices of persecuting the working bodies that made the revolutionary event possible.

The Understanding of the Genre: The Work of Crime Fiction

The stakes of the novel lie, then, on a reconceptualization of the (revolutionary) historical novel by experimenting with a view of Mexican modernity from the perspective of reproductive work. In other words, in the text modernity organizes itself—organizes its language—through the sexual division of labor. This view of history is at the service of producing intelligibility in contemporary times. And in fact, Rivera Garza writes for a neoliberal present marked by a growing feminization of survival, as Verónica Gago notes in an interview with Saskia Sassen: "More and more, migration to look for work, trafficking, and prostitution are the only option for survival for thousands of women all around the world. And they are the ones who bear the brunt of structural adjustment programs … Furthermore, the cuts in health and education spending also fundamentally impact women, since they are the ones who must take on and finance these aspects of care" (Gago).[12] Rivera Garza writes about the past to understand this present, particularly in Mexico, where these displacements and changes in workforce structures have triggered new forms of violence against women.

Rivera Garza's writing develops a series of formal responses that cover these questions about how contemporary violence is organized. Her essays in this regard are explicit, but I would like to explore her detective fiction, the genre that has largely cornered the market on literary representations of violence, especially relative to drug trafficking. For this reading, I evoke reflections arising from direct dialogue with my students. As it happens, crime fiction is the genre with which students are most familiar, due to its undeniable currency in popular culture. Thus, I will concentrate on how Rivera Garza intervenes traditional mechanisms of reading comprehension in detective fiction, and how she shows the violence that a certain type of reading comprehension generates.

Crime fiction is a genre traditionally founded on an imperative of rationalization, attribution of identities, criminalization of populations, and a notion of justice based on punishment and the reinstatement of an existing legal order. However, Rivera Garza's fiction dislocates all these imperatives by weakening the imperative to find the "guilty party." For this discussion, I will focus on the experience of an in-class collective dissection of a specific text, in this case, the short story "Simple placer, demasiado placer" (Simple Pleasure, Too Much Pleasure) published in *La frontera más distante* (The Farthest Border, 2008).

Summarizing this story is in itself a risk, a conjectural interpretation, since the sense of the plot is fairly feeble. The story starts with the classic discovery by a detective of a corpse, a naked, decapitated man on the side of the highway. The Detective sees the body from a taxi on her way to the airport for a business trip. Upon her return, she begins an inquiry into the case, only to discover that it has not been recorded in the Homicide Investigation Department's official files. The corpse has only one identifying feature: a jade ring carved as two intertwined snakes. Under murky circumstances, the Detective meets a woman with an identical ring. The Ring Woman then offers the Detective money to investigate the murder privately. The story ends with a financial transaction: the Detective admits to not having been able to discover absolutely anything about the case, and the Ring Woman, satisfied, pays her for her service.

At the formal level, the writing is incredibly elusive. The text begins with the following passage:

[S/he] would remember all of it unexpectedly and in detail. [S/he] would see the jade ring around the ring finger, and then immediately [s/he] would see the other jade ring. [S/he] would open the eyes wide and, without knowing why, [s/he] would stop talking. [S/he] wouldn't ask anything else. [S/he] would say: yes, very beautiful. It is. And [s/he] would run her fingertips over the delicate figure of the snakes. A caress. The hint of a caress. An unmoving hand below.[13]

The text reveals a series of challenges that only became apparent to me when I began to teach it. First, the use of the conditional—

its hypothetical aspect—already presents a challenge for a genre characterized by the reconstruction of facts or the interpretation of evidence. Are these reflections in the past or the present, or from another temporal aspect altogether, the potential? Second, the impossibility of determining definitively the grammatical subject of the sentences is also added, since in Spanish the subject is only implied by the verb. Nor are the antecedents of the possessives easily identifiable. Crime fiction as a genre that attributes identities—culprits/victims—or that attempts to attribute relations of property between characteristics and names remains in question. Although the reader might guess that this passage relates the Detective's thoughts about the corpse, this guess would only be a product of the *work* of reading, of an implication. In this first paragraph, we are shown the complicity that the classic detective story requires from the reader to establish a system of reading predicated on violent attributions:

> The detective novel constructs *an intellectual image of repression,* but its true repressive function does not lie in the anecdotal denouement of the plot, but in the projection of a superego capable of disciplining the distribution of the narrative elements in *the reader's consciousness . . .* The genre proposes an absolute transparency that is in itself repressive. This transparency, presupposed in the image of the detective, *subtly reproduces the panopticon, whose centralized viewpoint the reader accesses by identifying him/herself with the detective.* (Resina; emphasis mine)[14]

If we keep this in mind, we can then see Rivera Garza's wager on opacity as a political choice that attempts to make visible the operation of reading. As she would say, these are operations of writing where "the reign of authorship, in terms of who makes the meaning, has been radically displaced from the singularity of the author to the function of the reader."[15] The affective identification between readers and detective is a natural effect of the genre. But the Detective, acting as this disciplining awareness "of the distribution of the narrative elements," is already *corrupted.*

Corruption can be understood first as a linguistic phenomenon wherein the language that is supposed to identify the subjects gets dislocated, as demonstrated in the above example of the ambivalence of possessives. It is difficult to know absolutely whose hand it is, whose ring, whose are the actions described in the text. But even when the third-person voice describes the Detective's thoughts and speech acts, this organizing awareness is shown to be corrupted by a certain sensuality, by its bond with the body, an experiential dimension not commonly found in the investigations of classic crime novels. The ideological empiricism associated with the figure of the Detective appears here as a desire for material things: "I always wanted a ring like that," "Will you sell it?"[16] By turns, the Detective complains, gets tired, talks inappropriately about the demands of her job, about the money that corrupts her will to learn the truth. In the end, this is a story of seduction:

> –This ... is my work. This is how I earn my living. It's not a hobby, you might be interested to know.
> –I can pay you two or three times what you earn.
> –Make it four –she immediately answered ...
> Money. Money always did what it wanted with her ... Discovery and money. The chain of the natural world. As she climbed between the sheets she thought it wouldn't bother her at all if they were silk.[17]

At the end of the story, "The Detective visited her [the Ring Woman] to give her bad news: not a single fact, not a single finding, no information at all."[18] The traditional investigation fails; in Rivera Garza's police fiction, it is impossible to assign guilt. The Ring Woman then invites her to sit down, and immediately after that a character called Little Woman appears, removes the Detective's shoes and begins to give her a foot massage. During the massage, the Woman with the Ring answers her: "'Good work." The story ends with the Detective perplexed, her awareness (of herself, of her work) completely undermined, a catastrophe (for crime fiction): "The Detective bowed her head but raised her eyes. Her elbows were on her knees, the bills in her hand, and her feet in the warm, fragrant water. An odd image. Out of place. The corruption of the senses."[19] The story ends on the Detective's feet, the source of her guilty pleasure, her connection with the ground.

We could read this corruption allegorically, pointing obviously to the state of Mexican law where a headless body in a vacant lot would indicate the ghost of the 2008 war on drugs. Indeed, the case is not officially investigated because of "Lack of evidence . . . You know how it goes. One more execution. One of many."[20] The Detective's unconscious implication in the criminal order advances this reading of the State's silent collusion with organized crime— that chain of "natural" order where money is tied to self-interest. The impossibility of punishment for the crime and of enforcement of justice would correspond to a commitment to portray the total impunity from which Mexico suffers. However, "the corruption of the senses" points to a deeper epistemological dimension: beyond the moral acceptance of the term, it evokes the corruption of the *senses* of a textual body, or rather, of a textual corpus (the detective-fiction-as-genre) that traditionally seeks an impossible transparency. What appears already corrupted is a system of reading social reality predicated on the assignment of individual guilt, an order complacent with official discourses about crime. As a reader, identifying with the Detective's lost innocence represents, then, a collective taking charge of our ways of understanding the present violence.

I would like to end this section with a final comment on how the "improper" feminization of the narrative functions in her work are essential for the destabilization of the crime genre. This feminization is not played out through the construction of complex "feminine" characters but rather through the grammatical inscription of gender that is carried out only within language (Estrada). This inscription serves to destabilize crime fiction as a reading system that seeks to restitute a symbolic order, a patriarchal order in the sense that it is predicated on the reinstatement of law.

For example, Rivera Garza's most influential detective novel, *La muerte me da* (Death Strikes Me, 2007) is again constructed around the grammatical feminization of the main characters: the *female* Detective of the Homicide Investigation Department, the *female* Reporter, the *female* Informant, the *female* First Suspect, etc. However, this time the investigation revolves around a series of murders whose common thread is castration: all the victims are men. Thus, the novel probes a dissonance: in the Spanish language, "*la víctima* is always feminine." While being the object of (gender) violence means being grammatically feminine in Spanish, in the novel, the discourse of the media and law enforcement loses the ability to name facts effectively: "Everyone would become used to talking about the murderer in the feminine. No one would find, however, a suitable grammatical way to make *la víctima* masculine."[21]

Once again, it is about making an intervention on the social grammar of the text—as a tradition—and making the novel itself an investigation of the effects of such intervention, rather than a narration of the hunt for a culprit. So we should not simply assume that these castrations in the novel represent the author's literary revenge for the symbolic violence against women's bodies that crime fiction culture has traditionally stood for, although certainly the gesture makes visible in one fell swoop this aspect of the genre's historicity. Some critiques have mentioned that the novel is an oblique response to femicide in Mexico (Close 394). I, however, propose that beginning the text with castration indicates an invitation to read the crime fiction genre literally, in its nontranscendence, as a structure built of language. As the novel itself notes, "What really happens: the novel can't know that."[22] It is as if Rivera Garza is telling us that the traditional crime novel is structured around the fear of castration, around prohibition, limits, and punishment. And yet, for Rivera Garza we can only write differently *after* castration, on the far side of it, as the opening epigraph from Renata Salecl points out: "It may even be said that it is only because subjects are castrated that human relations as such can exist" (*La muerte me da* 13). Thus, as Joan Copjec argues, a feminist ethics does not rely on the construction of an autonomous order of meaning based on prohibition, but on a perspective that assumes the impossibility of building a completely autonomous order of meaning (253). In agreement with Glen Close, then, "What a literary narrative cannot provide, Rivera Garza seems to say, is that true knowledge or cognitive mastery of violence that the conventional detective hero still often claims" (409). In the end, a (male) character complains about the Detective's uselessness: "Then it's true that you never could find any evidence . . . Such a brutal case, and you with no evidence. Not even a motive. Or a weapon. Or a penis. Nothing. That's what your investigation came up with. Nothing."[23] And it seems that justice in Rivera Garza is not practiced as a simulacrum of police procedure; rather, it must always point to something beyond the text, outside the literary order, but also outside of legal discourse. As Copjec indicates, another ethics or another way of imagining justice is possible: "All we can suggest at this point is that the field of ethics has too long been theorized in terms of this particular superegoic logic of exception or limit. It is now time to devote some thought to developing an ethics of inclusion or of the unlimited ... Another logic of the superego must commence" (236).

Finally: The Work of the Author and the Literary Tradition

In *Los muertos indóciles* (The Disobedient Dead, 2013), Rivera Garza wonders, "What kinds of challenges does the exercise of writing face in an environment where the precariousness of work and the horrible sound of death constitute the substance of everyday life? What are the aesthetic and ethical dialogues that the act of writing, literally surrounded by dead people, throws us into?"[24] I would like to end this chapter with a concrete example of how her writing has generated discomfort for Mexican cultural institutions. Her latest book, *Había mucha neblina o humo o no sé qué* (There Was a Lot of Fog or Smoke or Who Knows What, 2016), is a chronicle—although it includes numerous instances of fiction—about the most influential Mexican writer of the twentieth century: Juan Rulfo (1917-1968). Despite being a lovely homage, the book became the center of a heated controversy when, on the centenary of Rulfo's birth in 2017, the president of the Rulfo Foundation, Víctor Jiménez, withdrew from the commemorative affair organized by the Autonomous University of Mexico (UNAM) because Rivera Garza was included on the schedule. He considered her book defamatory and prohibited the use of Rulfo's name in promoting the event. This then became a public dispute about the idea of the author as a figure that organizes the literary world as a regime of property and a system of production.

But what elements of the book did the Foundation find libelous? We could argue that they were precisely those elements associated with Rivera Garza's feminist perspective: her interest in the (re) productive labor that conditions every act of literary creation. The purpose of *Había mucha neblina* is clearly stated from the beginning: "What interests me most about Rulfo, just like everyone else, is his writing, but something even more: the content of his days as a writer . . . the material conditions that made it possible for a man born in 1917 in provincial Mexico to earn a living by writing." It is a book about the work of writing, but also about those other forms of work that accompany it and are seldom taken into consideration: "Indeed, in between doing the living and telling about living, one has to earn a living."[25]

Rulfo's writing illustrates the ravages wrought by modernization on the Mexican countryside, especially the displacement of rural laborers to urban centers. *Pedro Páramo* (1955), his only novel, narrates the history of the village of Comala, a place inhabited by the voices of a rural community of ghosts. At the stylistic level, the novel is decidedly experimental and represents the apex of Mexican high modernism. To explore the conditions of possibility that enabled the appearance of this very astonishing writing, Rivera Garza analyzes Rulfo's various jobs, particularly his role as advisor to the Papaloapan Commission, a modernizing project promoted by President Miguel Alemán (1946–1952). In the Commission's files, Rivera Garza finds Rulfo's photographs and descriptions of the Oaxacan indigenous communities, the oral and visual reports that would accompany the displacement of these people to make way for the construction of waterworks: "I still have the impression that the novelist's world is supported on the foundation of these two jobs."[26] It is this aspect that the Rulfo Foundation considered libelous, opining that Rivera Garza was accusing Rulfo of collaborationism. However, her writing explores something very different, which signals the experiential conditions through which a literary perspective is constructed: the writer's creation or genius is not *ex nihilo*, but stems from a concrete reality and a social relationship with others.

As part of her exploration, Rivera Garza visits the rural places where Rulfo had spent time for work-related reasons, tracing his itinerary to recuperate in some way the physical aspect: "I had been in his words, but now I wanted, God help me, to be in his shoes. And if that isn't love, then what is?" The route in her book leads to the town of San Juan Luvina, Oaxaca, where Rulfo got the inspiration for one of his most famous stories in *El llano en llamas* (*The Burning Plain*, 1953). Rulfo's own words and images of these Oaxacan communities accompany Rivera Garza's perspective, but she also takes detours, branching off, tracing other paths of reading. Accompanying is not repeating. It becomes a journey to cancel out the notion of cultural, geographic, and temporal "distance" in which modernizing projects were and continue to be constructed: "It is impossible to say the word *remote* without establishing the center from which it is enunciated ... I name you, says the speaker, and in naming you I distance you. Perhaps this is why in many of Mexico's modernizing plans from the mid-twentieth century the word *remote* underpins what is said or promised or about to be done."[27]

Upon arriving in San Juan de Luvina, Rivera Garza does not find desolation or distance but a well-attended party (sponsored by residents of Luvina now living in Los Angeles); she finds connections, communication, community, critical thinking, contemporaneity. The text incorporates not only the national historical memory that Rulfo constructed of these towns, but also how the towns remember Rulfo. However, it is not about "the paternalistic 'giving voice' of certain imperial subjects ... here, it is about writing practices that bring ... those others to the materiality of a text that is always, in this sense, forged relationally, that is, in community."[28]

But Rivera Garza's book is not only a travel chronicle; it is also a literal rewriting of Rulfo's texts. In the fourth chapter, Rivera Garza rewrites entire sections of *Pedro Páramo* to bring to light the fact that Comala is not just a deserted wasteland, but also a place full of sexual, joyful bodies where other forms of social organization and understanding of cultural and gendered identities can be perceived. Comala is a ruin, but it is also the site of an alternate sociability. While Mexican tradition has read *Pedro Páramo* as another form of the myth of male orphanhood and loneliness, Rivera Garza tells us that a different reading is possible, based on the way Rulfo actively incorporated female sexual desire in his texts: "While the cause has been the aloneness that isolates, the result will be the survival of a community that will otherwise be nothing but a box of ghosts. The future of Comala thus hangs on the liminal, nonnormative sexuality that already dominates its beds."[29] Rivera Garza asserts that through those bodies, Rulfo created an alternative reading of Mexican modernity. To illustrate this, she rewrites entire scenes of encounters as frankly feminist pornography. And indeed, for Rivera Garza, rewriting and curating is an essential practice of contemporary literature: "Reading rewritten paragraphs is a way of unreading . . . The one who rewrites, updates. The driving force of the rewriter is not nostalgia for the past, but the emergence of the present. This thing with no way out."[30]

Rivera Garza continues on present-day paths what Rulfo's writing bequeaths: a politics of memory for the bodies displaced by certain views of history. This is essential in a present marked by violence and the extreme impunity that benefits very specific sectors:

> Sometimes it seems like there are too many similarities between the vertical imposition of those modernizing projects that linked the Mexican economy with the global one throughout the twentieth century . . . and the economic and energy reforms imposed now by a neoliberal regime that involves both the Mexican State and that gang of savage capitalists that used to be known as *narcos*.[31]

To read the present violence, we need ways of writing that do not spectacularize violence without analyzing it—like narconarratives—but that go to the root of the interests that are again in play in the appropriation of resources from rural areas for transnational capital and on the displacement of communities through the violence of drug trafficking. The emergence of the present takes place precisely in those regions considered to be supposedly remote, there where capital is updated and communities are reorganized in ways still unimagined by those previously mentioned centers and their cultural institutions. Rivera Garza's book makes some people uncomfortable because it interrupts the transmission of a tradition by the codes of inertia, inviting us to interrupt the possibility of the past passing us by, unnoticed.

Thus, *Había mucha neblina* is not a libelous book; rather, it assumes a responsibility with present-day readers. What appears to be defamatory, then, is the question about work, production, property, and bodies: everything that relates to a feminist tradition that asserts that another mode of production, organization of social life, and communication is possible. What I have therefore learned to teach, accompanied by Rivera Garza, is that reading and writing in contemporary times is "the opposite of being alone."[32]

Notes

1. "No soy una defensora de la ignorancia, por supuesto. Pero en el mundo de la escritura, que es un mundo signado por la incertidumbre y el claroscuro, saber es, a menudo, saber demasiado" ("Saber demasiado").

2. "Saber en qué consiste el sentido temporal de tal contemporaneidad es, a decir de Gertrude Stein, el deber de todo escritor que no quiere vivir bajo la sombra del pasado o la imaginación del futuro" (*Los muertos indóciles* 31).

3. For this purpose, I follow the work of Kathi Weeks, who argues for the importance of not distinguishing between work and labor. Using Hannah Arendt's distinction "between labor as the activity that reproduces biological life and work as the creation of an object world" (14) runs the risk of creating a hierarchy of unequal value between them and making invisible the labor necessary for any work of art.

4. "La posibilidad de que este 'afuera' le imprima una nueva piel" (Guerrero 44).

5. "A diferencia de otras novelas históricas que narran las primeras dos décadas del siglo XX mexicano desde el ángulo de la revolución

[mexicana], ésta se dedica a contar las historias periféricas que han sido arrolladas por la narración hegemónica que surge en los años posteriores al triunfo constitucionalista" (Price).

6. For a reading of the discourses on how gender is produced in the novel and the instability of these roles, see Vinodh Venkatesh.

7. Here, I paraphrase Silvia Federici's assertion that "Reproductive work . . . is the work in which the contradictions inherent in 'alienated labor' are most explosive, which is why it is the ground zero for revolutionary practice, even if it is not the only ground zero" (2).

8. "¿Cómo se convierte uno en un fotógrafo de locos?" ("Reflejos" *Nadie me verá llorar*).

9. "Ver sin ser visto" ("La Diablesa" *Nadie me verá llorar*). "Joaquín desacostumbrado a oír la voz de los sujetos que fotografiaba, pensó que se trataba del murmullo de su propia conciencia" ("Reflejos" *Nadie me verá llorar*).

10. "–Te habías dado cuenta de que todas las equivocaciones empiezan por un nombre" ("La Diablesa" *Nadie me verá llorar*).

11. "En la ciudad de México, el doce por ciento de las mujeres entre quince y treinta años de edad eran o habían sido prostitutas alguna vez en su vida. Muchas eran huérfanas y solteras, auque las había también viudas, casadas y con hijos. Habían sido sirvientas, costureras, lavanderas, operarias y vendedoras ambulantes, cuyos salarios difícilmente rebasaban los veinticinco centavos diarios" ("La Diablesa" *Nadie me verá llorar*).

12. "Migración laboral, tráfico y prostitución son, cada vez más, salidas forzadas en el mundo entero para la supervivencia de miles de mujeres. Y es que sobre ellas se descarga el mayor impacto de los programas de ajuste estructural." "Además, el recorte de gastos de salud y educación también impacta fundamentalmente sobre las mujeres, ya que son ellas las que deben pasar a asumir y financiar esas dimensiones del cuidado." (Gago)

13. "Lo recordaría todo de improvisto y en detalle. Vería el anillo de jade alrededor del dedo anular y, de inmediato, vería el otro anillo de jade. Abriría los ojos desmesuradamente y, sin saber por qué, callaría. No preguntaría nada más. Diría: sí, muy hermoso. Lo es. Y pasaría las yemas de sus dedos sobre la delicada figura de las serpientes. Una caricia. El asomo de una caricia. Una mano inmóvil, abajo" (115).

14. "La novela policiaca construye una imagen intelectual de la represión, pero su verdadera función represiva no reside en el desenlace anecdótico de la trama, sino en la proyección de un superego capaz de disciplinar la dispersión de los elementos narrativos en *la consciencia del lector* . . . El género postula una transparencia absoluta que resulta represiva en sí misma. Esta transparencia, presupuesta en la imagen del detective, reproduce sutilmente el panóptico, cuya perspectiva central accede el lector identificándose con el detective" (39).

15. "El imperio de la autoría, en tanto productora de sentido, se ha desplazado de manera radical de la unicidad del autor hacia la función del lector" (*Los muertos indóciles* 22).

16. "Siempre quise un anillo así" (118); "¿Lo vendes?" (118).

17. "–Esto . . . es mi trabajo. Así me gano la vida. No es un *hobby*, por si te interesa saberlo. –Puedo pagarte dos o tres veces más de lo que ganas. –Que sean cuatro –respondió de inmediato . . . El dinero. El dinero siempre hacía de las suya con ella . . . El hallazgo y el dinero. La cadena del mundo natural. Cuando se metió bajo las sábanas pensó que no le molestaría en lo más mínimo que fueran de seda" (123).

18. "La Detective la visitaba para darle malas noticias: ningún dato, ningún hallazgo, ninguna información" (129).

19. "Buen trabajo" (130); "La Detective agachó la cabeza pero elevó la mirada. Los codos sobre las rodillas, los billetes en la mano, y los pies en el agua tibia, aromática. Una imagen extraña. Una imagen fuera de lugar. La corrupción de los sentidos" (131).

20. "–Falta de indicios … Ya sabes. Una ejecución más. Una de tantas" (127).

21. "La víctima siempre es femenina" (28). "Todos se acostumbrarían a hablar del asesino en femenino. Nadie encontraría, sin embargo, una forma gramatical adecuada para masculinizar a *la víctima*" (228).

22. "Lo que en realidad pasa: Eso no lo puede saber la novela" (107).

23. "–Entonces es cierto que nunca pudiste encontrar evidencias . . . Un caso tan brutal y tú sin evidencias. Ni motivo. Ni arma. Ni pene. Nada. Eso fue lo que produjo tu investigación. Nada" (263).

24. "¿Qué tipo de retos enfrenta el ejercicio de la escritura en un medio donde la precariedad del trabajo y la muerte horrísona constituyen la materia de todos los días? ¿Cuáles son los diálogos estéticos y éticos

a los que nos avienta el hecho de escribir, literalmente, rodeado de muertos?" (19).

25. "Me interesaba . . . lo que a todo mundo le interesa de Rulfo, que es su escritura, pero todavía algo más: la materia de sus días como escritor . . . las condiciones materiales que hicieron posible que un hombre nacido en 1917 en la provincia mexicana pudiera ganarse la vida escribiendo"(13-14). "En efecto, entre vivir la vida y contar la vida hay que ganarse la vida" (14).

26. "Sigo con la impresión de que el mundo del novelista continúa sosteniéndose sobre los cimientos de estos dos empleos" (15).

27. "Había estado en sus palabras pero ahora quería, válgame, estar en sus zapatos. Y si eso no es amor, ¿entonces qué es?" (16). "Es imposible pronunciar la pablara *remoto* sin establecer el centro desde el cual se enuncia . . . Yo te nombro, dice el hablante, y al nombrarte te alejo. Tal vez por eso en muchos de los planes modernizadores de mediados del siglo XX mexicano la palabra *remoto* apuntala lo dicho o lo prometido o lo que está por hacerse" (117).

28. "Lejos, pues, del paternalista 'dar voz' de ciertas subjetividades imperiales . . . se trata aquí de prácticas de escritura que traen a . . . esos otros a la materialidad de un texto que es, en este sentido, siempre un texto fraguado relacionalmente, es decir, en comunidad" (*Los muertos indóciles* 23).

29. "Si la causa ha sido la soledad que acorrala, el resultado será la supervivencia de una comunidad que, de otra manera, no podrá sino ser una caja de espectros. El futuro de Comala pende así de la sexualidad no normativa y liminal que domina ya sus lechos" (185).

30. "Leer párrafos reescritos es una forma de desleer . . . Quien reescribe, actualiza. El motor del reescritor no es la nostalgia por el pasado, sino la emergencia del presente. Esta cosa sin salida" (*Los muertos indóciles* 95).

31. "A veces me parece que hay demasiadas semejanzas entre la imposición vertical de esos proyectos modernizadores que articularon la economía mexicana con la mundial a lo largo del siglo XX . . . y las reformas económicas y energéticas impuestas ahora por un régimen neoliberal que involucra por igual al Estado mexicano y a esa gavilla de capitalistas salvajes que solían ser conocidos como *narcos*" (21).

32. "Lo opuesto a la soledad" (230).

Works Cited

Close, Glen. "*Antinovela negra*: Cristina Rivera Garza's *La muerte me da* and the Critical Contemplation of Violence in Contemporary Mexico." *MLN* 129.2, 2014, pp. 391-411.

Copjec, Joan. *Read My Desire: Lacan against the Historicist*. Verso, 2015.

Estrada, Oswaldo, editor. "Cristina Rivera Garza, en-clave de transgresión." *Cristina Rivera Garza: ningún crítico cuenta esto*. U of North Carolina; Eón, 2010.

Federici, Silvia. *Revolution at Point Zero: Housework, Reproduction, and Feminist Struggle*. PM Press; Common Notions, 2012.

Gago, Verónica. "El factor invisible." Entrevista con Saskia Sassen. *Página 12*, May 18, 2007. https://www.pagina12.com.ar/diario/suplementos/las12/13-3367-2007-05-18.html. Accessed July 15, 2017.

Guerrero, Javier. *Tecnologías del cuerpo: exhibicionismo y visualidad en América Latina*. Iberoamericana Vervuert, 2014.

Price, Brian L. "Cristina Rivera Garza en las orillas de la historia." *Cristina Rivera Garza: ningún crítico cuenta esto*. Edited by Oswaldo Estrada. U of North Carolina; Eón, 2010.

Resina, Joan Ramón. *El cadáver en la cocina: la novela criminal en la cultura del desencanto*. Anthropos, 2001.

Rivera Garza, Cristina. *La frontera más distante*. Tusquets, 2008.

_____. *Había mucha niebla o humo o no sé qué*. Random House, 2016.

_____. *La muerte me da*. Tusquets, 2010.

_____. *Los muertos indóciles: necroescritura y desapropiación*. Tusquets, 2013.

_____. *Nadie me verá llorar*. Tusquets, 2013.

_____. *No One Will See Me Cry*. Translated by Andrew Hurley. Curbstone, 2003.

_____. "Saber demasiado." Estrada, *Cristina Rivera Garza*.

_____. "The Criminalization of the Syphilitic Body: Prostitutes, Health Crimes, and Society in Mexico City, 1867-1930." *Crime and Punishment in Latin America: Law and Society since Late Colonial Times*. Edited by Ricardo D. Salvatore and Carlos Aguirre. Duke UP, 2001, pp. 147-81.

Silverstein, Stephen. "Ragpickers of Modernity: Cristina Rivera Garza's *Nadie me verá llorar* and Walter Benjamin's *Theses on the Philosophy of History.*" *Revista de Estudios Hispánicos* 47.3, 2013, pp. 533-59.

Venkatesh, Vinodh. "Transgresiones de la masculinidad: ciudad y género en *Nadie me verá llorar. Cristina Rivera Garza: ningún crítico cuenta esto.* Edited by Oswaldo Estrada. U of North Carolina; Eón, 2010.

Weeks, Kathi. *The Problem with Work: Feminism, Marxism, Antiwork Politics, and Postwork Imaginaries.* Duke UP, 2011.

RESOURCES

Further Reading

1980	*Respiración artificial* Ricardo Piglia (Argentina) *La misteriosa desaparición de la marquesita de Loria* José Donoso (Chile) *Sólo cenizas hallarás* Pedro Vergés (Dominican Republic) *La biografía difusa de Sombra Castañeda* Marcio Veloz Maggiolo (Dominican Republic)
1981	*La guerra del fin del mundo* Mario Vargas Llosa (Peru) *La vida exagerada de Martín Romaña* Alfredo Bryce Echenique (Peru)
1982	*La casa de los espíritus* Isabel Allende (Chile) *La tejedora de coronas* German Espinosa (Colombia) *La insurrección* Antonio Skármeta (Chile) *La última canción de Manuel Sendero* Ariel Dorfman (Chile)
1983	*Lumpérica* Diamela Eltit (Chile) *Luna caliente* Mempo Giardinelli (Argentina) *El entenado* Juan José Saer (Argentina)
1984	*Sin remedio* Antonio Caballero (Colombia) *Arturo, la estrella más brillante* Reinaldo Arenas (Cuba) *Colibrí* Severo Sarduy (Cuba)
1985	*El amor en los tiempos del cólera* Gabriel García Márquez (Colombia) *Frente a un hombre armado (Cacerías de 1848)* Mauricio Wácquez (Chile) *El desfile del amor* Sergio Pitol (Mexico)

| 1986 | *La nieve del almirante* Álvaro Mutis (Colombia) |
| | *Glosa* Juan José Saer (Argentina) |

1987	*Noticias del imperio* Fernando del Paso (Mexico)
	Una novela china César Aira (Argentina)
	Maitreya Severo Sarduy (Cuba)
	Los búfalos, los jerarcas y la huesera Ana Vásquez (Chile)

1988	*El imperio de los sueños* Giannina Braschi (Puerto Rico)
	O Alquimista Paulo Coelho (Brazil)
	El cuarto mundo Diamela Eltit (Chile)
	Cae la noche tropical Manuel Puig (Argentina)
	A sus plantas rendido un león Osvaldo Soriano (Argentina)

| 1989 | *Como agua para chocolate* Laura Esquivel (Mexico) |
| | *Un viejo que leía novelas de amor* Luis Sepúlveda (Chile) |

1990	*Agosto* Rubem Fonseca (Brazil)
	Una sombra ya pronto serás Osvaldo Soriano (Argentina)
	La visita en el tiempo Arturo Uslar Pietri (Venezuela)
	En estado de memoria Tununa Mercado (Argentina)
	Los fantasmas César Aira (Argentina)
	Realidad nacional desde la cama Luisa Valenzuela (Argentina)

1991	*La gesta del Marrano* Marcos Aguinis (Argentina)
	Santo oficio de la memoria Mempo Giardinelli (Argentina)
	Crónica de un iniciado Abelardo Castillo (Argentina)

| 1992 | *Antes que anochezca* Reinaldo Arenas (Cuba) |
| | *Tinísima* Elena Poniatowska (Mexico) |

La loca de Gandoca Anacristina Rossi (Costa Rica)
Vigilia del almirante Augusto Roa Bastos (Paraguay)

1993	*Cuando ya no importe* Juan Carlos Onetti (Uruguay) *Empresas y tribulaciones de Maqroll el Gaviero* Álvaro Mutis (Colombia) *El rastro* Jorge Gómez Jiménez (Venezuela) *Casa de campo* José Donoso (Chile) *Leopardo al sol* Laura Restrepo (Colombia) *Un campeón desparejo* Adolfo Bioy Casares (Argentina) *Los pichiciegos* Fogwill (Argentina)
1994	*Los vigilantes* Diamela Eltit (Chile) *Del amor y otros demonios* Gabriel García Márquez (Colombia) *In the Time of the Butterflies* Julia Álvarez (USA) *La pesquisa* Juan José Saer (Argentina) *La virgen de los sicarios* Fernando Vallejo (Colombia) *La guerra de Galio* Héctor Aguilar Camín (Chile)
1995	*Maqroll el gaviero* Álvaro Mutis (Colombia) *La nada cotidiana* Zoé Valdés (Cuba) *El cartero de Neruda (Ardiente paciencia)* Antonio Skármeta (Chile) *Santa Evita* Tomás Eloy Martínez (Argentina) *El miedo a los animals* Enrique Serna (Mexico) *Cartas cruzadas* Darío Jaramillo (Colombia) *No me esperen en abril* Alfredo Bryce Echenique (Peru)
1996	*El Cristo feo* Alicia Yánez Cossío (Ecuador) *Estrella distante* Roberto Bolaño (Chile) *Mal de amores* Ángeles Mastretta (Mexico) *El arte de la fuga* Sergio Pitol (Mexico) *Ella cantaba boleros* Guillermo Cabrera Infante (Cuba) *El jardín de al lado* José Donoso (Chile)

1997	*Plata quemada* Ricardo Piglia (Argentina)
	La noche es virgen Jaime Bayly (Peru)
	La muerte como efecto secundario Ana María Shua (Argentina)

1998	*Arráncame la vida* Ángeles Mastreta (Mexico)
	Yo-Yo Boing! Giannina Braschi (Puerto Rico)
	Los detectives salvajes Roberto Bolaño (Chile)
	Como un mensajero tuyo Mayra Montero (Cuba)
	El hombre, la hembra y el hambre Daína Chaviano (Cuba)
	El desierto y su semilla Jorge Barón Biza (Argentina)
	Como un mensajero tuyo (*The Messenger*) Mayra Montero (Cuba)
	Margarita está linda la mar Sergio Ramírez (Nicaragua)

1999	*Los años con Laura Díaz* Carlos Fuentes (Mexico)
	La orilla africana Rodrigo Rey Rosa (Guatemala)
	Rosario Tijeras Jorge Franco (Colombia)
	Porque parece mentira la verdad nunca se sabe Daniel Sada (Mexico)
	En busca de Klingsor Jorge Volpi (Mexico)
	La orilla Africana Rodrigo Rey Rosa (Guatemala)

2000	*La fiesta del chivo* Mario Vargas Llosa (Peru)
	Dois irmãos Milton Hatoum (Brazil)
	Una cierta nostalgia María Eugenia Ramos Suazo (Honduras)
	Salón de belleza Mario Bellatin (Mexico)
	La historia de Horacio Tomás González (Colombia)

2001	*La reina de América* Jorge Majfud (Uruguay)
	El desbarrancadero Fernando Vallejo (Colombia)
	Cumpleaños César Aira (Argentina)
	Eles eram muitos cavalos Luiz Ruffato (Brazil)
	La azotea Fernanda Trías (Uruguay)

2002	*Ojos, de otro mirar: poemas* Homero Aridjis (Mexico)
	Poesía Dulce María Loynaz (Cuba)
	El traductor Salvador Benesdra (Argentina)
	El vuelo de la reina Tomás Eloy Martínez (Argentina)
	Nove Noites Bernardo Carvalho (Brazil)
	El hijo de casa Dante Liano (Guatemala)
	Los impostores Santiago Gamboa (Colombia)
2003	*El paraíso en la otra esquina* Mario Vargas Llosa (Peru)
	El pasado Alan Pauls (Argentina)
	El delirio de Turing Edmundo Paz Soldán (Bolivia)
	La silla del Águila Carlos Fuentes (Mexico)
	Las películas de mi vida Alberto Fuguet (Chile)
	Diablo guardián Xavier Velasco (Mexico)
	Monkey Hunting Cristina García (USA-Cuba)
	Jardines de Kensington Rodrigo Fresán (Argentina)
	Angosta Héctor Abad Faciolince (Colombia)
2004	*2666* Roberto Bolaño (Chile)
	El testigo Juan Villoro (Mexico)
	La eternidad del instante Zoé Valdés (Cuba)
	El testigo Juan Villoro (Mexico)
	La burla del tiempo Mauricio Electorat (Chile)
	El inútil de la familia Jorge Edwards (Chile)
	Rosario Tijeras Jorge Franco Ramos (Colombia)
2005	*La novela luminosa* Mario Levrero (Uruguay)
	Adiós Hemingway Leonardo Padura Fuentes (Cuba)
	A.B.U.R.T.O. Heriberto Yépez (México)
	La grande Juan José Saer (Argentina)
	La otra mano de Lepanto Carmen Boullosa (Mexico)
	La sexta lámpara Pablo de Santis (Argentina)
	Memorias de mis putas tristes Gabriel García Márquez (Colombia)

2006	*El buscador de cabezas* Antonio Ortuño (Mexico)
	La isla de los amores infinitos (*The Island of Eternal Love*) Daína Chaviano (Cuba)
	Abril rojo Santiago Roncagliolo (Peru)
	Las genealogías Margo Glantz (Mexico)
	Saga. A História de Quatro Gerações de uma Família Japonesa no Brasil Ryoki Inoue (Brazil)
	Yawara! A Travessia Nihondin-Brasil Júlio Miyazawa (Brazil)
	Bonsái Alejandro Zambra (Chile)
	Corpo Estranho Adriana Lunardi (Brazil)

2007	*The Brief Wondrous Life of Oscar Wao* Junot Díaz (USA-Dominican Republic)
	Jamás el fuego nunca Diamela Eltit (Chile)
	A guerra dos bastardos Ana Paula Maia (Brazil)
	La vida no es una tómbola Siu Kam Wen (Peru)
	Radio Ciudad Perdida Daniel Alarcón (Peru-USA)
	O Sol Se Põe em São Paulo Bernardo Carvalho (Brazil)
	Historia secreta de Costaguana Juan Gabriel Vásquez (Colombia)
	Un chino en bicicleta Ariel Magnus (Argentina)
	El lugar del cuerpo Rodrigo Hasbún (Bolivia)

2008	*O Súbito (Banzai, Massateru!)* Jorge J. Okubaro (Brazil)
	Tirana memoria Horacio Castellanos Molla (Honduras)
	La iluminación de Katzuo Nakamatsu Augusto Higa (Peru)
	Os Livros de Sayuri Lúcia Hiratsuka (Brazil)

2009	*Las grietas de Jara* Claudia Piñeiro (*A Crack in the Wall* 2013) (Argentina)
	España, aparta de mí estos premios Fernando Iwasaki (Peru)
	El verano largo Siu Kam Wen (Peru)
	El viajero del siglo Andrés Neuman (Argentina)

Un lugar llamado Oreja de Perro Iván Thays (Peru)
Señales que precederán al fin del mundo. Yuri Herrera (Mexico)

2010	*El país de las mujeres* Gioconda Belli (Nicaragua) *La hora de los monos* Federico Falco (Argentina) *Fiesta en la madriguera* Juan Pablo Villalobos (Mexico)
2011	*Verde Shangai* Cristina Rivera Garza (Mexico) *United States of Banana* Giannina Braschi (Puerto Rico) *Nihonjin* Oscar Nakasato (Brazil) *Betibú* Claudia Piñeiro (Argentina) *Norte* Edmundo Paz Soldán (Bolivia) *El daño no es de ayer* Ignacio Padilla (Mexico) *El espíritu de mis padres sigue subiendo en la lluvia* Patricio Pron (Argentina) *Los ingrávidos* Valeria Luiselli (Mexico)
2012	*Plegarias para un zorro* Enza García Arreaza (Venezuela) *El viento que arrasa* Selva Almada (Argentina)
2013	*La libertad total* Pablo Katchadjian (Argentina) *Muerte súbita* Álvaro Enrique (Mexico) *Rojo semidesierto* Joel Flores (Mexico) *¡Alemania, Alemania!* Felipe Polleri (Uruguay) *Todos Nós Adorávamos Caúbois* Carol Bensimon (Brazil) *La tarde de los sucesos definitivos* Carlos Manuel Álvarez (Cuba) *En medio de extrañas víctimas* Daniel Saldaña París (Mexico)
2014	*Tríptico de la infamia* Pablo Montoya (Colombia) *La historia de mis dientes* Valerie Luiselli (Mexico)

Nossos Ossos Marcelino Freire (Brazil)
Distancia de rescate Samanta Schweblin (Argentina)
Canción de tumba (Julián Herbert)
Después del invierno Guadalupe Nettel (Mexico)

2015	*Metástasis McFly* Pedro J. Acuña (Mexico)
	Los accidentes Camila Fabbri (Argentina)
	Mongolia Julia Wong (Peru)
	Los trabajos del amor Damián González Bertolino (Uruguay)
	Puente adentro Arnoldo Gálvez (Guatemala)
	No te ama Camila Gutiérrez (Chile)
	Un rojo aullido en el bosque José Adiak Montoya (Nicaragua)
	El invierno con mi generación Mauro Libertella (Argentina)
	Coronel lágrimas Carlos Fonseca (Costa Rica/Puerto Rico)
	Los echamos de menos Óscar Guillermo Solano (Mexico)
	Umami Laia Jufresa (Mexico)
	Antifaces Jennifer Thorndike (Peru)
2016	*El futuro es un lugar extraño* Cynthia Rimsky (Chile)
	Una canción de Bob Dylan en la agenda de mi madre Sergio Galarza (Peru)
	Nuestro mundo muerto Liliana Colanzi (Bolivia)
	Las tierras arrasadas Emiliano Monge (Mexico)
	Qué vergüenza Paulina Flores (Chile)
	Tláloc, piedra de agua Ave Barrera (Mexico)
	Acerca de Suárez Francisco Ovando (Chile)
	Borrador final Marcela Ribadeneira (Ecuador)
	Os maus modos Carol Rodrigues (Brazil)
	Black Out María Moreno (Argentina)
2017	*Los jóvenes no pueden volver a casa* Mario Martz (Nicaragua)

Bibliography

Alarcón, Norma. *Bibliography of Hispanic Women Writers.* Chicano-Riqueño Studies, 1980.

André, María, and Eva Bueno, editors. *Latin American Women Writers: An Encyclopedia* Routledge, 2008.

Avelar, Idelber. *The Untimely Present: Postdictatorial Latin American Fiction and the Task of Mourning.* Duke UP, 1999.

Balderston, Daniel, and Mike Gonzalez, editors. *Encyclopedia of Latin American and Caribbean literature, 1900-2003.* Routledge, 2004.

Barnstone, Willis. *Literatures of Latin America: From Antiquity to the Present.* Prentice Hall, 1999.

Bassnett, Susan, editor. *Knives and Angels: Women Writers in Latin America.* Zed Books, 1990.

Bethell, Leslie, editor. *A Cultural History of Latin America: Literature, Music, and the Visual Arts in the 19th and 20th Centuries.* Cambridge UP, 1998.

Beverley, John. *Against Literature.* U of Minnesota P, 1993.

Bhalla, Alok. *Latin American Writers: A Bibliography with Critical and Biographical Introductions.* Envoy, 1987.

Bleznick, Donald. *A Source Book for Hispanic Literature and Language: A Selected, Annotated Guide to Spanish, Spanish-American, and Chicano Bibliography, Literature, Linguistics, Journals, and Other Source Materials.* 3rd ed. Scarecrow, 1995.

Boland, Roy C., and Sally Harvey, editors. *Magical Realism and Beyond: The Contemporary Spanish and Latin American Novel.* Vox/AHS, 1991.

Bloom, Harold, editor. *Modern Latin American Fiction.* Chelsea House, 1990.

Brower, Keith H. *Contemporary Latin American Fiction: An Annotated Bibliography.* Scarecrow, 1989.

Bryant, Shasta M. *A Selective Bibliography of Bibliographies of Hispanic-American Literature.* 2nd ed. U of Texas at Austin, 1976.

Calimano, Ivan E. *Index to Spanish Language Short Stories in Anthologies.* SALALM Secretariat, General Library, U of New Mexico, 1994.

Castillo, Debra A. *Talking Back: Toward a Latin American Feminist Literary Criticism.* Cornell UP, 1992.

Castro-Klaren, Sara, editor. *Companion to Latin American Literature and Culture.* Blackwell, 2008.

Chamberlain, Bobby J. *Portuguese Language and Luso-Brazilian Literature: An Annotated Guide to Selected Reference Works.* MLA, 1989.

Cohen, John Michael. *Latin American Writing Today.* Penguin, 1967.

Colvile, Georgiana M. M. *Contemporary Women Writing in Other Americas.* Mellen, 1996.

Condé, Lisa P., and Stephen M. Hart, editors. *Feminist Readings on Spanish and Latin-American Literature.* Mellen, 1991.

Cortés, Eladio. *Dictionary of Mexican Literature.* Greenwood, 1992.

Corvalan, Graciela N. V. *Latin American Women Writers in English Translation: A Bibliography.* Latin American Studies Center, California State U, 1980.

De la Campa, Roman. *Latin Americanism.* U of Minessota P, 1999.

Fenwick, M. J. *Writers of the Caribbean and Central America: A Bibliography.* Garland, 1992.

Fernández Moreno, César, Julio Ortega, and Ivan A. Schulman, editors. *Latin America in Its Literature.* Translated by Mary G. Berg, Holme and Meier, 1980.

Flores, Ángel. *Spanish American Authors: The Twentieth Century.* Wilson, 1992.

Forster, Merlin H., editor. *Tradition and Renewal: Essays on Twentieth-Century Latin American Literature and Culture.* U of Illinois P, 1975.

Foster, David William. *Argentine Literature: A Research Guide.* 2nd ed. Garland, 1982.

_____. *Brazilian Literature: A Research Bibliography.* Garland, 1990.

_____. *Chilean Literature: A Working Bibliography of Secondary Sources.* Hall, 1978.

_____. *Cuban Literature: A Research Guide.* Garland, 1985.

_____. *Cultural Diversity in Latin American Literature.* U of New Mexico P, 1994.

_____. *Latin American Writers on Gay and Lesbian Themes: A Biocritical Sourcebook*. Greenwood, 1994.

_____. *Manual of Hispanic Bibliography*. 2nd, rev. and expanded ed. Garland, 1977.

_____. *Mexican Literature: A Bibliography of Secondary Sources*. 2nd ed. Scarecrow, 1982.

_____. *Peruvian Literature: A Bibliography of Secondary Sources*. Greenwood, 1981.

_____. *Puerto Rican Literature: A Bibliography of Secondary Sources*. Greenwood, 1982.

_____. *The Twentieth Century Spanish-American Novel: A Bibliographic Guide*. Scarecrow, 1975.

_____. *The Twentieth-Century Spanish-American Novel: A Bibliographic Guide*. Scarecrow, 1975.

_____. editor. *A Dictionary of Contemporary Brazilian Authors*. Center for Latin American Studies, Arizona State U, 1982.

_____. editor. *A Dictionary of Contemporary Latin American Authors*. Center for Latin American Studies, Arizona State U, 1975.

_____. editor. *Handbook of Latin American Literature*. Garland, 1992.

_____. and Daniel Altamiranda, editors. *The Twentieth-Century Spanish-American literature since 1960*. Garland, 1997.

_____. and Virginia Ramos Foster, editors. *Modern Latin American literature (A Library of Literary Criticism)*. Ungar, 1975.

Franco, Jean. *An Introduction to Spanish-American Literature*. 3rd. ed. Cambridge UP, 1994.

_____. editor. *The Decline and Fall of the Lettered City: Latin America in the Cold War*. Harvard UP, 2002.

_____. *An Introduction to Spanish American Literature*. Cambridge UP, 1994.

_____. *Plotting Women: Gender and Representation in Mexico*. Columbia UP, 1989.

_____. *Spanish American Literature since Independence*. Ernest Benn, 1973.

Freudenthal, Juan R. *Index to Anthologies of Latin American Literature in English Translation*. Hall, 1977.

Gallagher, David Patrick. *Modern Latin American Literature*. Oxford UP, 1973.

González Echevarría, Roberto, editor. *The Oxford Book of Latin American Short Stories*. Oxford UP, 1997.

González Echevarría, Roberto, and Enrique Pupo-Walker, editors. *The Cambridge History of Latin American Literature*. Cambridge UP, 1996.

Goodrich, Diana Sorensen. *The Reader and the Text: Interpretative Strategies for Latin American Literatures*. Benjamins, 1986.

Goslinga, Marian. *Caribbean Literature: A Bibliography*. Scarecrow, 1998.

Gracia, Jorge, editor. *Philosophy and Literature in Latin America: A critical Assessment of the Current Situation*. SUNY P, 1989.

Harss, Luis, and Barbara Dohmann. *Into the Mainstream: Conversations with Latin American Writers*. Harper, 1967.

Herdeck, Donald E., et al. *Caribbean Writers: A Bio-Bibliographical-Critical Encyclopedia*. Three Continents, 1979.

Higgins, James. *A History of Peruvian Literature*. Cairns, 1987.

Hulet, Claude. *Brazilian literature*. Georgetown UP, 1974-75.

Jackson, Richard L. *The Afro-Spanish American Author: An Annotated Bibliography of Criticism*. Garland, 1980.

Johnson, Harvey Leroy, editor. *Contemporary Latin American Literature: A Conference Held under the Auspices of the Committee on Latin American Studies, University of Houston*. U of Houston, 1973.

Kaminsky, Amy K. *Reading the Body Politic: Feminist Criticism and Latin American Women Writers*. U of Minnesota P, 1993.

Kanellos, Nicolás. *Biographical Dictionary of Hispanic Literature in the United States: The Literature of Puerto Ricans, Cuban Americans, and Other Hispanic Writers*. Greenwood, 1989.

King, John, editor. *Modern Latin American Fiction: A Survey*. Faber, 1987.

Klein, Leonard S., editor. *Latin American Literature in the 20th Century: A Guide*. Ungar, 1986.

Kristal, Efraín, editor. *The Cambridge Companion to the Latin American Novel*. Cambridge UP, 2005.

Krstovic, Jelena, editor. *Hispanic Literature Criticism*. Gale, 1994.

Leonard, Kathy S. *Index to Translated Short Fiction by Latin American Women in English Language Anthologies.* Greenwood, 1997.

Lindstrom, Naomi. *Twentieth-Century Spanish American Fiction.* U of Texas P, 1994.

Lichtblau, Myron I. *The Argentine Novel: An Annotated Bibliography.* Scarecrow, 1997.

Lockhart, Darrell B., editor. *Jewish Writers of Latin America: A Dictionary.* Garland, 1997.

Luis, William, editor. *Modern Latin-American Fiction Writers.* Gale, 1992.

_____. *Voices from Under: Black Narrative in Latin America and the Caribbean.* Contributions in Afro-American and African Studies. Greenwood, 1984.

Minc, Rose S., editor. *Latin American Fiction Today: A Symposium.* Montclair State College and Hispamérica, 1979.

MacAdam, Alfred J. *Modern Latin American Narratives: The Dreams of Reason.* U of Chicago P, 1977.

Magill, Frank N. editor. *Masterpieces of Latino Literature.* HarperCollins, 1994.

Magnarelli, Sharon. *The Lost Rib: Female Characters in the Spanish-American Novel.* Bucknell UP, 1985.

Martin, Gerald, editor. *Journeys through the Labyrinth: Latin American Fiction in the Twentieth Century.* Verso, 1989.

Martínez, Julio A. *Dictionary of Twentieth-Century Cuban Literature.* Greenwood, 1990.

Marting, Diane E., editor. *Women Writers of Spanish America: An Annotated Bio- Bibliographical Guide.* Greenwood, 1987.

Martínez, Julio A. *Dictionary of Twentieth Century Cuban Literature.* Greenwood, 1990.

Messinger Cypess, Sandra, David R. Kohut, and Rachelle Moore. *Women Authors of Modern Hispanic South America: A Biography of Literary Criticism and Interpretation.* Scarecrow, 1989.

Meyer, Doris, and Margarite Fernandez Olmos, editors. *Contemporary Women Authors of Latin America.* Brooklyn College P, 1983.

Miller, Beth, editor. *Women in Hispanic Literature: Icons and Fallen Idols.* U of California P, 1983.

Millington, Mark I., and Paul Julian Smith, editors. *New Hispanisms: Literature, Culture, Theory*. Dovehouse, 1994.

Moss, Joyce, and Lorraine Valestuk. *Latin American Literature and Its Times*. Gale, 1999.

Paravisini-Gebert, Lizabeth, and Olga Torres-Seda, compilers. *Caribbean Women Novelists: An Annotated Critical Bibliography* Greenwood, 1993.

Paz Soldán, Edmundo, and Debra A. Castillo, editor. *Beyond the Lettered City: Latin American Literature and Mass Media*. Garland, 2000.

_____. *Latin American Literature and Mass Media*. Psychology Press, 2001.

Peacock, Scot, editor. *Hispanic Writers: A Selection of Sketches from Contemporary Authors*. 2nd ed. Gale, 1999.

Plimpton, George, editor. *Latin American Writers at Work*. Modern Library, 2003.

Pratt, Mary Louise, editor. *Imperial Eyes: Travel Writing and Transculturation*. Routledge, 1992.

Preuss, Mary M., editor. *Past, Present, and Future: Selected Papers on Latin American Indian Literatures*. Labyrinthos, 1991.

Rela, Walter, compiler. *A Bibliographical Guide to Spanish American Literature: Twentieth Century Sources*. Greenwood, 1988.

Rice Corina, Lynn Ellen. *Spanish-American Women Writers: A Bibliographical Research Checklist*. Garland, 1983.

Rogers, Elizabeth S., editor. *In Retrospect: Essays on Latin American Literature*. Spanish Literature, 1987.

Román-Lagunas, Jorge. *The Chilean Novel: A Critical Study of Secondary Sources and a Bibliography*. Scarecrow, 1995.

Ryan, Bryan, editor. *Hispanic Writers: A Selection of Sketches from "Contemporary Authors."* Gale, 1991.

Shaw, Bradley A. *Latin American Literature in English Translation: An Annotated Bibliography*. New York UP, 1976.

Siskind, Mariano. *Cosmopolitan Desires. Global Modernity and World Literature in Latin America*. Northwestern UP, 2014.

Smith, Paul Julian. *The Body Hispanic: Gender and Sexuality in Spanish and Spanish American Literature*. Clarendon, 1989.

_____. *Representing the Other: "Race," Text, and Gender in Spanish and Spanish American Narrative*. Clarendon, 1992.

Smith, Verity, editor. *Concise Encyclopedia of Latin American Literature*. Fiztroy Dearborn, 2000.

_____. *Encyclopedia of Latin American Literature*. Fitzroy Dearborn, 1997.

Solé, Carlos A., and María Isabel Abreu. *Latin American Writers*. Scribner's, 1989.

Solé Carlos, A., and Klaus Müller-Bergh, editors. *Latin American Writers. Supplement I*. Scribner's, 2002.

Sommer, Doris. *Foundational Fictions. The National Romances of Latin America*. U of California P, 1991.

Stavans, Ilan, editor. *Mutual Impressions: Writers from the Americas Reading One Another*. Duke UP, 1999.

Stern, Irwin. *Dictionary of Brazilian Literature*. Greenwood, 1988.

Valdés, Mario J., and Djelal Kadir, editors. *Literary Cultures of Latin America: A Comparative History*. Oxford UP, 2004.

Tompkins, Cynthia Margarita. *Latin American Postmodernisms. Women Writers and Experimentation*. UP of Florida, 2006.

Williams, Raymond Leslie, editor. *The Postmodern Novel in Latin America: Politics, Culture and the Crisis of Truth*. St. Martin's, 1995.

Wilson, Jason. *An A To Z of Modern Latin American Literature in English Translation*. Institute of Latin American Studies, 1989.

Woodbridge, Hensley Charles. *Guide to Reference Works for the Study of the Spanish Language and Literature and Spanish American Literature*. 2nd ed. MLA, 1997.

_____. *Spanish and Spanish-American Literature: An Annotated Guide to Selected Bibliographies*. MLA, 1983.

Zubatsky, David S. *Latin American Literary Authors: An Annotated Guide to Bibliographies*. Scarecrow, 1986.

About the Editor

Ignacio López-Calvo is Professor of Latin American literature at the University of California, Merced. He is the author of more than seventy articles and book chapters, as well as eight books on Latin American and US Latino literature and culture: *Saudades of Japan and Brazil: Contested Modernities in Lusophone Nikkei Cultural Production* (U of Colorado P, forthcoming), *Dragons in the Land of the Condor: Tusán Literature and Knowledge in Peru* (Arizona UP, 2014), *The Affinity of the Eye: Writing Nikkei in Peru* (U of Arizona P, 2013), *Latino Los Angeles in Film and Fiction: The Cultural Production of Social Anxiety* (U of Arizona P, 2011), *Imaging the Chinese in Cuban Literature and Culture* (UP of Florida, 2007), *"Trujillo and God": Literary and Cultural Representations of the Dominican Dictator* (UP of Florida, 2005), *Religión y militarismo en la obra de Marcos Aguinis 1963-2000* (Mellen, 2002), and *Written in Exile. Chilean Fiction from 1973-Present* (Routledge, 2001). He has also edited the books *Latinx Writing Los Angeles: Nonfiction Dispatches from a Decolonial Rebellion* (U of Nebraska P, forthcoming), *The Humanities in the Age of Information and Post-Truth*, coedited with Christina Lux (Northwestern UP, forthcoming Spring 2018), *The Humanities in a World Upside Down* (Cambridge Scholars, forthcoming), *Critical Insights: Roberto Bolaño* (Salem, 2015), *Roberto Bolaño, A Less Distant Star: Critical Essays* (Palgrave, 2015), *Critical Insights: Magical Realism* (Salem, 2014), *Peripheral Transmodernities: South-to-South Dialogues between the Luso-Hispanic World and "the Orient"* (Cambridge Scholars, 2012), *Alternative Orientalisms in Latin America and Beyond* (Cambridge Scholars, 2007), and *One World Periphery Reads the Other: Knowing the "Oriental" in the Americas and the Iberian Peninsula* (Cambridge Scholars, 2009), and coedited *Caminos para la paz: literatura israelí y árabe en castellano* (2008). He is the coexecutive director of the academic journal *Transmodernity: Journal of Peripheral Cultural Production of the Luso-Hispanic World* and the the coexecutive director of the Palgrave Macmillan Book series "Historical and Cultural Interconnections between Latin America and Asia."

Contributors

Rudyard Alcocer is the Forrest and Patsy Shumway Chair of Excellence in Romance Languages and associate professor of Latin American literature and culture in the Department of Modern Foreign Languages and Literatures at the University of Tennessee, Knoxville, where he is the founding director of the Latin American and Caribbean Studies Faculty Seminar. He is the author of *Time Travel in the Latin American and Caribbean Imagination: Re-reading History* (Palgrave Macmillan, 2011), *Narrative Mutations: Discourses of Heredity and Caribbean Literature* (Routledge, 2005), and *Celluloid Chains: Slavery in the Americas through Cinema* (coedited; forthcoming from University of Tennessee P).

Mark Anderson is associate professor of Latin American literatures and cultures at the University of Georgia. He conducts research primarily on Mexican, Colombian, and Brazilian cultural texts dealing with crisis, natural disaster, and ecocritical topics. He is author of *Disaster Writing: The Cultural Politics of Catastrophe in Latin America* (Charlottesville, VA: University of Virginia Press, 2011) and coeditor of *Ecological Crisis and Cultural Representation in Latin America* (Lanham, MA: Lexington Books, 2016).

Gene H. Bell-Villada (Ph.D., Harvard, 1974) is Professor of Romance Languages at Williams College. He is the author of *Borges and His Fiction: A Guide to His Mind and Art* (U. of North Carolina, 1981; second edition, revised and expanded, U. of Texas, 1999) and *García Márquez: The Man and His Work* (U. of North Carolina, 1990; second edition, revised and expanded, also UNC, 2010; translated into Turkish and Spanish). In 2004 he served as a consultant for the Oprah's Book Club selection of *One Hundred Years of Solitude*. His wide-ranging study, *Art for Art's Sake & Literary Life: How Politics and Markets Helped Shape the Ideology and Culture of Aestheticism, 1790-1990* (U. of Nebraska, 1996), was a finalist for the 1997 National Book Critics Circle Award and was translated into Serbian and Chinese. The author of two volumes of fiction, he has also published a memoir, *Overseas American: Growing up Gringo in the Tropics* (U. Press of Mississippi, 2005). His latest authored book is *On

Nabokov, Ayn Rand and the Libertarian Mind: What the Russian-American Odd Pair Can Tell Us about Some Values, Myths and Manias Widely Held Most Dear (Cambridge Scholars, 2013). His most recent edited volume is entitled *Gabriel García Márquez in Retrospect: A Collection* (Lexington, 2016).

Melissa A. Fitch, a second-generation Mexican-American from the United States/Mexico borderlands region, is a Latin American and US Latino cultural studies professor and a scholar focused on the area of Latin American-Asian studies. Her work encompasses the period marked by the rise of mass media at the turn of the last century in the United States to the present day influence and pervasiveness of social media and digital culture around the world. Her work includes many parts of Asia, but the fulcrum of her research and writing since 2006 encompasses the mutual cultural influences between Latin America and the world's two most populous countries, China and India. She is particularly interested in seminal concepts that have emerged in the last decade related to social media, political activism, globalization, and transnationalism. She examines how the portrayals of Latin American and Latino culture that emerged from the United States have continued to exercise influence on modern representations of the region coming from the two Asian powerhouses. She is currently a University Distinguished Professor and 1885 Distinguished Scholar of Spanish and Portuguese cultural studies at the University of Arizona. Born in Los Angeles, California, and educated at Arizona State University, where she received her PhD in 1995. She is the author of *Side Dishes: Latin/a American Women, Sex, and Cultural Production* (Rutgers UP, 2009) and *Global Tangos: Travels in the Transnational Imaginary* (Bucknell UP, 2015). She is also a coauthor of *Culture and Customs of Argentina* (Greenwood, 1998). She has been editor-in-chief of the academic journal *Studies in Latin American Popular Culture* (U of Texas P) since 2002. Her essays have also appeared in numerous academic journals.

David William Foster (PhD, University of Washington, 1964 [BA, 1961; MA, 1963 University of Washington]) is Regents Professor of Spanish, Humanities, and Women's Studies at Arizona State University. He served as chair of the Department of Languages and Literatures from 1997-2001. In spring 2009, he served as the Ednagene and Jordan Davidson Eminent

Scholar in the Humanities at Florida International University. His research interests focus on urban culture in Latin America, with emphasis on issues of queer gender construction and sexual identity, as well as Jewish culture. He has written extensively on Argentine narrative and theater, and he has held Fulbright teaching appointments in Argentina, Brazil, and Uruguay. He has also served as an Inter-American Development Bank Professor in Chile. Most recent publications have included *Glimpses of Phoenix: The Desert Metropolis in Written and Visual Media* (McFarland, 2013) and *Latin American Documentary Filmmaking: Major Texts* (U of Arizona P, 2013). He has recently published monographs on Argentine and Brazilian graphic narrative (U of Texas P) and Chicano photography (U of Pittsburgh P). He is past president of the Latin American Jewish Studies Association.

Shigeko Mato (PhD, University of New Mexico, 2000) teaches Spanish and Latin American Literature and Culture at the School of International Liberal Studies, Waseda University, Tokyo. She has published several articles and book chapters on contemporary Japanese Peruvian literature in Peru, the United States, and Japan. Currently, she is working on a book project related to Japanese migration to Peru and Japanese Peruvians' reverse migration to Japan. She is also the author of *Cooptation, Complicity, and Representation: Desire and Limits for Intellectuals in Twentieth-Century Mexican Fiction* (Peter Lang 2010).

Moisés Park is Assistant Professor of Spanish in the Department of Languages and Cultures at Baylor University and holds a PhD in Spanish with a Designated Emphasis in Critical Theory from the University of California, Davis. His research interests are Latin American literature and film, masculinity studies, Otherness, Orientalism and popular culture. He is author of more than ten articles and book chapters, as well as a book on contemporary Chilean literature and film, *Desire and Generational Conflicts in Contemporary Chilean Narrative and Cinema* (Peter Lang, 2014). His first poetry book was published in 2017, *El verso cae al aula* (Editorial Amanuense Chile).

Paula C. Park's research interests are Latin American literary/cultural productions from the twentieth and twenty-first centuries, Philippine literature in Spanish and English, Orientalism and Asian diasporas in the Hispanic world, exile writers, media culture, and sound studies. Her articles on these topics have been published or are forthcoming in *Hispanic Review, Hispanófila, Comparative Literature and Culture Web, Transmodernity, Revista Filipina,* and *Symploke.* She also has a chapter on Cuban writer Severo Sarduy's radioplays in the edited volume *TransLatin Joyce: Global Transmissions in Ibero-American Literature* (Palgrave, 2014). Park's current book project focuses on the literary, cultural, and diplomatic relations between the Philippines and Latin America from 1898 to 1965.

Traci Roberts-Camps is a professor of Spanish at University of the Pacific. Her areas of specialization include Latin American women film directors, twentieth-century Latin American literature, and Mexican women novelists. She is the author of *Latin American Women Filmmakers: Social and Cultural Perspectives* (2017) and *Gendered Self-Consciousness in Mexican and Chicana Women Writers: The Female Body as an Instrument of Political Resistance* (2008). She has published book chapters and articles on a variety of Latin American women film directors, including Marisa Sistach, Dana Rotberg, María Novaro, and Lucía Puenzo, and on novelists such as Rosario Castellanos, Cristina Rivera Garza, and Bárbara Jacobs.

Sandra Sousa holds a PhD in Portuguese and Brazilian Studies from Brown University. Currently, she is assistant professor at the University of Central Florida, where she teaches Portuguese Studies. Her research interests include colonialism and postcolonialism; Portuguese colonial literature; race relations in Mozambique; war, dictatorship, and violence in contemporary Portuguese and Luso-African literature; and feminine writing in Portuguese, Brazilian, and African literature. She is the author of *Ficções do Outro: Império, Raça e Subjectividade no Moçambique Colonial* (Esfera do Caos, 2015) and coedited *Visitas a João Paulo Borges Coelho. Leituras, Diálogos e Futuros* (Colibri, 2017).

Laura Torres-Rodríguez holds a PhD from the University of Pennsylvania and is currently an assistant professor at New York University. Her research interests are in Mexican literature and visual culture since 1890; Latin American intellectual history; Orientalism and transpacific studies; and Latin American feminist traditions. Her current book-length project *Orientaciones transpacíficas: la modernidad mexicana y el espectro de Asia* establishes the centrality of references about East and South Asia in the twentieth-century Mexican aesthetic and cultural debates on modernity. She is currently the book review editor of *Transmodernity: Journal of Peripheral Cultural Production of the Luso-Hispanic World.*

Antonio Luciano Tosta is an associate professor of Brazilian Literature and Culture at the University of Kansas. He is the author of *Confluence Narratives: Ethnicity, History, and Nation-Making in the Americas* (Bucknell UP, 2016). The manuscript won the 2016 Vice Chancellor for Research Book Publication Award at the University of Kansas. He coedited *Luso-American Literature: Writings by Portuguese Speaking Authors in North America* (Rutgers UP, 2011) and *Brazil: Nations in Focus* (ABC/ CLIO, 2015). His essays have appeared as book chapters and in journals in the United States, Brazil, England, and Canada. He has a PhD in Comparative Literature and Master's Degrees in Comparative Literature and Portuguese and Brazilian Studies from Brown University, a Master's Degree in Comparative Literature from the State University of New York at Buffalo, and a Bachelor's and a *Licenciatura* degrees in English from the Federal University of Bahia in Brazil. He is currently working on two book projects. The first is tentatively entitled *Brazilian-American Literature and U.S. Brazilian Literature: Transamerican Politics, Postcolonial Readings*, and the second *The Unlettered City: Human Geography, Subalternity, and Spaces of Oppression in Iberian and Latin American Literature and Film.*

Index